POWER OF READING

POWER OF READING

From Socrates to Twitter

Frank Furedi

BLOOMSBURY

LONDON · OXFORD · NEW YORK · NEW DELHI · SYDNEY

Bloomsbury Continuum
An imprint of Bloomsbury Publishing Plc

50 Bedford Square   1385 Broadway
London   New York
WC1B 3DP   NY 10018
UK   USA

www.bloomsbury.com

Bloomsbury, Continuum and the Diana logo are trademarks of Bloomsbury
Publishing Plc

First published 2015

British Library Cataloguing-in-Publication Data
A catalogue record for this book is available from the British Library.

Library of Congress Cataloguing-in-Publication data has been applied for.

ISBN: HB: 978-1-4729-1477-4
ePDF: 978-1-4729-1479-8
ePub: 978-1-4729-1478-1

2 4 6 8 10 9 7 5 3 1

Typeset by Integra Software Services Pvt. Ltd.
Printed and bound in Great Britain by CPI Group (UK) Ltd, Croydon CR0 4YY

To find out more about our authors and books visit www.bloomsbury.com.
Here you will find extracts, author interviews, details of forthcoming events and
the option to sign up for our newsletters.

To my father Laszlo,
who inspired me to love reading

CONTENTS

PREFACE

Reading has transformed human consciousness and changed the world. Aside from serving as a powerful medium of communication and a source of pleasure, it opened the gate to knowledge about virtually everything that is important. Throughout the Anglo-American world, reading is confused with literacy. Literacy is a skill oriented towards the decoding of written texts, and in a modern society that relies so much on communication this is an essential skill to possess. But reading is much more than literacy. Reading involves interpretation and imagination; it is a cultural accomplishment through which meaning is gained. Reading 'between the lines' allows readers to use their imagination and knowledge to understand and gain meaning from the text in front of them.

Apprehensions about the state of literacy are frequently coupled with warnings about the demise of books and the allegedly deleterious influence of the internet on our capacity to read. Those who lament the decline of the culture of reading are often rebuffed as cultural dinosaurs. It has become fashionable in some quarters to claim that in the world of ubiquitous connectivity, the book reader will be left behind by those setting out to find meaning through the resources provided by an ever-changing, instantaneous media-rich environment.

I intuitively felt that both sides of the debate about the future of reading and digital technology were one-sided and probably wrong. It was unlikely that the fate of the culture of reading would be determined by a new media technology: something else had to be at work. Since the act of reading has always had meaning that was influenced by prevailing cultural assumptions, I decided to embark on a historical reading of reading, to explore how its meaning for people and its impact upon them have been perceived throughout history. Here, I attempt to outline the complex and often contradictory meanings associated with this important endeavour.

Although I am a sociologist by trade, I draw on the perspective of history to emphasize contrasting themes as well as recurrent patterns in order to outline the distinct and unique features of a reading culture in the midst of the current transition from print to digital technology. My conclusion is that the culture of reading faces some serious challenges, but the drivers of these problems are not to be found in the domain of technology. The principal challenge we face is to revitalize the ethos that values reading as a cultural accomplishment in its own right. I can think of no better place to start than in our schools. Instead of training children to gain literacy skills, we should educate them to become readers.

The research for this book was facilitated by a grant from The British Academy and an Emeritus Fellowship from the Leverhulme Trust. I am grateful for their financial support. My colleagues Dr Jennie Bristow and Dr Ellie Lee were always a source of stimulating criticism. Nick Cater provided helpful advice on how to focus some of my arguments. My copy-editor Richard Mason did a great job on the text. Jamie Birkett of Bloomsbury was always helpful with his advice. I am indebted to my commissioning editor, Robin Baird-Smith, who from the start understood the importance of tackling this project and encouraged me at every stage.

Cadogna
Lombardy, Italy, 14 May 2015

INTRODUCTION

Why is reading in the twenty-first century such a problem? When the word 'literacy' appears in the news, it tends to be followed by some disquieting account of its precarious standing. The activity of reading has become entangled in numerous apparently diverse disputes, and the public language through which it is discussed frequently draws upon the rhetoric of crisis. The teaching of reading has become highly politicized, and in Anglo-American societies it has become a focus for intemperate arguments frequently referred to as 'the Reading Wars'.

At the same time, the diagnosis for reading difficulties has become extensively medicalized. A growing number of people are declared to be suffering from one or more reading-related conditions, such as dyslexia. It is frequently claimed that the arrival of digital media has reduced attention spans, leading to gloomy predictions of the 'end of the book' and the 'death of the reader'.

The narrative of gloom that characterizes this cultural obituary of the reader stands in contrast to the manner in which the practice of reading was once regarded in literate societies. Great thinkers celebrated reading as a solution to the predicaments they faced; in the Judaic and Christian traditions, reading attained the status of a moral virtue, a medium for gaining access to the Truth. From the Renaissance onwards, the voyage of discovery of the self was guided by reading. The Enlightenment embraced the reader as the arbiter of rationality and progress. Democrats and revolutionaries looked upon reading as a moral and intellectual resource for the conduct of a vibrant public life and as a tool of social transformation.

By the eighteenth century, the idea of the 'love of reading' took hold in many parts of the Western world, with reading increasingly regarded as a practice that was valued in and of itself. In the nineteenth century, reading was perceived as a source of self-improvement, motivating many people to learn to read by themselves or with the help of family members. Even throughout most of the twentieth century, literacy was seen both as a means of achieving enlightenment or pleasure, and as an instrument for helping to solve problems associated with poverty and economic stagnation.

So what has changed? Ours is not the first epoch to express anxieties and concerns about the role of reading and its impact on society. As we note in the chapters that follow, reading has always served as a focus of controversy and apprehension. Yet the common thread running through the ever-growing list of contemporary concerns indicates a more disturbing trend – the apparent difficulty that modern societies have in affirming their cultural values. Many influential voices have become deeply ambivalent about the value and future of reading. Even educators and literacy theorists have called into question the authoritative cultural status enjoyed by literacy.

The invention and proliferation of new types of literacies – visual literacy, aural literacy, computer literacy, emotional literacy, sexual literacy, ecoliteracy, media literacy, multicultural literacy, financial literacy – implicitly calls into question the unique status and cultural authority of Literacy. The representation of reading as one literacy among many renders it banal.

The aim of this book is to explore the historical origins and influences that inform how we think about reading in order to understand what is distinct about the way in which society regards this practice today. It questions the current tendency to devalue and de-authorize the reader, arguing that despite technological innovation and the influence of new media, the humanist ideal of the discriminating reader capable of autonomous judgement should serve as the cultural ideal of the present day.

Current concerns about the deleterious influence of digital technology and the internet on literacy and the reader are misplaced. The cultivation of individual identity through reading provides enormous possibilities for personal development, and the challenge confronting society today is cultural and political, rather than technological.

THE SOCRATIC PARADOX

Plato, writing through the mouth of Socrates, issued the first health warning for would-be readers. He was troubled by the spread of literacy, in part because he believed that it would remove from individuals the responsibility of remembering. Socrates used the Greek word *pharmakon* – 'drug' – as a metaphor for writing, conveying the paradox that reading could be a cure or a poison.[1] In centuries to come, this paradox would crystallize into a tension between reading as a useful medium of enlightenment and communication, and as a channel through which disturbing questions facing the moral order would be raised.

Socrates warned that written ideas had the potential to acquire a life of their own. Oral dialogues, such as those between Socrates and his acolytes, were conducted between individuals of similar standing and with a shared ethos, in a contained and secure cultural environment. The reactions and behaviour of a distant reader, on the other hand, could not be scrutinized. Socrates asserted that writing is indiscriminate in that it 'roams about everywhere': it does not discern between readers who can understand and benefit from its communication, and those who will become misled and confused by it. He warned that writing reaches those with 'understanding no less than those who have no business with it'.[2] In line with the paternalistic worldview of his era, Socrates assumed that in the wrong hands a little knowledge was a threat to social order.

In the context of the political culture of Socrates' Athens, those who had no business reading the written word were the vast majority of the public, the uneducated. From his perspective, even words of wisdom could, when written down, serve as a catalyst for confusion. He observed that problems would occur if the questions raised by a written manuscript were not dealt with in the presence of someone with wisdom. Pointing to such communications, Socrates argued that 'when it is faulted and attacked unfairly, it always needs its father's support; alone, it can neither defend itself nor come to its own support.'[3]

Socrates' disapproval of the written text was based in part on a conviction that the pursuit of the truth was so demanding that only a few Athenian citizens could be trusted with its undertaking. He insisted that knowledge 'is not something that can be put into words like other sciences';

it is only 'after long-continued intercourse between teacher and pupil, in joint pursuit of the subject', that true knowledge finds its way to the soul.[4] Plato's main concern appears to be not so much the written text but its circulation to a mass audience:

> If I thought they could be put into written words adequate for the multitude, what nobler work could I do in my life ... to bring to light the nature of things for all to see? But I do not think that the 'examination', as it is called of these questions would be of any benefit to men, except to a few, i.e., to those who could with little guidance discover the truth by themselves. Of the rest, some would be filled with an ill-founded and quite unbecoming disdain, and some with an exaggerated and foolish elation, as if they had learned something grand.[5]

In today's self-consciously inclusive democratic public culture, Socrates' inclination to restrict people's freedom to read material of their own choosing and in circumstances of their own making would be seen as anathema. Yet even in the twenty-first century, the public are often represented as powerless victims of media manipulation by tabloid journalism or by the subliminal techniques of advertisers. Such concerns have become amplified in the age of the internet.

A SOURCE OF MORAL DISORIENTATION

The ancient Greek philosopher hit upon an important insight. Once the written word was allowed to 'roam about everywhere', the world would never be the same.

Reading provides people with access to different views and ideas about their predicament, and fosters an attitude that encourages readers to view their world in new ways. It is through reading that a consciousness oriented towards change emerges and a sensibility towards novelty gains definition. The act of reading always contains the potential for subverting taken-for-granted assumptions. It also offers the promise of giving meaning to human experience. But since the written text invites its own critique, the meaning gained through reading often proves to be a temporary one. The history of reading indicates that it raises more questions than answers.

The elusive quality of the quest for meaning leads one generation after another to declare that 'there is too much information out there'. This complaint pre-dated not only the invention of the internet but also that of the printing press. The Roman poet Juvenal, who died in the early second century AD, was worried about information overload, as was the fourteenth-century humanist writer Petrarch, who complained that there were far too many scribes at work in their day. The Dutch Renaissance humanist philosopher Erasmus protested about 'the swarms of new books'.[6] In 1600, Barnaby Rich, an English writer, lamented that 'one of the great diseases of this age is the multitude of books that doth so overcharge the world that it is not able to digest the abundance of idle matter that is every day hatched and brought into the world'.[7]

The perception that the proliferation of published texts had a significant downside was fairly widespread by the seventeenth century. Pointing to a glut of printed texts, one English critic argued that they were 'begotten only to distract and abuse the weaker judgments of scholars'.[8] In this sense, the sentiment that far too much is being published has always expressed insecurities about the human capacity to understand the surrounding world.

Too many books were taken to mean too much choice, which in turn raised questions about which text could be trusted to possess genuine authority. That is one reason why, from ancient times to the modern era, moralistic advice on reading tended to warn against the dangers of extensive reading. The Roman Stoic philosopher Seneca advised that the 'reading of many books is a distraction' that leaves the reader 'disoriented and weak', and asserted 'you must linger among a limited number of master-thinkers, and digest their works, if you would derive ideas which shall win firm hold in your mind'.[9] Seneca's advice was widely advocated until recent times.[10] Presumably limiting the diversity of books would spare the reader from confronting the existential uncertainties thrown up by competing points of view.

The outlook of ancient, medieval and even early modern communities was disposed to take the written text very seriously. The written manuscript was often endowed with sacred or quasi-sacred qualities, as evidenced by swearing on the Bible or the ritual touching of a book. During the first millennium BC, the phrase 'for it is written' acquired sacred authority. Precisely because of its sacred status, the written text required the attention of a group of priests and scribes who were charged with interpreting and commenting on them. So long as this task could be restricted to a small group of specialist interpreters of the text, reading did not need to be perceived or represented as a serious social problem. The authority of what was 'written' remained relatively unproblematic.

By the seventeenth century, the culture of literacy had established a significant presence in Europe. The expansion of the practice of reading called into question the authoritative version of the written text. Once readers gained access to the written text they no longer had need of priests and interpreters, and could choose for themselves which interpretation they opted for. At first the growth of reading did not undermine the authority of the written text itself – merely a particular interpretation of it. Disputes about the interpretation of sacred texts marked the first phase of an emerging contestation of moral authority. However, such competing interpretations sometimes crystallized into newly authored commentaries on texts, which claimed to be authoritative in their own right. That reading would encourage the questioning of the sacred, which in turn would promote heresy, was the principal reason why the medieval Church discouraged it.

The Humanist Renaissance encouraged readers to pursue their activities in private. The shift towards private reading directly contributed to the emergence of the consciousness of the individual. In private, individual readers were free to explore and question prevailing ideas and conventions. Private reading promoted the flourishing of the internal life of readers, and served to consolidate their sense of selfhood. It fostered an atmosphere of experimentation and reflection that allowed some readers to adopt views inconsistent with the prevailing norms. In this cultural environment, 'common orthodoxy had to yield to individual opinion, as each reader became an authority'.[11]

Medieval Christianity was the first institution confronted with the challenge of how to affirm the sacred status of the text whilst marginalizing the corrosive influence of popular reading. By the fifteenth century it was struggling to uphold its doctrinal orthodoxy and moral authority in the face of criticism from opinionated lay readers of the vernacular Bible. The failure of the Church to resolve this challenge led to its split between

Protestantism, which upheld the sacred authority of the written text, and Catholicism, which embraced the authority of custom and tradition.

Sir Thomas More eloquently articulated the Catholic Church's reaction to what was perceived as the morally corrupting influence of reading. Although initially open to the idea of translating the Bible into the vernacular, More eventually became hostile to it because he feared that it would 'stir up disputation rather than piety among the common people'.[12] His premonition that reading would serve as a source of moral contestation proved to be prescient. Reading, which involves the act of interpretation, often led people to draw conclusions that challenged the prevailing moral order.

READING TROUBLES

The paradox of literacy, which was first raised by Socrates, has yet to be resolved. Indeed, it is difficult to avoid the conclusion that the matter will never be settled. Despite the current tendency to regard literacy as a skill, reading has always been more than the mechanical act of decoding texts. It is a way of acquiring knowledge, a vehicle for self-improvement, a source of enjoyment, and a medium for gaining meaning. It is the principal gateway through which questions of value are internalized, articulated and clarified.

From its origins, the written word affirmed but also threatened moral norms. Protagoras, the sophist who questioned the existence of gods, was one of the first philosophers to discover the seriousness with which a community could feel threatened by the written word. He was tried for impiety in Athens in 411 BC. Protagoras allegedly argued that 'concerning Gods I am not able to know either that they do exist or that they do not exist'.[13] For this act of impiety he was exiled and his books burned in the marketplace. His writings were deemed to be a threat to civic virtue, and would-be readers needed to be protected from their corrupting influence.

The burning of Protagoras' writings established a precedent for future censors of morally troubling texts. It is well known that suspicion and intolerance towards the reading public characterized the response of many religious and political institutions, but what is often overlooked is that even philosophers and movements who espoused liberal and democratic values also shared some of the misgivings of their political foes. For example, Enlightenment thinkers who believed in the power of education and reason were nevertheless not always confident that the public could read in a responsible manner and draw the 'right' conclusions. It was as if ideals that were true and enlightening when studied by the wise few turned into dangerous thoughts when read by the untutored many.

Despite their advocacy of moral autonomy, many Enlightenment thinkers took for granted that the reading public lacked the ability to discriminate between truth and falsehood. It was feared that the avail-ability of cheaply produced popular fiction would estrange people from the fine words of their educated superiors. Their objection was not to reading as such, but to the reading of material that distracted people from appreciating the promise of the Enlightenment. In the late eighteenth and early nineteenth centuries, such distractions were often pathologized in the language of addiction, and the main target was the novel. It was alleged that these tales of romance and adventure provided no benefit to the reader; indeed, they encouraged people to read 'excessively'. Reading 'for its own sake' was presented as not only a purposeless but also a potentially corrupting activity.

The narrative of associating reading with the pathology of addiction communicates three important recurring themes. The first is a lack of confidence in the capacity of elite culture to influence and direct the reading taste of the wider public. The second is contempt toward popular tastes, which expresses itself with the certainty that the public will be drawn to the most debased and corrupting literary influences. The third theme inflates the power of the written word to control and direct human behaviour, with members of the public presented as literally helpless to resist the manipu-lative influence of that written word. Against such an omnipotent and irresistible force, it was argued, the worthy literature of Enlighteners simply could not compete.

Today, when advocates of literature frequently lament the decline of the habit of reading, it may seem odd that not so long ago apprehensions were directed at the perils of indiscriminate reading. Yet from its inception, reading was perceived as a risky activity that could compromise well-being. 'Be careful,' warned Seneca, 'lest this reading of many authors and books of every sort may tend to make you discursive and unsteady.'[14]

The aesthetic critique of 'reading for its own sake' and reading 'too many books' can be interpreted as an attempt to influence public taste and to gain support for the cultural authority of educated elites. By the eighteenth century, with the rise of printing and publishing and the emergence of a sizable reading public, it was no longer possible to prevent people from gaining access to books. Moreover, reading was increasingly represented as a cultural accomplishment that would assist the education and enlightenment of humankind. But Western society could not quite accommodate itself to the idea that all readers and all forms of readings ought to be valued. Reading has never been an accomplishment that human society could take for granted, and even when it enjoyed significant cultural affirmation, it was a focus of unease and even a source of panic.

From the eighteenth century onwards, book reviews, notices and abstracts sought to provide guidance to readers. At their best such initiatives sought to educate, inform and contribute to the emergence of a critical and sophisticated public. But 'helpful advice' about how to read and discriminate between good and bad literature often acquired the tone of a sermon, promoting the moralizing agenda of its authors.[15]

By the nineteenth century, reading had become a source of controversy amongst the cultural political elites. Those of a conservative or reactionary disposition regarded reading – particularly when practised by the masses – as a source of instability and moral peril. Others calculated that reading would help instil the solid virtues and values of polite society to an ever-widening section of the public. Those on the radical end of the political spectrum hoped that reading would serve as a tool of education, social emancipation and liberation. But whatever the differences that separated them, they all believed that the reader had to be taken very seriously. The reading public was assigned great importance and the challenge was to influence and, if necessary, control their taste and opinions. They all sought to tame and discipline mass literacy.[16] But of course, readers were not always prepared to be tamed.

Until late in the nineteenth century, the pathologization of reading tended to be expressed through an explicitly self-consciously moralistic tone. Romantic fiction was described as 'moral poison' and critics stressed its debauching and corrupting effects.[17] Such sentiments were still widely voiced in the first half of the twentieth century. Indicting readers who were addicted to the consumption of 'light reading', the literary critic Q. D. Leavis suggested that the term 'dissipation' was a most useful way of describing this 'vice'.[18]

Moralizing about people's reading habits and problems has often been expressed in the language of disease, through a narrative of medicalization. The narrative of medicalization led to the rise of conditions like 'reading-mania', the 'reading-bug', 'book-addiction' or 'reading-fatigue'. The contemporary condition of 'internet addiction' is simply the latest version of the centuries-old tendency to stigmatize apparently disturbing reading behaviour through the diagnosis of a psychological illness.

The narrative of medicalization can also account for problems that are the very opposite of compulsive reading. Whereas in the past anxieties were frequently directed at too much reading, today they are directed at too little reading. The vocabulary of medicalization represents reading as an inherently unnatural activity: indeed, according to an American historian of reading, this practice is 'one of the most unnatural activities in which man has ever engaged'.[19] Experts commenting on reading problems regularly repeat the claim that reading is alien to human nature.

Neuroscience has now been mobilized to support the thesis that 'we are not born to read'.[20] One advocate of this narrative observed that accounts of problems and illnesses associated with reading back in the eighteenth century may well have been based on an early appreciation of the 'sheer physicality of the process' of reading: 'They may have intuitively understood what our technology permits us to newly discover, that reading is a demanding activity that shapes you in mind and body.'[21]

During the early twenty-first century, the problem of reading has shifted to a focus on people's *inability to read*. An entire generation of young people has been diagnosed with an inability to concentrate on the written text. Numerous experts and educators allege that it is simply impossible or unrealistic to expect 'digital natives' and young people to bother to read a book, and the deficit of their attention spans is often blamed on digital technology or the distractions of consumer culture. Socrates' claim that writing weakened the reader's mind anticipates the current crop of internet-related inattention syndromes.

And so today, it is the failure to pick up a book that serves as a marker for a health problem. According to Andrew Solomon, the rising rates of depression and escalating levels of Alzheimer's disease can be attributed to the decline of reading; indeed, he contends that the crisis in reading in the United States is a crisis in national health.[22]

The narrative of medicalization has thus been reframed so that reading has been transformed into a promoter of good health. Advocates of reading insist that it improves your mind-reading skills;[23] that it can help reduce stress – according to some researchers you only need to read silently for six minutes 'to slow down the heart rate and ease tension in muscles';[24] and that it provides an antidote to depression.[25] Reading is no longer a 'moral poison' but a magical cure-all.

Although society frets about the literacy crisis in the classroom and culture-brokers warn about the decline of serious reading, the main focus of twenty-first-century reading troubles is the internet. Old troubles that were originally diagnosed as afflictions faced by readers of manuscripts have been rediscovered and amplified as risks associated with the consumption of digital culture. Seneca's call to restrain the habit of reading has been recycled in a language that warns that 'our ability to learn can be severely compromised when our brains become overloaded with diverse stimuli online'.[26] Panics regarding literacy, the reading of literature, the threat to culture posed by texting and the social media, and online pornography, are just some of the symptoms of problems associated with reading in the digital age.

Outwardly, the current debates on reading in the digital age appear as a caricatured version of the controversies of the past. But as the following chapters indicate, history does not simply replicate the past and our reading troubles say much that is distinctive of our era.

1

THE CULTURAL CONTRADICTIONS OF LITERACY

Reading has always been a subject of moral ambiguity, as recognition of the usefulness of literacy has coexisted with anxieties about its impact on readers. Over the centuries ambivalence towards literacy crystallized into a constant preoccupation with what is today referred to as 'the media effect'. That is why so many of the reservations raised by Plato continue to find an expression in the age of the internet and digital communication. The idealization of the love of reading runs in parallel with profound disquiet about its influence on the moral order.

WRITERS WARNING ABOUT WRITING

When he received the Heinrich Böll Prize from the City of Cologne in 1985, the German author Hans Magnus Enzensberger decided to devote his acceptance speech to praising the virtues of illiteracy. Clearly uncomfortable with the educational ethos of his time, he drew attention to what he perceived as the cultural loss that accompanies the rise of literacy, stating: 'I envy the illiterate his memory, his capacity for concentration, his cunning, his inventiveness, his tenacity, his sensitive ear.' Enzensberger asserted that he was not indulging in nostalgic fantasies about the 'noble savage' of the past: 'I am speaking not about romantic phantoms but about people I have met.'[1] In his praise of illiteracy Enzensberger drew attention to its 'contribution' to human culture, by which he meant the invention and dissemination of myths, children's fables and songs. 'Without oral tradition, there would be no poetry; without illiterates, no books,' he claimed.[2]

Motivated by the sensibility of late modern cultural populism, Enzensberger's ambivalence towards literacy took issue with its use as a method of social control. Writing from a different, and self-consciously elitist, outlook, the Spanish liberal philosopher José Ortega y Gasset warned that 'dulled by the habituality of reading which is now almost second nature to us, we enjoy the evident advantages of the written word – the printed, in fact – and we have lost consciousness of the wastes and dangers which it brings'. The main danger that concerned Ortega y Gasset was the threat that the written text posed for the 'oral world' and for 'the most human marvels of all, which are dialogue, and rhetoric – the only true magic'.[3]

Like Enzensberger, Ortega y Gasset was a prodigious author of written texts. That he chose to communicate his preference for the magic of the oral dialogue through the form of a written essay indicated that his celebration of the 'human marvel' of the oral world coexisted with the recognition that writing was more than just a practical necessity. In the end he was prepared to accept that the loss of the magic of the dialogue was a price worth paying for the gains realized through the technology of the written text, writing that: 'The relative impersonality and dehumanization of the written word, at the same time that it makes the elocution ghostlike, lends it a distance and anonymity, an "objectivity", which are indispensable for the trans-mission of, for example, theories.'[4]

The language through which this begrudging acceptance of the book was expressed echoes a long-standing sense of alienation from what some experience as the cold and disenchanted realm of mechanically produced written texts. This sensibility continues to influence deliberations on the media in the age of digital technology.

Arguments that associate harmful influence with reading and writing often suggest that these are unnatural or inhuman ways of communicating and internalizing knowledge, which denude the act of meaning and feeling. Such concerns originated with the very discovery of the techniques of reading and writing: no sooner did reading emerge as a novel human practice than critics began to warn against its perilous consequences.

Although Western civilization is associated with the tradition of Great Books, a coherent statement of suspicion about writing and reading occurred much earlier than the positive reflections by its greatest advocates. It was Plato, whom Ortega y Gasset described as the 'first "writer of books"', who put forward the first coherent and elaborate argument against the written text. Some of the greatest figures of world literature – Miguel de Cervantes, Samuel Johnson, Samuel Taylor Coleridge, Anthony Trollope, George Eliot, Edith Wharton, Wilkie Collins, Thomas Hardy, Jane Austen, Virginia Woolf and many others – thought and wrote about the risks of reading.

The paradox of writers warning about writing expresses the contradiction between intent and effect. Whatever writers' stated aim or aspiration, the effect of their communication cannot be predicted. For Plato, one important contrast between Greek oral and written culture was the scale of associated risks. He perceived the loss of control over the direction and impact of the written text as a threat to the stability of his community.

THE MEDIA EFFECT

Public communication through prophecies, myths, poems and stories – oral and written – have been a source of concern since the beginning of human history. Plato's warnings about the effects of poetry and of writing represented a response to the cultural uncertainties thrown up in the Greek city states, but they resonate with the modern imagination and influence contemporary reactions to different varieties of media.

Maryanne Wolf, an American cognitive neuroscientist, frequently draws on Socrates to reinforce her argument about the debilitating effect of the internet on the so-called reading brain. She is convinced that Socrates' warnings about the risks posed by the written text are particularly relevant for thinking about the transition from print and digital media and its impact on children, explaining that: 'Socrates' perspective on the pursuit of information in our culture haunts me every day as I watch my two sons use the Internet to finish a homework assignment, and then they tell me they "know all about it".'

As a result of this experience, says Wolf, she felt 'an unsettling kinship with Socrates' futile battles so long ago': 'I cannot help thinking that we have lost as much control as Socrates feared 2,500 years ago over what, how, and how deeply the next generation learns.'[5] Wolf's twenty-first-century concerns have as their focus adult anxieties about the status of children: 'I came to see that Socrates' worries about the transition from an oral culture to a literate one and the risks it posed, especially for young people, mirrored my own concerns about the immersion of our children into a digital world.'[6]

Plato was deeply apprehensive about the likely impact of written texts on the children who read them. But it would be strange to attribute to Plato the preoccupation that parents now have regarding the education of their offspring. Unlike the ambitious modern parent, Plato's principal concern was not the development and interest of the child, but the maintenance of social order in his republic. As he pointed out in the *Laws*, 'in a truly good city a son would not belong to his genitor at all, but only to the polis'.[7]

As someone who was committed to carefully vetting and controlling the socialization of young children in his ideal city state, Plato was not only preoccupied with what youngsters read but also with what they heard. In *The Republic* he asserted that because the 'young and tender' were so 'malleable' they could be easily misled by stories, and he called for the supervision of storytellers, seeking to persuade nurses and mothers to tell their children 'the ones we have selected, since they will shape children's souls with stories much more than they shape their bodies by handling them'. Plato warned that in his ideal city state 'many of the stories they tell now' must be 'thrown out'.[8] His call to censor the stories and poems was based on the conviction that the 'young can't distinguish what is allegorical from what isn't, and the opinions they absorb at that age are hard to erase and apt to become unalterable'.[9]

Plato was not merely worried about the effects of written communication, but also about orally transmitted tales and poems. Not even the magnificent poetry of Homer and Hesiod escaped Plato's censorious gaze. *The Republic* took exception to those poets for giving a 'bad image of what gods and heroes are like'. Plato was critical of Hesiod for showing gods fighting each other, and for his account of how the son of Cronus punished his father for his transgression, which Plato believed could incite young people to challenge paternal authority. Plato thought that such stories, even if they were true, had to be 'passed over in silence, not told to foolish young people'.[10] He also took exception to Homer's description of the horrors of life in the underworld of Hades because he feared that such passages would cause warriors to fear dying in battle. Plato asked, 'Can someone be unafraid of death, preferring it to defeat in battle or slavery, if he believes in a Hades full of terrors?'[11]

Plato was not simply concerned about the content of Homer's poems but also about the capacity of poetry to influence the human imagination in a way that undermined the strength of his city state. From this perspective, the more subtle and powerful a poem, the greater the threat it posed. His criticism of Homer was not that his poems lacked artistic creativity, but that, on the contrary, they possessed great artistic merit. 'It isn't that they aren't poetic and pleasing to the majority of hearers,' he noted, 'but that, the more poetic they are, the less they should be heard by children, or by men who are supposed to be free and to fear slavery more than death.'[12]

Plato regarded poetry as corrosive because it had the potential to capture people's imagination and influence their souls. Through its focus on emotional states, poetry distracted people from reason and habit.[13] As the cultural historian Barry Ife remarks, the 'crux of Plato's case against the immorality of art is therefore that the sympathetic indulgence through art in emotions which we would be ashamed to admit in real life has an adverse effect on the character by undermining resistance to adversity and temptation'.[14]

Plato's warnings about the dangers of poetry were underpinned by the conviction that most people lacked the moral and intellectual resources necessary for avoiding its disorienting influence. He asserted that poetry was 'likely to distort the thought of anyone who hears it, unless he has the knowledge of what it is really like, as a drug to counteract it'.[15] Since only a small number of educated citizens were likely to possess an antidote to poetry's damaging effects, Plato believed that it was better to expel all but the officially sanctioned ceremonial poets from the city state. Thus the metaphor of a poisonous illness was used at a very early stage to highlight the dangers of communication.

Plato's representation of poetry as a subversive influence on conventional norms offered a paradigm on which subsequent critiques of art and media would draw. The risks of an all-consuming media became a recurring theme, and even cultures and societies that acclaimed its positive benefits were concerned about its potential dangers. Concern with the power of poetry shows that oral culture anticipated the emergence of what today is characterized as the 'media effect' – the uncertain and possibly disorienting consequence of the images, ideas and suggestions communicated through art and technologies of communication.

The 'effect' that matters most to those interested in this threat has been the way in which the media influences people's outlook, values and behaviour. The French philosopher Jacques Derrida is right to conclude that, for Socrates, the 'question of writing opens as a question of morality', adding that 'it is truly *morality* that is at stake, both in the sense of the opposition between good and evil, or good and bad, and in the sense of mores, public morals and social conventions'.[16] Since morality is forever disputed, reading has always been an activity subjected to contradictory social attitudes.

THE AMBIGUITY OF LITERACY

Whatever concerns Plato had about what people heard paled into insignificance compared with his anxiety about what they read. Why? Because literacy penetrates and shapes human thought. It transforms people's mentality, alters the way they think, and can, in certain circumstances, shape their identity. Plato sensed not only that reading and writing had a powerful effect on people but that these activities also changed them.

It is difficult to be certain of how strongly Plato believed in the epistemological superiority of dialogue over writing. He insisted that it was difficult to write about profound philosophical issues, for such knowledge could not be 'put into words like other sciences'.[17] Yet despite expressing these misgivings Plato had no inhibitions writing extensively about some of the most fundamental and difficult philosophical questions facing Greek society. 'Paradoxically,' observes the media theorist Walter Ong, Plato could formulate 'his preference for orality over writing, clearly and effectively only because he could write'.[18] Plato's philosophical system, his analytical thought, was 'possible only because of the effects that writing was beginning to have on mental processes'.[19]

Arguably it was the assistance that writing contributed to the capacity to conceptualize and analyse that helped Plato mount his critique of writing. Indeed, 'Plato's entire epistemology was unwittingly a programmed rejection of the old oral, mobile, warm, personally interactive lifeworld of oral culture', which was best 'represented by the poets, who he would not allow in his Republic', writes Ong.[20]

Those who present Plato as an unambiguous advocate of orality suffer from a lack of sensitivity to the historical circumstances of his time. In classical Greece writing existed on the margins of society and though it was becoming increasingly influential, the subsequent polarized conceptions of oral versus written cultures had not yet crystallized.[21] This emerged over centuries of development, and only acquired a coherent form in the early modern era.

It is likely that Plato intuited that the powers unleashed by the technology of writing were likely to be even greater than those of oral communication, and also far more difficult to contain. That is why he had Socrates explicitly condemn the technology of writing. Yet the very manner in which this condemnation was communicated – through a written text – indicated that even its author could not reject literacy in its entirety. Socrates' use of the word *pharmakon* – 'drug' – as a metaphor for writing captured the ambiguous status of literacy. Like all drugs, writing had the potential to be poisonous but could also offer a cure. Derrida argued that Plato was convinced that 'there is no such thing as a harmless remedy' and therefore the '*pharmakon* can never be simply beneficial'.[22]

Through the use of the metaphor of a drug, Plato laid the foundation for the association of reading and writing with artificial or unnatural characteristics. The implication conveyed through the linking of writing with artificiality was to underline its unnatural, fabricated, contrived and even fake attributes. This physical-moral condemnation of writing served to highlight the virtues of oral communication – specifically its natural and human qualities. Yet, its very artificiality served to endow writing with a consciousness and sense of purpose that assisted the development and constant refinement of ideas. Through its impact on readers, the unnatural act of developing abstract ideas not only changed the way people thought: it also transformed human nature.

The ancient Greek dramatist Menander (342–291 BC) warned that those who teach women how to read and write are 'feeding a vile snake on more poison'.[23] But warnings about the dangers of reading in ancient Greece existed side by side with a positive appreciation. Some philosophers and politicians regarded the written text as a medium that would protect the people from the arbitrary interpretation of oral custom and laws. Aristotle believed that 'writing the laws down' encouraged 'justice or fairness' and was 'an essential basis for democracy',[24] and it was for this reason that he criticized the leaders of Sparta who determined cases by their own 'judgement and not by written law'.[25] Similar sentiments were voiced by the Sophist thinker Gorgias, who asserted that 'written laws are the guardians of the just'.[26]

Although in late fourth- and fifth-century Athens it was widely believed that the written law was integral to the conduct of democratic life, oral dialogue and communication continued to enjoy great cultural status. According to a study of the relationship between the spoken and written word in the classical period, 'written laws were regarded as inferior to "unwritten laws," not merely by the Antigone of Sophocles and by Thucydides in the Funeral Oration of Pericles but by ordinary men'.[27] It is likely that even Aristotle regarded 'the written word' as inferior to 'the spoken word'.[28]

The ambiguous relationship between the written and spoken word found a striking expression in a text written by the fourth-century BC Sophist Alcidamas of Elaea. The purpose of this statement was to attack competing Sophist orators who relied on speaking from written speeches. Alcidamas wrote that writing could be easily 'assailed' and had no special merit 'because it may be easily and readily practised by anyone of ordinary ability'. To this very 'ordinary' practice he juxtaposed the extraordinary accomplishments of those unique individuals who could speak extemporaneously.

What is interesting about Alcidamas' otherwise pompous text is that it attempted to provide an account of the differential cultural significance that Greek society attached to writing and speaking. Inadvertently his condemnation of the written speech offers a coherent statement about the contradictory attitude held by classical culture towards literacy. Alcidamas did not entirely reject writing but believed that it 'should be practised as an ancillary pursuit'. From his standpoint, writing had its uses and was suitable for those 'woefully deficient in rhetoric and philosophy', who 'may be called poets rather than Sophists'.[29]

The sensibility of cultural conservatism expressed by Alcidamas echoed some of Plato's sentiments. However, Alcidamas was far more explicit in acknowledging that writing was acceptable as an 'ancillary pursuit'. The lack of cultural status accorded to writing and reading at this point in time also had a basis in the limited development of this new technology. The shortage of writing material, such as animal skin and papyrus, limited the scope for the elaboration of ideas through written texts, therefore reading was continually constrained by this material reality. Written statements by philosophers tended to be communicated as 'summary pronouncements of the philosophers' doctrine'. Such summaries were likely to have been 'published as a guide to the philosopher's system' and 'to be used as a supplement to oral teaching'.[30] In such conditions, since the 'reading of the literate Athenian was confined to limits that we would think narrow', the appreciation of the technology of writing was likely to be pragmatic rather than aesthetic.

Derrida argued that Plato's 'diatribe against writing' was directed 'above all against sophistics'. But what Plato feared, even if indirectly, was the risk of uncontrolled dissemination of the written text.[31] The conservative reaction against writing readily blended in with the political impulse to restrain the influence of democracy. But despite the central role that orators played in the public life of Athens, the influence of literacy steadily gained in standing. 'The age of Aristotle is an age of readers and libraries', concludes a study of this subject, observing that with Aristotle, the Greek world 'passed from oral instruction to the habit of reading'.[32]

Despite the relative lack of cultural validation for writing, the effectiveness and practical usage of this technology ensured that its influence would steadily expand. According to historical sources before 600 BC, very few Greeks could read – but from this point onwards literacy became more common as writing acquired a greater public function. It was around the time of Plato (c.427–c.347 BC) 'that the Greek language advanced to the point where one could begin to address abstract concepts adequately for the first time', and it is likely that writing assisted this process of linguistic and conceptual clarification.[33]

In Athens the transition from an oral to a written tradition occurred between the fifth and fourth centuries BC. Although Greece remained an oral rather than a literate society, there is evidence that writing was no longer confined to the production of public texts, such as legal documents; the private reading of texts (papyrus rolls) was relatively common amongst the elites. Aristotle personified the ferocious reader who used his private library to pursue his research and philosophical investigation. Writing and reading fostered a climate in which critical thought and scepticism flourished, leading to a veritable intellectual revolution.[34] The cultural power of reading was expressed by the Greek dramatist Menander, when he stated: 'those who can read see twice as well'.[35]

The acceptance of writing and reading was based on pragmatism. Writing and reading provided a powerful medium of communication and helped validate knowledge; they served to lubricate public life and helped administrative and bureaucratic institutions to manage their affairs. The written text existed in an uneasy and uncertain relationship with the oral word: it had considerable authority, but the day when the love of reading would become common was still far off. Alexander the Great may have been an exceptional figure in this respect. When he died in Babylon in 323 BC, he was said to be clutching the scrolls of Homer's *Iliad*. By this time, reading and the pursuit of knowledge were seen as closely intertwined activities.

ENDURING SUSPICION TOWARDS LITERACY

At first sight it appears curious that Plato's critique of writing and the wider suspicion directed by classical Greek culture towards this medium continue to be a focus of interest to this day. Both opponents and advocates of the internet have alluded to the Socratic critique of the technology of writing and to the unique natural qualities of the world of orality. Indeed it sometimes appears as if the further we are from the ancient and medieval world, the more oral culture appears to excite the jaded literary imagination.

The Cluetrain Manifesto, published in 2000 by enthusiasts of the dot. com business ethos, aimed to cast the internet corporate world in the role of a benevolent facilitator for the rediscovery of the authentic human voice. This influential business manual sought to humanize the otherwise impersonal transactions of the marketplace by likening it with the dialogical interactions of the ancient Greek bazaar. Thus the selling point of the internet is that it works like a high-tech agora:

> What if the real attraction of the internet is not its cutting-edge bells
> and whistles, its jazzy interface, or any of the advanced technology

that underlies its pipes and wires? What if, instead, the attraction is an atavistic throwback to the prehistoric human fascination with telling tales?

The *Manifesto* answers its questions by appealing to the sense of alienation and estrangement 'wrought by homogenized broadcast media, sterilized "mass culture" and the enforced anonymity of bureaucratic organization'.[36]

The *Manifesto's* celebration of what it depicts as the atavistic qualities of oral culture is presented as an expression of a timeless quest for rediscovering the 'human voice'. It declares that the 'Web is simply liberating an atavistic human desire, the longing for connection through talk', and adds 'that's the one constant throughout our evolution from caves to mud huts to open-air-bazaars'.[37] This depiction of the internet as a 'space in which the human voice could be rapidly rediscovered' presupposes that the development of the different media technologies that preceded it has served to suppress the fundamental aspiration after orality.

The *Cluetrain Manifesto* does not refer directly to Plato's critique of writing. But it presents the legacy of the Greeks as the cultural precursor of its celebration of the internet. Doc Searls, one of the authors of the *Manifesto*, declared with unreserved bombast that 'democracy, mathematics and politics are all viral memes that were born in the agora, the Greek marketplace', and that 'while empires and civilisations rose and fell the conversational fires started by Pythagoras, Socrates and Aristotle have only continued to spread'.[38]

While *The Cluetrain Manifesto* praises the internet for its capacity to facilitate active engagement through conversation, others criticize digital technology for rendering communication artificial and passive. Walter Ong, who is drawn to the 'agonistic mentality' of oral cultures, has observed that the arguments used by Plato's Socrates against writing apply with equal force to the internet. Ong wrote that Socrates 'holds it against writing that the written word cannot defend itself as the natural spoken word can'; for unlike writing, 'real speech and thought always exist essentially in a context of give-and-take between real persons'. Hence Ong concludes that 'writing is passive, out of it, in an unreal, unnatural world' – and 'so are computers'.[39]

Plato's critique of writing, and his enthronement of dialogue as the path to clarity and truth, have continued to resonate with those uneasy about the workings and consequences of the new media. The enduring appeal of Plato's reflections on the relationship between writing and speaking was its condemnation of the unnatural, mechanical or artificial attribute of communications technology. Time and again the sensibility of disenchantment with the unnatural and mechanical dimension of human experience has raised its head in relation to writing and reading. Indeed it is arguable that it was in reaction to the invention of writing that the now classical anti-technological and romantic sensibility emerged, albeit in an embryonic form.

The conviction that reading poses a risk to human well-being continues to retain a degree of influence over the sphere of education. In the nineteenth and twentieth centuries, texts devoted to teaching children how to read often reminded their consumers that reading is an unnatural accomplishment. At the turn of the twentieth century, Granville Stanley Hall, the pioneering educator and first president of the American Psychological Association, adopted this approach in his influential text *How to Teach Reading: And What to Read in School*. 'From antiquity to the present time, many thoughtful men have declared writing to be not only inferior to speech, but a spurious form of knowledge,' stated Hall. After recapitulating some of the traditional reservations expressed about writing, Hall raised his own criticism of bookishness: 'Reading, in emancipating men from their physical and mental environment, often weakens local pride and local interest, and creates a distaste for what is nearest, and what, therefore, should be pedagogically first.' Hall warned that teaching the unnatural art of reading may well be a mixed blessing, concluding that 'finally, we sometimes find a habit of passionate reading in children that not only interferes with the physical development, but destroys mental and moral independence, and may be called as morbid'.[40]

A decade after Hall's publication, Edmund Burke Huey, another central figure in early twentieth-century reading pedagogy, advocated a child-centred approach that postponed the teaching of reading until relatively late on the grounds that children needed protection from its unnatural and harmful effects.[41] Echoing Plato, Huey argued against the 'premature reverence for books', which he believed led to neglecting one's own thinking and to the 'atrophied', 'naïve originality of the children', who become 'slaves to "what is written"'.[42]

'How many children are becoming Socrates' nightmare?' asked an author in *The New York Times*, before informing her twenty-first-century readership that 'we know' that no human being was born to read.[43] Although this author's concern was with the perils of children consuming texts online, the allusion to Socrates indicated that even in an age of mass literacy, some still consider reading to be a form of human activity that is not quite natural.

The portrayal of writing as artificial assumes that something genuine, authentic, natural or human will be damaged or lost through its usage. In the case of Plato, writing was indicted because of its harmful effect on the functioning of the brain, specifically on memory. In its most dramatic form this sense of cultural loss is expressed in the romanticization of illiteracy and the deprecation of literacy. Historically, nostalgia for the loss of oral or traditional virtues has been associated with the anti-modernist conservative imagination. Stanley Hall was strident in his assertion of this sentiment, stating that he could not 'refuse all quality of admiration for men who lived before Gutenberg' or for those 'doughty medieval knights who despised the petty clerk's trick of writing'. His sympathy was with the man of action rather than with those who indulge in the 'slavish and unmanly' activity of reading. So in *How to Teach Reading* he concluded:

> Thus I have gradually almost come to the opinion that many of our youth would develop into better health, stauncher virtue, and possibly better citizenship, and a culture in every way more pedagogical and solid, had they never been taught to read, but some useful handicraft, and the habit of utilizing all the methods of oral education within reach, instead.[44]

Hall's indirect celebration of non-literacy expressed the mood of disenchanted anti-modernist conservatives at the turn of the twentieth century. By the 1960s such sentiments were no longer confined to old-fashioned traditionalists. Disappointment with the workings of modernity fostered a climate of cultural relativism where a radical romantic repudiation of modern life often coincided with a display of reverence towards oral culture.

The sense of nostalgia towards communities whose life had not yet been distorted by literacy is evident in the work of one of the most fashionable social theorists of the 1960s and 1970s, the French social anthropologist Claude Lévi-Strauss. In his study *Tristes Tropiques*, he presents the loss of innocence as in part the consequence of the acquisition of writing. This romantic perspective recognized the practical advantages of reading and writing but argued that these benefits come at a high cost to our humanity. It contended that the shift from an oral culture to the written text, particularly in its printed forms, is paralleled by a loss of the capacity for emotional self-expression.

This view was eloquently expounded by one of the most influential figures in modern communication studies, the philosopher Marshall McLuhan. His writings convey a powerful sense of disenchantment with print culture and literacy, which he appears to perceive as stultifying, individualistic and intensely alienating. McLuhan idealized the oral person and regarded those socialized into a literate culture as inferior versions. He believed that the modern, technologically driven literate world created people who lack the emotional depth of their oral ancestors.

McLuhan adopted the classical model of the modern–primitive contrast for interpreting the different stages of historical development. However, his account justified a preference for the emotional world of his version of the primitive Noble Savage. McLuhan updated and developed Socrates' claim that the technology of writing lacked the depth and richness of dialogue, and would therefore weaken the spirit of those who practised it. While he recognized that this technology possessed important advantages that ensured its ascendancy, McLuhan worried that the technology of the printed word imposed a regime of routine on the human soul:

> Civilization is built on literacy because literacy is a uniform processing of a culture by a visual sense extended in space and time by the alphabet. In tribal cultures, experience is arranged by a dominant auditory sense-life that represses visual values. The auditory sense, unlike the cool and neutral eye, is hyper-esthetic and delicate and all-inclusive. Oral cultures act and react at the same time. Phonetic culture endows men with the means of repressing their feelings and emotions when engaged in action. To act without reacting, without involvement, is the peculiar advantage of Western literate man.[45]

McLuhan's indictment of literacy is far more expansive than the objections raised by Plato. Plato's comments on writing constituted a response against a practice that had become visibly influential but had not yet quite gained a powerful presence in Greek society. The twentieth-century world of McLuhan was one where literacy served as a defining feature of cultural life, and his statement touched on what he perceived as its corrosive impact on the fundamental dimension of the human condition.

McLuhan identified the rise of the printing press during the Renaissance period as the moment when literacy began to exact significant human costs on community life. His is a reaction to the positive valuation that the Enlightenment attached to the power of the printed texts; he viewed literacy as a threat to traditional communities and the organic way of life associated with them. One of the underlying themes of McLuhan's writing is a lament for the pre-Renaissance and pre-print medieval era:

> A culture based upon the printed book, which has prevailed from the Renaissance until lately, has bequeathed to us – along with its immeasurable riches – snobberies which ought to be cast aside. We ought to take a fresh look at tradition, considered not as the inert acceptance of a fossilized corpus of themes and conventions, but as an organic habit of re-creating what has been received and is handed on.[46]

His call to re-appropriate the oral tradition was not simply directed at the 'snobberies' of print culture but also at what he perceived as its negative spiritual and social consequences.

McLuhan's call for a 'reactionary' orientation towards literacy resonated with the romantic spirit of the 1960s, particularly with the emerging counter-culture. The British classicist Eric Havelock drew attention to this widespread fascination with the pre-literate imagination. In his essay 'The Modern Discovery of Orality', Havelock noted that around 1963 a 'modern consciousness' of orality 'appears to burst' on the scene. He concluded that this reaction was integral to a wider repudiation of a shallow consumerist culture.[47]

The remarkable impact of McLuhan's arguments about Western intellectual life in the 1960s and 1970s was enhanced by a growing mood of scepticism towards the Enlightenment ideals of development and progress. As the hopes invested in modernity turned into scepticism and estrangement, so attitudes towards the pre-Enlightenment epoch changed. The positive claims made on behalf of literacy were called into question and oral culture was rediscovered as a source of precious human attributes. Numerous critics denounced the association of literacy with positive connotations and illiteracy with negative ones. The spirit of this era expressed a mood that called into question the long-standing distinction between people who were deemed to be civilized and those who were primitive. The very ideal of civilizational progress was often dismissed as an unacceptable manifestation of racial superiority.

At this conjuncture, the very suggestion that a literate culture was superior to an illiterate one was denounced as at best insensitive and at worst a symptom of ethnocentrism. As Walter Ong notes, the term 'illiteracy' was becoming increasingly unacceptable because it communicated the idea of a 'lack or deficiency'; such terms were gradually being replaced by 'a more positive understanding of earlier states of consciousness', and a 'less invidious and more positive term to use as a substitute for illiteracy was oral'.[48]

The term 'oral' bypassed the negative connotations of illiteracy and by implications called into question the representation of literacy as an unambiguously progressive development. In academic circles, it was frequently argued that the significance which previous generations attached to the transformative impact of literacy was ideological and wrong. The verdict that 'literacy was overrated' was widely echoed by the influential revisionist theories of the last quarter of the twentieth century.[49]

BEGRUDGING RESPECT

Yet despite the sceptical attitudes that are often expressed about the value of literacy, in the real world reading and writing are taken very seriously, and they remain accomplishments that are highly valued. Even McLuhan conceded: 'The achievements of the Western world, it is obvious, are testimony to the tremendous values of literacy.'[50] However, his begrudging acknowledgement of the 'tremendous value of literacy' was immediately qualified by a significant 'but': 'but many people are also disposed to object that we have purchased our structure of specialist technology and values at too high a price'.[51]

McLuhan's representation of literacy as an agent of technological dehumanization was not endorsed by mainstream intellectual and educational opinion, but it did have a significant impact on the cultural debates in Western societies at that time. Previous optimistic predictions about the capacity of literacy to transform people's lives for the better gave way to the realization that on their own, reading and writing had only a limited influence on social change.

Disillusionment with the modernist promise of literacy intermeshed with disenchantment about a society that appeared so enamoured with technological development that it had lost its human soul. Technophobia, coupled with a romantic yearning for the natural, provided a cultural context for the devaluation of the printed word. Outlining the shallow generalizations about the effects of literacy at this time, the sociologist Kenneth Levine commented that:

> Print has been portrayed as an isolating and individuating force, weakening networks of kin and other primary attachments and partially displacing their social-psychological support for the self with remote sources of identification and an enhanced sense of personal determination.[52]

The 1960s revolt against literacy constituted a reaction to the authority of the printed text and its claim to a supreme position in the hierarchy of communication. The contestation of cultural authority, which had been an ongoing theme in the twentieth century, had direct implications for the status of literacy.

Nostalgia for non-literate oral traditions was and remains a symptom of the diminished authority of the written text. However, nostalgia can rarely be converted into a positive cultural force. Whatever reservations such sentiments express about reading, there is no real appetite for displacing it with oral communication. As Ong notes:

> Orality is not an ideal, and never was. To approach it positively is not to advocate it as a permanent state for any culture. Literacy opens possibilities to the word and to human existence unimaginable without writing. Oral cultures today value their oral traditions and agonize over the loss of these traditions, but I have never encountered or heard of an oral culture that does not want to achieve literacy as soon as possible.[53]

Modern society is inconceivable without reading and writing. Yet although these accomplishments have inspired humanity for centuries, they continually face challenges to their cultural authority.

CONCLUSION

The apprehensions that Socrates expressed about the shift from an oral to a written culture are frequently alluded to in current discussions about the displacement of the printed by the digital text. Umberto Eco described Socrates' reaction as an expression of 'an eternal fear: the fear that a new technological achievement could abolish or destroy something that we consider precious, fruitful, something that represents for us a value in itself, and a deeply spiritual one'.[54] However, the tendency to draw parallels between contemporary concerns about the demise of print culture and Socrates' warnings about the dangers of writing tends to flatten out the uniqueness of historical experience.

Modern society's ambivalence towards technological innovation is based on centuries of experience with its disorienting consequences. There was no such experience for Socrates to draw on, and though he feared that writing would lead to the weakening of human memory, he was much more concerned with the destabilizing consequences of writing for Athenian culture and society. Over the centuries, attitudes towards reading underwent significant modifications and, as we shall see, tended to reflect issues that were historically specific to their time.

The crystallization of Plato's critique into an anti-modernist romantic repudiation of literacy was not the outcome of a process of steady evolution. Once the potential of literacy was grasped, it was welcomed by numerous communities in different historical circumstances. From the Renaissance onwards, literacy gained significant cultural significance to the point that by the early nineteenth century the term 'love of reading' was widely used and signified the idealization of literacy.

The idealization of the 'love of reading', which really took off in the eighteenth century, has during the past five decades or so mutated into the instrumental acceptance of reading.[55] However, the written text always signified more than impersonal characters. It also conveyed the passions and the spirit that motivated authors to express themselves in a written form. Readers have always sought to find meaning from the texts they held in their hands. Egyptian hieroglyphics were perceived to possess magical powers; centuries later, the religious texts of the Jews, Christians and Muslims were also endowed with sacred properties. During the centuries that followed, the 'phrase "for it is written" came to take on authoritative, indeed divine, significance'.[56] In succeeding epochs the book was often associated with mystical, revelatory and later powerful therapeutic qualities.

The sacralization of the text inevitably endowed reading with a variety of culturally and morally valued characteristics. Even with the rise of mass literacy, reading was still regarded as one of the most highly significant cultural accomplishments, and rarely as merely a physical activity. It was and continues to be perceived as a medium that can transform attitudes, affect the emotions, enlighten, indoctrinate, subvert, seduce or corrupt. That is why reading was so often subject to the contradictory sentiments of love and hate.

2

READING IN SEARCH OF MEANING

Literacy is often presented as a medium of communication, but reading and writing were often experienced as more than just useful techniques. Almost from its inception, reading was regarded as a cultural accomplishment that provided important insights for both individuals and their communities. The association of reading with the sensibility of revelation lent reading a spiritual and sometimes a mystical dimension. Religions such as Judaism and Christianity defined themselves through their relationship to a holy text, and reading was sacralized as a result. Saint Augustine's reflections on reading indicate that the reading of such texts not only assisted the quest for the Truth but also helped readers to gain self-knowledge.

With the rise of humanism and the advent of the Renaissance, the spiritual dimension of reading acquired an increasingly individual and personal form. Over the centuries, the activity of reading gradually shifted from its purposeful instrumental quest for God's truth to an practice that was considered (at least by a significant minority) as essential for the cultivation of the self. In the long run the outcome of these developments was the crystallization of the ideal of the *love of reading*.

NOT JUST PRACTICAL

Writing, like most technologies, was invented to serve a practical need. According to Plato's mythical account, the Egyptian divinity

Theuth – the 'father of writing' –justified his invention on the ground that 'once learned, [it] will make the Egyptians wiser and will improve their memory'.[1] Although Plato and others had doubts about the wisdom of relying on the information and guidance provided by the written word, the usefulness of this technique was recognized by those charged with the storing, processing and distribution of data and information. For the Egyptians, writing served two main purposes: 'administration and monumental display'.[2] Literacy was confined to those charged with overseeing religious and bureaucratic institutions.

Writing and reading were adopted by different groups of political and cultural elites because they were perceived as effective instruments of communication. The Roman civilization, which emphasized the usefulness – *utilitas* – of ideas, embraced reading and writing in a self-consciously instrumental manner. In classical Rome most writing played a functional role, communicating information and assisting the management of accounts, business, and the running and coordination of the Empire. Reading was regarded as a useful and well-rewarded skill that could bolster an individual's material prospects. In Petronius' *Satyricon*, the rag merchant Echion refers to the ability to read legal documents and observes that *Habect haec res panem* – 'this thing has bread in it'.[3]

Even in the age of Shakespeare, Elizabethan reading remained 'above all utilitarian' and 'radically analytical'.[4] A century later, in Stuart England, individual readers continued to regard their activity as a means for the attainment of knowledge and information that was useful for their careers and advancement.[5] The utilitarian attitude towards reading continued to characterize Western reading culture into the eighteenth century, where reading tended to be perceived principally as a technical skill directed towards a practical purpose; and the invention of the idea of functional literacy in the twentieth century indicates that the instrumental validation of reading continues to the present.

But reading was also a cultural activity. Humanly constructed signs conveyed meanings that had to be both mechanically decoded and culturally interpreted. It is likely that Egyptian hieroglyphs that were inscribed on coffins, tomb walls and monuments served to communicate exhortations to the gods. Funerary inscriptions found on the walls of the antechamber of the Pyramid of Unas at Saqqara 'described the ruler's perilous journeys through the underworld to this rightful place among the gods'.[6] Although such inscriptions conveyed the political message of the powerful, they also drew attention to the spiritual and sacred character of the deceased.

Alongside the instrumental attitude towards reading, many regarded the written word as a source of wisdom, moral truth and even pleasure. The discovery of ribald graffiti poking fun at well-known individuals on the walls of the surviving buildings of the ancient Roman city of Pompeii indicates that by the first century AD writing and reading had become integral to popular culture.[7]

The Romans were ambivalent about poetry, which they regarded as beautiful but at the same time frivolous. According to one account, for the Romans 'reading was a useful activity only if it led to writing and especially if the writing proved to be *morally* useful'.[8] Although the Romans favourably contrasted *utilitas*, the 'doctrine of usefulness', to that of *voluptas*, 'pleasure', they were also drawn to the aesthetic side of reading. The lyric poet Horace claimed that there was an advantage in both advising and delighting the reader at the same time; poets who were 'both pleasing and useful for life' were the ones most likely to succeed.[9]

Writing sometime around AD 63, the Stoic philosopher Seneca described the pleasure and relaxation that he gained from reading. Seneca may not have been the first writer to describe the irresistible attraction of the book but he was one of the first to grasp its powerful impact on the human psyche. His advised the new reader to exercise care and avoid being distracted by the temptation to jump from one text to the next. Seneca called on young readers to focus attention on a limited number of books authored by master thinkers.[10] The pleasures and excitement of reading conveyed the promise of an elevated emotional experience; but as with all pleasures, Seneca argued, it tempted the individual reader to lose sight of the boundary that separates spiritual order from moral chaos.[11]

Seneca's call for restraint was probably influenced by his distaste for the public reading 'mania' that appeared to afflict the early Roman Empire. This period saw the emergence of the *recitatio* – public literary readings conducted by prose writers and poets. Authors and publishers used the *recitatio* as a form of (self-)promotion, which 'grew to be the curse of literature';[12] readings by self-important and vain individuals became the target of sarcastic humour. According to the Roman satirist Martial, not even public toilets were off-limits for intrusive public readers. In one of his sarcastic epigrams Martial wrote:

> You read to me as I stand, you read to me as I sit,
> You read to me as I run, you read to me as I shit.
> I flee to the baths; you boom in my ear.
> I head for the pool, you won't let me swim.
> I hurry to dinner, you stop me in my tracks.
> I arrive at the meal, your words make me gag.[13]

Yet for public readers in search of an audience for their written thoughts, their performance was no joke. Authorship had become associated with authority and the reading of books had acquired a formidable cultural status. It is significant that the Latin term for authority, *auctoritas*, is closely linked with the concept of the author or authoring. In classical Latin, the author is an authority whose statements are regarded as authoritative.[14] The association of the role of the author with that of *auctoritas* suggests that Roman society associated writing and reading with status and prestige.

Anyone studying Seneca's thoughtful epistle 'On Discursiveness in Reading' today might be tempted to overlook the fact that reading in ancient Rome represented an experience quite unlike our own. People read scrolls, called *volumina*, made from about twenty sheets of papyrus glued together, which were difficult to handle and read and were also easily damaged. Roman texts were written without word divisions and changes of speakers were not always indicated. Reading involved the laborious act of deciphering the text out loud. It was not until the Middle Ages, when words became separated on written texts, that significant groups of readers could conduct their activity in a silent and private manner.

As the practice of the *recitatio* indicates, reading in the Roman Empire was very different to the individual, often solitary, activity of our times. Although Rome around the time of Augustus was more literate than most societies, it is doubtful that more than 10 per cent of the population could read. The impressive culture of literacy – Virgil, Horace, Ovid – coexisted with one in which memory and oral communication retained an important role in public life. Consequently, through oral practices such as the *recitatio*, people could be literate 'in the sense of "knowing books" in a "second-hand" way'.[15]

The experience of Roman culture indicates that a reader does not simply read written texts. Readers also listen to the sound of their own voices and those of others, they imagine, interpret and search for clues and meanings. According to the numerous definitions offered by the *Oxford English Dictionary*, a reader was once seen as an 'expounder or interpreter of dreams' and of 'occult signs'. The *OED* draws attention to the 'ancient reader of signs and portents' to signify the historical association of this activity with the act of interpretation. As a historical and cultural accomplishment, the act of reading transcends the literal internalization of the text. Reading often becomes disconnected from the physical text. An individual described by the novelist James Joyce in his *Dubliners* as a 'reader of faces' or by the novelist Edward Bulwer-Lytton as a 'profound reader of men's character' shares at least one important characteristic with the careful literal reader of the text – the search for meaning.[16] As we argue in this chapter, one of the curious outcomes of this quest is that it often changes how readers think and also challenges how they perceive themselves.

The meaning of reading and what people do with the written text is contingent on the historical circumstances within which this activity occurs. The challenge faced by the Roman reader attempting to decipher an unwieldy handwritten scroll is very different to one faced by a nineteenth-century individual perusing a novel or the twenty-first-century teenager glued to a computer screen. Situational constraints, such as the technology available for written communication, cultural attitudes towards ideas, and the spread of literacy are just some of the influences that guide how people read.

RELIGION AND THE SACRALIZATION OF THE TEXT

One of the most significant cultural influences on the evolution of the Western sensibility towards reading in the pre-modern era was the pursuit of religious enlightenment and truth. From clay tablets to the development of handwritten scrolls on papyrus and later on parchment, to the emergence during the first and second centuries AD of a new form of the book, the codex – a group of pages made of papyrus or parchment – texts were always attributed with magical and sacred properties.[17] The written word was correlated with sacred knowledge, and reading was regarded as a spiritual experience that could serve as a prelude to revelation. The earliest adopters of literacy, who were frequently priest-scribes and religious groups, and institutions encouraged the sacralization of the text.

For most of the major religions of the world, the written text provided a medium for conserving sacred knowledge and guiding believers. Until the late eighteenth century, religious literature dominated and shaped reading in Western civilizations. In many parts of the globe, especially within Islamic societies, religious themes still exercise a weighty influence over reading. The interaction between the technology of reading and writing and religion has led to the mutual reinforcement of the authority of both, with the written text often serving as a metaphor for the representation of sacred religious identity. The mere articulation of a phrase from a religious text can directly communicate divine and authoritative guidance and direction.

Jews describe themselves as 'People of the Book', to underline their 'cultural and religious identity rooted fundamentally in Torah, the original book of the Law',[18] and highlight their relationship to the Torah and other expressions of sacred law, such as the Mishnah and the Talmud. Muslims use the term 'People of the Book' to represent those who follow revealed scriptures, such as Christians and Jews. It is likely that the systematic sacralization of readings had its origins within ancient Jewish culture. Unlike the Greeks, who paved the way for the validation of cultural reading, Jews turned it into a sacred act; the 'written word ... became fundamental to the Jewish identity'.[19]

The sacralization of reading developed further with the rise of Christianity. The emergence of Christianity and its consolidation in the West was closely connected to the technology of text production. As Alan Jacobs suggests, the codex 'recommended itself to early Christianity for four primary reasons: *economy, portability, integrity* and *sequentiality*'.[20] The codex provided a medium through which a copious amount of material could be integrated into one book. This new format allowed religious texts, such as the Scriptures, to be read in their integral unity, and allowed the reader to gain access to any section of the text without the trouble of unrolling a series of interconnected scrolls. It also helped Christianity to spread its influence, and the written word became a source of authority for this new religion.

The enormous significance that Christian theologians attached to writing and the written text altered the way that reading was perceived in the Roman Empire. The reading of texts gained authority as the medium through which important events in the present and the future could be intuited or understood. The practice of understanding the future through stars, deities, weather, omens and magic gave way to the insights provided through reading texts. By 'late antiquity, the rise of a reading culture among Christians gradually put limits on the range of validity of other forms of understanding the future'.[21]

CHRISTIAN READING

For Christian readers, the sacred status of the written word lent reading a distinctly spiritual and transformative dimension. Reading was prescribed as an experience that could lead to the revealed truth and individual salvation. The idea of conversion or salvation through the proper reading of the Bible was integral to the Christian outlook of late antiquity and the medieval period. Arguably the most systematic and certainly the most eloquent account of the meaning of reading for the early Christian reader is to be found in the writings of St Augustine of Hippo (354–430). Augustine's exploration of this subject 'gave birth to the West's first developed theory of reading',[22] and his study *On Christian Doctrine* (427) served as the foundation for literary theory during the Middle Ages.[23]

Throughout the Middle Ages, Augustine's writing on the subject influenced the way in which people perceived the meaning that reading constituted in their lives. Some of the leading early humanists such as Dante (1265–1321) and Petrarch (1304–1374) were directly influenced by Augustine's reflections on the subject. The modern-day reader of Augustine's *Confessions*, written in 397–8, will find that this is a text which not only sought to theorize what reading did to the human imagination, but also offered an early example of the contemporary literary genre of the Confessional. The author's personal transformation from sinner to saint was revealed through an exposition of a journey of salvation achieved through reading.

Unlike Plato, Augustine claimed that memory did not provide a sufficient foundation for understanding the past. Augustine recognized that the power of memory was prodigious but claimed that it did not provide the resources necessary for understanding the will of God. 'My God, my true Life, what, then, am I to do,' he asked, before answering: 'I shall go beyond this force that is in me, this force which we call memory, so that I may come to you.'[24] Since neither God nor the Truth reside in memory, Augustine argued for the need to journey beyond memory through contemplation and the reading of the Scriptures. For this Church Father, reading served as a prelude for salvation and the revelation of God's wisdom. Augustine 'argued that if the contemplative frame of mind is our only experience of the blessed life while we are alive, the person most likely to achieve temporary happiness is the reader'.[25]

Augustine depicted reading in an instrumental manner as a religious duty – an activity that served as a means to an end. For Augustine and other Church Fathers, the purpose of reading was to gain greater self-knowledge and understanding of God's wisdom. From this standpoint reading served as a means of education and despite its sacred status the Bible was viewed as an instrument to that end.[26] But reading was also acknowledged to offer a spiritual experience, one that engaged the human body and the senses, and that was potentially a source of pleasure. Although he expressed his ideas through a religious narrative, Augustine fully recognized the emotional and aesthetic dimension of this experience. The reader of Augustine's account of his views on reading will be struck by the frequency with which the instrumental mutates into an aesthetic appreciation of the attainment of spiritual insight.

The Confessions frequently deals with the psychological and physical effects of reading that may dramatically overcome the reader. Augustine reported that he was overwhelmed by the intensity of his emotional response to the reading of Cicero's *Hortensius*, which he perceived as a catalyst to a life-changing event. Reading Cicero converted him to philosophy. The passions that reading excited in Augustine, though expressed through the idiom of religion, can strike a modern readership as dramatically similar to the emotional upheavals associated with accounts of falling in love. 'How I cried out to you, my God, when I read the Psalms of David,' exclaimed Augustine. Deploying the biblical metaphor of Fire, he exclaimed how the Psalms 'set me on fire with love of you'.[27]

Augustine's spiritual journey through reading reached its climax when he turned to the writings of the Apostle Paul. Enraptured by the passionate experience of reading these words, Augustine became a Christian convert. Referring to this portentous moment of revelation he declared, 'it was wonderful how these truths came home to me when I read *the least of your apostles* and the thoughts of your work had set my heart trembling'.[28] This feverish emotional and physical reaction to the Scriptures indicates that for Augustine and, by implication, for the genuine Christian reader, much is at stake.

Augustine himself does not go so far as to represent reading explicitly as a 'means of spiritual transformation'. Outwardly, he endorses the instrumental status of reading. But spiritual progress through literary contemplation meant that reading itself was endowed with spiritual qualities. Accordingly, Augustine's religious conversion required that he 'become a convert to reading itself'.[29] Augustine frankly acknowledged that reading changed who he was.

The conviction that the truth can be found through reading the right books recurs through the *Confessions*. However, the kind of reading that can gain access to the truth is one that is neither simply technical nor merely driven by an appetite for knowledge and curiosity. Nor is the exercise of reason a sufficient guide to reading: indeed Augustine's *Confessions* can in places be interpreted as an exercise in self-criticism about his youthful curiosity-led reading, his scepticism and validation of reason. He admonishes himself for adopting a sceptical and questioning reading practice and for failing to 'bow' his head to the Bible and 'to follow where it led'.[30]

For Augustine the act of genuine Christian reading represents an act of commitment to faith. From this perspective the limits of reasoning can be overcome through the faithful reading of the authoritative text. He asserted that 'since we are too weak to discover the truth by reason alone', we 'need the authority of sacred books'.[31]

Augustine justified his prescription of reading as an act of faith on the grounds that the mysteries of God could not be understood through reasoning alone. His version of Christianity requires that faith precede reason in order to allow all people to develop a spiritual relationship with God. He observed that 'the Church demanded that certain things should be believed even though they could not be proved, for if they could not be proved, not all men could understand the proof'. He believed that without trusting the Church 'we should accomplish absolutely nothing in this life'.[32]

Augustine's affirmation of faith and trust was integral to a concept of reading that regarded it as a spiritual quest. The reader could gain only

a limited insight from the mechanical act of decoding the text. The text
had to be read spiritually in order to gain insight into truths that could
not be accessed merely through the technical act of decoding. Augustine
indicated that though Scripture can be read by all with 'ease', it also 'has a
deeper meaning in which its great secrets are locked away'.[33] These secrets
require that reading be conducted as a spiritual and contemplative activity.
Consequently, for the Christian reader, reading constituted an act of interpretation for accessing meaning and truth. A study of Christian literary
theory concludes that since 'meaning resides finally in the person and is not
intrinsically a property of mere words', reading 'responsibly' is an 'ethical
activity'.[34]

The challenge facing Christian readers was to go beyond the letter of
the text and immerse themselves in its spirit. Inspired by St Ambrose, the
Bishop of Milan whom Augustine met in AD 384 and who often stated
his preference for the spiritual over the written law, Augustine believed
that Christian reading 'lifted the veil of mystery, and disclosed the spiritual
meaning of texts which taken literally, appeared to contain the most
unlikely doctrines'.[35] During most of the Middle Ages the Augustinian
approach to reading, which has been described by one scholar 'as seeking
epiphanies between the lines', exercised a dominant influence in cultural
life.[36] Augustine understood that texts had a literal meaning and that
'the spiritual sense was always based on the literal and that every text had
a literal meaning'; but he regarded spiritual reading as the medium for
gaining enlightenment.[37]

The search for meaning through reading between the lines often gave
this activity a mystical and religious significance. The knowledge gained
about God's work and intention and the experience of revelation had
a life-changing impact. Reading thus constituted an important psychological experience of personal change through which the faithful gains
self-knowledge. Augustine's account of finding faith and gaining salvation
was paralleled by his personal transformation. Following the teaching of
Ambrose, Augustine came to understand that the reader:

> ... could distinguish between what Paul called the 'spirit' and the 'letter'
> as a parallel to the 'inner' and the 'outer' self. Texts and selves interpen-
> etrated: it became possible to look upon the building of a new self as an
> exegetical and interpretive process.[38]

This penetration of the text into the internal world of the individual represented a moment of revelation into both God's design and the state of the self.

EARLY TRACES OF THE SELF

In most accounts of the development of self-consciousness, the emergence of the individual is associated with the rise of the Renaissance in Italy. Jacob Burckhardt's influential study argues that around the close of the thirteenth century, Italy 'began to swarm with individuality' and that the subjective side of humanity began to assert itself to the point that 'man became a spiritual *individual*'.[39] The ascendancy of Humanism was interlinked with a more subjective form of reading.[40] Yet although secular subjectivity and individual self-consciousness is rightly interpreted as an accomplishment of the Renaissance, it is possible to gain a glimmer of the search for self-awareness in Augustine's writings and those of other thinkers in the early medieval era.

Spiritually motivated reading that was oriented towards the acquisition of meaning and the truth led to a journey that encouraged the emergence of a sensibility oriented towards the self. The *Confessions* uses the mode of self-reflection in the hope of acquiring greater knowledge and self-awareness. Thus, the act of conversion and the acquisition of an understanding of God's design through reading had not only a religious but also a therapeutic function. At one point Augustine refers to God as the 'physician of my soul', and later implores the Almighty to help him discover his true self.[41]

As one study of Augustine's search for self-knowledge contends, 'one of the techniques for describing the self that evolves during the later ancient period involves the real or imagined use of reading and writing.'[42] As reading became enmeshed with the emergence of the sensibility of the self, it became a central medium for the gradual realization and expression of conscious subjectivity.[43]

One important legacy of the *Confessions*, and more widely of the evolving genre of religious biographies, is that they drew attention to the persona of the reader. Integral to this experience was the coexistence of spiritual enlightenment with self-education and understanding. Reading between the lines, interpreting signs, and monitoring emotional reactions to the text heightened the sense of subjectivity.

At least for a small group of Christian readers, engagement with the mysteries of the text gave them access to their internal life. This journey of self-enlightenment did not have merely a religious significance: it also served to cultivate a secular sensibility, which during the Renaissance would be perceived as that of the individual self.

One of the most frequently recounted episodes in the history of reading is Augustine's encounter with Bishop Ambrose in AD 384. In a widely debated passage in the *Confessions*, Augustine reports his surprise at coming across this holy man who is deeply absorbed in silently reading a book: 'When he read, his eyes scanned the page and his heart explored the meaning, but his voice was silent and his tongue was still.'[44] Augustine's astonishment at seeing someone reading in silence has been subsequently interpreted as evidence that, until this point in time, silent reading was rare if not unknown. The nineteenth-century German scholar Eduard Norden saw this passage as proof that reading aloud was the norm throughout antiquity; in response, others contend that silent reading must have been well known to ancient audiences, since characters can be seen to be reading silently onstage in plays by Euripides and Aristophanes.

The debate about the timing of the emergence of silent reading continues to this day. However, what is not in doubt is that the gradual ascendancy of silent reading by solitary individuals occurred centuries after the publication of the *Confessions*. The technical precondition for the spread of silent reading was the introduction of the practice of separating words in a text. This practice probably originated in Ireland and gradually expanded to the European continent during the course of the ninth, tenth and eleventh centuries. Word separation, notes the historian Paul Saenger, was 'the singular contribution of the early Middle Ages to the evolution of Western written communication'.[45] In the absence of word separation, people uttered the text out loud in order to understand it, while reading in silence was very difficult and certainly not a practical way of absorbing meaning.

It is likely that by the eleventh century, word separation had been widely adopted by monasteries in France. One important stimulus for silent reading was the emergence of a corpus of complex ideas associated with scholasticism, which required a mode of comprehension that was more effective than reading out loud. The gradual spread of silent reading amongst religious orders developed alongside the evolution of a 'more rigorous intellectual life in the twelfth and early thirteenth centuries in the *studia* of Cistercian abbeys' and the cathedral schools from which universities would emerge.[46]

The powerful influence that reading in silence exerted on cultural life was matched by its stimulus in the development of individual self-consciousness. The potent emotional experience of Augustine's spiritual reading could acquire a more unrestrained force through silent and private acts that were far less subject to external surveillance and attention. The act of interpretative reading carried out in silence greatly assisted the reader who was inclined to withdraw from the world. This shift from the external to the internal world allowed readers to insulate themselves from the pressures of everyday life and explore their subjectivity.

The role of silent reading was pivotal in promoting the cultural importance of private study and individual reflection. Studies indicate that the individual self became a matter of interest to a select group of cultural readers as early as the twelfth century. When Bernard of Clairvaux, one of the founders of the Cistercian order, told a correspondent that 'he can be known through his writings', he drew attention to the identity-forming potential of reading and writing.[47]

Over the centuries, silent reading became entwined with a shift in the focus of people's emotional and intellectual energies from the theological to the psychological realm. By the latter part of the Middle Ages, 'the effect books had on private sensibility was increasingly emphasized'. Alongside a growing awareness of this sensibility there emerged new attitudes towards private life. Reading constituted a new way of conceptualizing the individual by 'delineating the separate realm of private and public performance', states an important study of this historical moment.[48] It is at this point in time that the figure of the reader, possessing a distinct identity and cultural status, makes its appearance. In the late Middle Ages the idea of reading was 'characterized by the conviction that books serve as vehicles for establishing both self-awareness and self-actuation'.[49]

That the search for spiritual truth through reading would eventually lead to the discovery of the very secular individual self was an unexpected consequence of the growing usage of this channel of communication. Silent reading assisted the exploration of the imagination and of thinking the unthinkable, providing a vehicle for uncensored communication.

It helped create a world unregulated by public bodies and moral rules. This was a world where day-dreaming, erotic fantasies, heretical thoughts and subversive ideals could flourish. The growth of religious heretical movements in the eleventh century coincided with the spread of silent reading. Although it was still confined to a small minority of people, silent reading was increasingly identified by the Church as very threatening and the subversive. The book was frequently castigated as a 'silent heretic'.[50]

HUMANIST READING

Augustine's reflections on reading serve as a testimony to the power and the importance of this practice. His autobiographical account of spiritual transformation bestowed upon reading a lofty ethical quality. As a means for accessing the mysteries of religious texts and revealing the needs of the soul, Augustine represents reading as a singularly potent medium for the attainment of self-knowledge and the cultivation of self-identity. From the standpoint of the history of reading, Augustine is an important figure not only because of what he wrote on the subject but also because he emerged in the Middle Ages as the idealized personification of the Reader.

What is historically significant about the *Confessions* was its capacity to capture the reader's imagination. Augustine's use of the confessional mode of writing transcended the sphere of the otherworldly to the point that it could resonate with the innerwordly concerns of the emerging self. It was in this vein that the Benedictine monk Goscelin of Saint-Bertin, in his *Liber Confortatorius* of the early 1080s, advised his spiritual daughter Eve to adopt the *Confessions* as the model for meditation: 'Do not consider of less account among the rest the book of Augustine's *Confessiones*, which may pour divine affection into you more deeply.'[51] Goscelin's advice to his protégée offers an important insight into the psychology of medieval religious thought and spiritual practice. For Goscelin the unique power of the *Confessions* to touch the soul constituted the virtue of this form of emotional communication.[52]

Linda Olson's study on the influence of Augustine on medieval women readers noted that the monastic community saw the confessional mode as 'a particularly effective genre for exciting the "affection" of readers'.[53] She cited the example of Adam of Dryburgh, writing in the second half of the twelfth century, who described the confessional mode that he borrowed from Augustine for his *De triplici genere contemplationis* as a 'particularly effective mode for exciting the "affection" of his readers'.[54] The leading medieval scholastic theologian Anselm of Canterbury regarded the confessional as an important genre for exciting those reading it into the love of God.[55]

The *Confessions* exercised considerable influence on the outlook of the early humanist writers and philosophers. Dante's *Vita Nuova* (1295), which recounted his emotionally charged spiritual transformation, echoes the personal journey of Augustine. Petrarch goes a step further and in his influential *Secretum*, written between 1347 and 1353, he directly evokes the spirit of Augustine through an imaginary dialogue with the author of the *Confessions*.[56] The strength of Petrarch's emotional identification with a text written over 900 years previously is fuelled by the conviction that all can experience its account of the transformative power of reading. For Petrarch, reading serves the project of self-examination.[57]

Despite Petrarch's emotional identification with Augustine and his spiritual quest for meaning, his carefully elaborated account of the relationship between reading and the self is motivated by personal impulses. It is with Petrarch that the outline of the figure of the modern reader begins to takes shape. The manner in which Petrarch approached the *Confessions* was shaped by his heightened sense of individual self-consciousness. Brian Stock claims that Petrarch reinterpreted the *Confessions* to represent it as 'about the conflict within the self'. From this embryonic 'modernist' perspective, the act of reading was redirected towards the individual self. Reading itself emerged as its own reward.

The influence of Augustine on Petrarch's self-identity as reader acquired its most moving and emotionally charged expression in the Italian poet's famous account of his ascent of Mont Ventoux in April 1336. In his letter written around 1350, Petrarch dramatically intertwines his description of a physically arduous climb with the insights afforded him by his reading practice. Despite his longing for sight of the distant panorama, when he reached the top of the mountain his attention turned to a copy of Augustine's *Confessions*, which he always carried with him. He recalled how his eye fell on a passage where Augustine wrote that 'men go about to wonder at the heights of the mountains, and the mighty waves of the sea, and the wide sweep of rivers, and the circuit of the ocean, and the revolution of the stars, but themselves they consider not'. Reading these words convinced Petrarch to re-focus his energy from the beauty of the mountain to the locus of his emotional concern: 'I turned my inward eye upon myself.'[58]

When individuals began to turn their inward eye upon themselves, reading acquired a more individualistic and secular dimension. For Petrarch, reading became a 'means of meditating and engaging the world itself; it becomes, moreover, a way of knowing the self.'[59] Given its capacity to enlighten the self, reading served to confer a highly valued identity on those who participated in this spiritually and emotionally rewarding quest. That is why poets and philosophers begin to present themselves to the world through the figure of the reader. The self-drawn image of Petrarch on top of Mont Ventoux reading Augustine's *Confessions* idealizes the reader as a pilgrim on a voyage of self-discovery. For late medieval authors such as Chaucer, Christine de Pisan and Petrarch, the performance of reading represented a statement of identity and a claim to moral authority.

For Petrarch and other humanists, self-understanding demanded a withdrawal from the world. Reading in solitude bore some resemblance to the spiritual withdrawal associated with monastic life. However, his idea of withdrawal was very different to that of the ancient holy hermits living in isolation in the desert. An important shift has occurred and 'for the first time since antiquity, it is the secular library and not the monastic cell that is the image of this solitude'.[60]

As reading turns towards attending to the needs of the self and becomes implicated in the formation of self-identity, it acquires an increasingly psychological and cultural dimension. Now the Christian reader is also a cultural reader, for whom religious duties and individual salvation interweave with the emotionally demanding project of self-realization. The literary subjectivity that emerged regarded the reading of religious texts as its model for the transformative capacity of reading in a secular context.

READING WITH REASON

The religious and psychological impulses that encouraged the revelatory orientation towards reading evolved alongside attitudes that sought to demystify the meanings that could be uncovered from the text. In medieval approaches towards reading, the tension between interpretation and the literal meaning of the word tended to be resolved in favour of the former. The emphasis in early Christian reading on disclosing the spiritual rather than the literal meaning of the text was in part a reaction to the weight that the Jewish tradition attached to the 'letter of the law'. It was in this vein that the Apostle Paul's warning – 'the letter killeth but the spirit giveth life' (II Corinthians 3:6) – was interpreted by the faithful. Augustine reminded his readers that Ambrose often repeated Paul's warning, and added that when texts are read literally their spiritual meaning will be misunderstood.[61]

Until the late Middle Ages, religious reading tended to be focused on uncovering the meaning that lay behind the word. This lent the act of reading a quality that was not only spiritual but also mystical. The gift of being able to see through the letters of the text was regarded as an ideal to be achieved by the Christian reader. 'Blessed are the eyes which see divine spirit through the letter's veil,' noted Claudius, the Catholic Bishop of Turin.[62] David Olson's important study of the development of reading and writing suggests that for scholars in the early medieval era, 'the actual words or forms are merely the tip of the conceptual iceberg, the real meanings lying far beneath the surface and detectable only by internalization and meditation'.[63]

This highly subjective orientation towards the text indicated that meaning was as much an accomplishment of feeling and intuiting as it was of exercising the capacity to reason. It was the emotional impact of words and texts, and the insights and visions they stimulated, that provided some of the spiritual resources for interpretative reading. For such readers the literal meaning of a text was 'scarcely worth seeking since as far as Christians were concerned, it was the spiritual sense that mattered'.[64]

The unrestrained subjectivity and mysticism fostered by a spiritual interpretation and the tendency to devalue literal reading was never fully embraced by scholars. Augustine regarded the spiritual sense of the text as more significant than its literal one, but he nevertheless 'defended the notion that the spiritual sense was always based on the literal and that every text had a literal meaning'.[65] By the thirteenth century the tendency to take seriously the literal meaning of texts was reinforced by the demands of intellectual and cultural life in Europe. The rediscovery of Aristotle in the thirteenth century, and the idea of a law rooted in nature and comprehensible through reason, gained influence over European intellectual life. The development and appreciation of a more rigorous approach towards science and knowledge promoted a more scholarly attitude towards reading and interpretation.

The advocacy of a more literal approach to reading was associated with a growing interest in scholarly research. The Abbey of St Victor in Paris played a leading role in the elaboration of a more rigorous approach towards the interpretation of religious texts. Hugh of St Victor (d.1141) and his student Andrew of St Victor (d.1175) guided the abbey's scholarly orientation towards the reading of texts. Hugh insisted that meaning was settled 'not by prayer and meditation resulting in epiphany' but by an appeal to 'new sources of evidence based on textual, historical and geographical research'.[66]

Thomas Aquinas (1225–1274), the Italian Dominican theologian and philosopher who introduced Aristotle to Christian Europe, was also occupied with encouraging a more literal approach towards reading. He forcefully argued that the 'literal meaning' has to be taken seriously by the reader because it constituted the meaning that was intended by the writer. In his influential study *Summa Theologica* (1267), Aquinas insisted that the literal sense of a text is revealed logically prior to how it is interpreted. This was particularly the case in the domain of scientific knowledge where 'things are signified by words'.

Aquinas recognized that in the Holy Scriptures words could have different meaning (senses) and that words can signify other things. Nevertheless, he argued that the 'literal sense', which is what 'the author intends', provides the foundation for the spiritual understanding of the Bible, and that the inter-pretative reading of the Bible led to confusion and disorientation: 'Hence it is plain that nothing false can ever underlie the literal sense of Holy Writ.'[67]

David Olson believes that a major change occurred between the Middle Ages and the Renaissance, which can be interpreted as a 'matter of learning to read in a new way'. How reading was understood 'changed from that of "epiphanies" or revelations of meanings to the methodical recognition of authorial intentions'.[68] Aquinas drew a distinction between authorial intention – a legitimate object of scientific study – and the spiritual revelation, which was the focus of theology.

The tension between literal and interpretative reading is a recurring theme in Western culture. The attempt to understand the meaning of the text is always complicated by the fact that what matters is not simply what appears on the pages of the written text but also how this is taken by the reader. As one commentator on the subject has asserted, 'the history of reading may be seen, in part, as a series of attempts to recognise and cope with what is *not* represented in a script'.[69]

TAKING READING SERIOUSLY

It was during the Renaissance, which first emerged with full force in Florence in the fourteenth century, that reading acquired the attributes and virtues associated with it in its modern form. At this point in time the majority of Europeans were illiterate – but merchants, professionals and aristocrats perceived literacy as an important cultural marker of distinction. Literacy levels in Florence – estimated at between 24 and 35 per cent – were exceptionally high.[70]

Petrarch, who was described by Burckhardt as 'one of the first truly modern men', adopted an active approach towards reading. Until the fourteenth century, reading tended to be a passive activity involving readers looking for meaning – hidden or literal – in the text. Petrarch and other humanist readers regarded texts as material to be worked on, taken apart, re-appropriated through making notes, and compared with other texts. These were readers who regarded texts as materials to be used and assimilated through the application of reason. Sometimes readers felt an obligation to question the veracity of texts and to search for the original sources, which the books purported to express.

Humanist readers prided themselves on their independence of thought. They adopted an active approach to taking notes and were prepared to question the authenticity of the texts they consulted. They often ignored the venerated commentaries that were handed down to them from the Middle Ages and opted to search for the original texts. The historian Laura Amtower contrasts the Middle Ages, when the book 'represented an authority beyond challenge and beyond scrutiny', with the fourteenth and fifteenth centuries, when reading became humanized.[71] The more active and critical approach of humanists towards the text altered the relationship between the reader and the book.

The adoption of a more active approach towards texts did not mean readers had ceased to be subjected to their power. Rather, reading was perceived in a more multidimensional manner. Readers were beset by a variety of influences: they were expected to read more analytically and reasonably, but Renaissance culture also encouraged a rich subjective sensibility towards reading. Illustrations in manuscripts often depict people holding or gazing at the mystery of an open book. Such illustrations associate the act of reading with a spiritual or ethical significance, and the book serves as a medium through which a very personal act of revelation may occur.

Both the objective (reasoning) and the subjective (spiritual) sides of reading evolved alongside each other. Burckhardt's fascinating account of the historical emergence of the individual showed that Renaissance culture was hospitable to both an '*objective* treatment and consideration of the state' as well as to a '*subjective*' sensibility that celebrated the 'spiritual *individual*'. Niccolò Machiavelli's famous letter to his friend Francesco Vettori, written on 10 December 1513 whilst living in exile, demonstrates how for this realist and political theorist, reading provided a passage to an imaginary world. Machiavelli recounted how on his walks in the countryside he always had a book by one of the great poets under his arm, and noted that 'I read of their amorous passions and their loves, I remember my own and enjoy myself for this thinking.' But it was at night-time that his reading turned into a ritual that assisted him both to transcend the pain of his exile and to offer the insights that would culminate in the writing of some of his most important philosophical studies:

> When evening has come, I return and go into my study. At the door I take off my clothes of the day, covered with mud and mire, and I put on my regal and courtly garments; and decently reclothed, I enter the ancient courts of ancient men, where, received by them lovingly, I feed on the food that alone is mine and that I was born for. There I am not ashamed to speak with them and to ask them the reasons for their actions; and they in their humanity reply to me. And for the space of four hours I feel no boredom, I forget every pain, I do not fear poverty, death does not frighten me. I deliver myself entirely to them.[72]

Machiavelli's use of the metaphor of feeding on the 'food that alone is mine' highlights both the personal and physical attributes of his reading. At the same time this performance of reading helps Machiavelli to develop and clarify his ideas through turning his internal dialogue into a conversation with the past.

Machiavelli followed the path of the humanist thinkers who represent themselves as active readers. He explained that 'because Dante says that to have understood without retaining does not make knowledge, I have noted what capital I have made from their conversations'. The notes he took from his reading and his reflections on them led to what he called 'a little work' – one of the first works of modern political theory – that today is known as *The Prince*. Arguably, for Machiavelli reading constituted a lifeline that connected his existential quest for self-knowledge to the intellectual legacy of the past. It also provided aesthetic and spiritual nourishment for the sustenance of his subjectivity.

From a sociological point of view, the significant development from the fourteenth century onwards, and especially in the fifteenth and sixteenth centuries, was the emergence of the self-conscious reader. At this point, what readers do begins to become important, and this activity assumes an important role in the construction of the identity of the self.[73] The manuscripts of this era are 'inundated with images not just of books, but of people reading the books';[74] and images depict reading as an activity that possessed a profound spiritual and ethical significance. The portrait of a person reading, holding a book, or surrounded by manuscripts communicated the ideal of a culturally accomplished individual devoted to lofty moral sentiments.

The striking figure of the Florentine poetess Laura Battiferri (1523– 1584), who is painted as self-consciously displaying her opened manuscript of the sonnets of Petrarch, is meant to signal her symbolic connection with the famous humanist who lived two centuries previously. In this painting (c.1560) the artist Agnolo Bronzino represents the open book not as a prop but as an extension of Battiferri's personality.[75] Another painting by Bronzino, titled *Allegorical Portrait of Dante*, depicts the poet holding open a very large book of his *Paradiso*. The portrait is as much about the book as it is about Dante.[76]

Paintings of readers and their books served to reinforce the idealization of this activity as a unique aesthetic, spiritual and potentially revelatory experience. From the fourteenth century onwards, this experience was perceived through a heightened sense of individual subjectivity. Petrarch serves as an exemplar in this respect. For him 'reading becomes a means of authorizing the self, teaching the individual through his own empathetic response to react ethically to material dilemmas'.[77]

TO THE LOVE OF READING

Renaissance writers frequently portrayed themselves in their role as readers. This performance of veneration for the written text served to draw attention to the moral capacity for leading a disinterested and contemplative life. The German theologian Thomas à Kempis (1380–1471) exhorted his readers to revere books with a religious fervour: 'Take thou a book into thine hands as Simon the Just took the Child Jesus into his arms to carry Him and kiss Him.' He added that 'when thou hast finished reading, close the book and give thanks for every word out of the mouth of God; because in the Lord's field thou hast found a hidden treasure.'[78]

Petrarch's *The Life of Solitude* (1346), which outlined a confessional of his quest for self-realization, also celebrated books 'in whose substance and whose authors one has pleasant, unfailing companions'. These companions are 'ready at his bidding to go into public or return to his house'; they are ready to 'converse, to teach the secrets of nature, the memorable deeds of history, the rule of life and the contempt of death, moderation in prosperity, fortitude in adversity, equanimity and steadfastness in all our actions'.

Petrarch observed that the companionship offered by books does not exact a high material price, since 'they do not ask for food or drink and are content with scant raiment and a narrow portion of the house'. Yet 'they afford their hosts inestimable treasures of mind, spacious houses, brilliant attire, delightful entertainment, and most savoury food'.[79] The unique significance of reading is eloquently affirmed by Geoffrey Chaucer in his poem *The Legend of Good Women*, written in the 1380s:

> And as for me, though my learning's slight,
> In books for to read is my delight,
> And to them I give faith and full credence,
> And in my heart hold them in reverence
> So heartily that pleasure is there none.[80]

By the fourteenth century, declarations of love of books sometimes assumed a formulaic affectation amongst prose writers and poets.

Richard de Bury's essay *Philobiblion*, written in 1344 but not published until 1473, is said to be the 'earliest English treatise on the delights of literature'.[81] *Philobiblion* reads like a devotional celebration of the book.

De Bury, who served as the Bishop of Durham and travelled widely as a diplomat, personified the book-lover of the late Middle Ages. *Philobiblion* says very little about de Bury's actual experience of reading: his real interest is evidently the collection of books rather than their study. He was an enthusiastic *bibliophile* who was more concerned with encouraging scholarship than in pursuing it himself. There is something ravenous about de Bury's devotion to collecting books. His biographer William de Chambre claimed that books surrounded de Bury in all of his residences, and that 'so many books lay about his bed-chamber, that it was hardly possible to stand or move without treading upon them'.[82]

De Bury must have anticipated that his unrestrained appetite for collecting books could become a target of criticism, for he explicitly defends himself from the charge of excess in the Prologue to *Philobiblion*, declaring that his 'ecstatic love' for books led him to abandon 'all thoughts of other earthly things' so that he could give himself up 'to a passion for acquiring books'. The purpose of writing *Philobiblion* was to let posterity understand his intent and 'for ever stop the perverse tongues of gossipers'; he hoped that his account of his passion would 'clear the love we have had for books from the charge of excess'.[83]

De Bury's representation of books as the love-object of his semi-sacred passion resonated with a cultural imagination that regarded them as symbols of prestige and cultural status. By presenting its author as *the* lover of books, *Philobiblion* offers an early example of the eagerness with which some sought to cultivate a highly respected identity through their possession of, and relationship with, books.

Conspicuous reading and conspicuous book collecting expressed an aspiration to display proof of possessing highly sought cultural status and accomplishments. These activities served to distinguish the figure of the reader and the lover of books from the rest of society. The presentation of the self through the book was perceived as a medium through which individuals could elevate themselves and legitimize their persona with cultural capital. One study noted that 'merchants and other members of the middle strata must have been aware that bookishness was an effective way conspicuously to display the refinements increasingly associated with their noble social superiors and thus earn the kind of social approval that rarely derives from the possession of "naked" wealth'.[84]

Most historical accounts date the development of the narrative of the love of reading in Europe to the eighteenth century.[85] According to their analysis, the ascendancy of this narrative of the love of reading was preceded by the introduction of printing and the growth of literacy. No doubt the love of reading in the eighteenth century gained a powerful cultural affirmation from Europe's nobility and became an ideal that also influenced the popular imagination. However, the idealization of the book emerged over centuries of reflection about the meaning of reading.

As we have seen, since late antiquity reading had been perceived as a sacred or quasi-sacred activity that could serve as a prelude to revelation about the higher truths as well as about the self. From the thirteenth century onwards, reading was gradually regarded as a worthy cultural activity in its own right and became an object of identification, affection and sometimes love. By the time the figure of the individual reader emerged onto the stage of history, this activity had acquired significant cultural capital and possessed the capacity to confer a much-valued identity on the student of books.

It is important to situate the narrative of the love of reading in its rightful historical context. Until the eighteenth century, and arguably until later in the nineteenth century, the love of reading was integral to a cultural script internalized by a relatively small minority in Western society. At a time when the majority of people were not literate, the love of reading served as a distant ideal that could influence the emotional life of relatively small groups of aristocrats, educated professionals and prosperous merchants. But it was an ideal that became culturally significant during the Renaissance and in the centuries to follow. Even though for most literate people reading served a practical and utilitarian function, its idealization as a richly rewarding spiritual and enlightening experience had a significant presence in public life.

3

THE DEMOCRATIZATION OF READING AND THE PROLIFERATION OF READERS

The Protestant Reformation and the introduction of movable-type printing to Europe by Johannes Gutenberg around 1440 transformed the culture of reading. This chapter examines how a series of developments – the rise of the Reformation, the growth of literacy, a growing recognition of the authority of individual conscience, and the evolution of a new public of readers – interacted with the introduction of printing. The so-called 'printing revolution' turned the question of the role and status of the reader into a public issue, as the way in which readers reacted to the texts they consumed became a matter of concern to religious and political authorities. It also raised questions about the impact of the media that continue to be a focus of controversy to this day.

THE PROLIFERATION OF READERS

The dramatic increase in the numbers of literate individuals and the emergence of a mass reading public resulted from two historically momentous developments: the introduction of printing, which led to the print revolution; and the Protestant Reformation. During the centuries that followed, the printed text served as a medium through which Western societies gained information about everything that mattered. Cultural and political life was increasingly mediated through printed texts, and the collective views of readers were often represented as the new power of *public opinion*. The period from the Renaissance to the ascendancy of the Enlightenment constitutes a unique era in the history of reading. Whereas the previous chapter discussed the evolution of the idea that reading mattered, this chapter explores the era when *readers* began to feel that they constituted a powerful public force.

The flourishing of an intellectually dynamic cultural climate in the Renaissance stimulated the adoption and application of the technology of printing. An upsurge of interest in the reading of texts, old and new, created a demand for books. This intertwined with the eruption of the battle of ideas that was unleashed by the Reformation. As a technology, printing allowed the Reformation to expand beyond a small number of localities, which were under the direct influence of its prominent leaders, such as Martin Luther and John Calvin. Lutheranism has been frequently represented as the 'child of the printed book'.[1] Such statements underline 'the central role that books and printing played in this history-changing religious cultural creation'.[2]

Printed religious texts promoting the Protestant Reformation found a readership in virtually all the regions of Europe. This was 'the first movement of any kind, religious or secular, to use the new presses for overt propaganda and agitation against an established institution'.[3] The effectiveness of printed propaganda was recognized by the Catholic adherents of the Counter-Reformation, who in turn decided to harness the power of this new technology to challenge the influence of Protestant doctrine. In France and elsewhere, supporters of the Counter-Reformation flooded 'the market with an enormous quantity of religious tracts'.[4]

The close association between printing and the ferment in the domain of religion and culture ensured that this innovation became closely associated with the spread of controversial new ideas. The religious conflicts and the doctrinal disputes that enveloped sixteenth-century European society also reinforced and deepened its valuation of reading. In France and elsewhere, 'the history of mass literacy, like that of school, is rooted in the conflictual yet mutually-supportive confrontation between the Reformation and the Counter-Reformation'.[5] In the minds of many, reading was now perceived as a public duty.

During the centuries that followed the Reformation, reading and literacy were regarded as accomplishments that were synonymous with progress, cultural and scientific development, democracy and political emancipation. The formidable social forces unleashed by the expansion of literacy were recognized even by those who were determined to resist the pull of progressive ideas. The Catholic Church and the Counter-Reformation took very seriously the authority of the written text to influence readers, and sought to harness its influence to promote their own objectives. At the same time, the Catholic Church and Counter-Reformation attempted to censor and control publications considered dangerous or heretical, launching the Index of prohibited books in 1564 and seeking to regulate the reading of controversial books and translations of the Scriptures.[6]

The introduction of printing to Western Europe coincided with the emergence of other historically significant trends, whose cumulative outcome was the modernisation of culture and society. The growth of printing 'coincided with multiple challenges to received opinion' and saw the rise of 'new habits of critical thinking'.[7] The Renaissance era saw the growth of demand for books by groups of inquisitive readers who possessed an appetite both for classical texts and for new information.

The introduction of printing ensured that books would no longer be scarce commodities. Before printing, there were only a few thousand manuscript books in circulation in Europe. Collections were meagre and even the holdings of the library of the Vatican did not exceed 2,000 such texts.[8] Fifty years after printing was introduced, towards the end of the fifteenth century, the number of books had risen to more than 900,000. The technology of printing resonated with the spirit of times, and through its capacity to publish large numbers of books it served as a resource on which the unfolding cultural revolution of Europe could draw. As Richard Abel argues, the 'introduction of printed books in multiple copies' in the late fifteenth century led to a sudden 'upsurge in the generation and testing of ideas'.[9] Abel characterizes printing as 'an entirely novel and powerful knowledge-generating engine' – one that 'brought into being a new and previously unforeseen intellectual and ethical world'.[10]

Books were no longer published for a tiny minority of clerics, scholars and aristocrats. Until 1500, around 60 to 65 per cent of the books printed were in Latin; thirty years later, books printed in the vernacular far exceeded those in Latin.[11] The shift from Latin and Greek towards the vernacular had important cultural implications for the construction of national reader-ships. It meant that readers began to identify themselves with those who shared the same language and gradually a national readership was born. Books were also produced for different groups of readers and stimulated the development of 'new reading publics'.

The printing revolution helped democratize reading and contributed to the liberation of culture from 'the control of clerics and scribes'.[12] The historian Susan Achinstein observes that in England the 'spread of the printed word down the social scale is a remarkable story of the early modern period'.[13] Literacy was still very much a marker of people's position and status in the social hierarchy, and the labouring poor and agricultural workers had little opportunity to learn how to read. However, by the seventeenth century an estimated 30 per cent of adult males in England, and 60 per cent in London, could read. The rate of literacy was much lower for women. Although still far from achieving universal literacy, the dramatic increase in the size and influence of the reading public meant that society as a whole came under the sway of the culture of printing. Through printed notices and public readings, even non-literate people came under its influence. As one cynic put it in 1592, 'every red-nosed rhymester is an author, every drunken man's dream is a book'.[14]

New genres of publications were created to meet the demand for reading material from different layers of society, including those who possessed only a rudimentary level of literacy. According to Achinstein:

> For those with the barest literacy, there were ballads, newsbooks, singlesheet broadsides, chapbooks, jestbooks; a variety of religious materials – Bible stories, sermons, catechisms, primers, devotional works; and almanacs – by 1640, sales of almanacs had reached 400,000 copies, sufficient to supply one quarter of all households.[15]

The age of the mass media had arrived, and with it a golden age of litera-ture. This period saw the development of Baroque poetry, the growth of theatre, and the publication of some enduring European literary master-pieces. William Shakespeare published *Hamlet* in 1603 and *King Lear* in 1605. The production of these plays coincided with the publication of

Don Quixote (1605) by Miguel de Cervantes. In France, Pierre Corneille published *Le Cid* in 1637. Molière and Jean Racine wrote their great plays in the 1660s.

The expansion of publishing and literacy did not only mean that more people could have access to written culture. It also meant that the way people read and the meaning they attached to reading altered as well. The erosion of the literate elite's monopoly on written culture helped create a new public of readers who did not necessarily share the views of their superiors. The circulation of new publications conveying novel thoughts and ideals gained a powerful influence over public life, and fostered a climate of controversy and debate.

The English Civil War (1642–51) can be described as a war of words conducted through printed texts: in 1600 the English press produced 259 separate texts, but by 1642 the output of the press had increased to 2,968. This explosion of printed publications was fuelled by controversy and political polarization. All the parties to the Civil War recognized the power of the written texts and for the first time in English history, 'the press became the vehicle for open political conflict'.[16] The reader had become the target of what was sometimes described as the pamphlet war, and many supporters of the old order denounced the new public of readers who drew conclusions that were antithetical to their cause.

During the sixteenth and seventeenth centuries, reading became increasingly individualized. There was a perceptible shift from people reading aloud to members of their families, friends or groups and towards private and silent reading. Oral culture still played a significant role in the lives of working people, but its status had become marginalized. The new individualized forms of reading could be experienced as liberating, for within the confines of their private space individuals could freely peruse the pages of a book and come to their own interpretation and conclusions.

The active and critical approach towards reading that was adopted by humanist readers like Petrarch became more widely practised. Many historians claim that in the post-Gutenberg era readers adopted a more questioning approach and were less likely to defer to the authority of the text. The availability of a large number of different texts fostered a climate in which at least some readers began to question and reinterpret the content of texts.[17] Leading thinkers of the sixteenth and seventeenth centuries encouraged readers to adopt a pragmatic and active stance towards books. 'Read not to contradict and confute; nor to believe and take for granted; nor to find talk and discourse; but to weigh and consider', advised Francis Bacon.[18]

It soon became apparent that readers would not always interpret texts in line with official orthodoxy. It was impossible for either officialdom or the Church to control how the public of readers reacted to an essay. That is why the initial enthusiasm that Protestant theologians showed towards the mass reading of the Bible often gave way to hesitancy: they feared that individual readers of the Bible would travel down the road of heresy. The philosopher John Locke recognized this new state of affairs when he wrote that the printing of the Bible 'chopped and minced' and led to the 'splintering of faith and encouraged individual interpretation'. He noted that readers were no longer bringing 'their opinions to the sacred Scriptures, to be tried by that "infallible rule", instead they were bringing "the sacred Scripture" to their opinions, to bend it to them, to make as they can'.[19]

The printing revolution therefore saw the reconstitution of the reader as a more individualized, active and publicly relevant individual. Writers adapted their work to the new audience, expecting their readers to consume their texts in the privacy of their homes. Bacon celebrated studies because they offered a space for 'privateness and retiring'.[20] From the late Renaissance onwards, authors developed the strategy of attempting to influence their readership by directly appealing to idealized reader identities. The Preface often served as a device for drawing a connection with the reader, by appealing to 'the Christian Reader', 'the courteous Reader', 'the discreet Reader', the 'Impartial Reader', or the 'Knowing Reader'. In this way authors invited their readers to embrace an identity projected through the text, so as to guide their reading in a desirable direction.

One of the most audacious attempts to construct a new identity for the reader is to be found in the English poet John Milton's radical representation of England as a nation of critical readers. In *Areopagitica*, his important defence of press freedom, Milton self-consciously celebrated the capacity of readers to exercise rational judgement. Throughout this text the poet challenged the claim made by supporters of censorship that the public lacked the intellectual resources to evaluate the merits of what they read, joking that if 'English citizens were thought to be "slow and dull" then "the whiff of every new pamphlet would stagger them out of their catechism"'.[21]

Although Milton's sentiments were shared by only a relatively small minority, the question he posed about the capacity of the nation's readers for critical thought had become a focus of widespread concern.

THE REFORMATION – READING TURNED INWARDS

The idealization of the project of universal literacy has its origins in the cultural imagination of the Reformation. It represented literacy as a religious duty, and in many parts of Europe influenced by the Lutheran Church, families were charged with the responsibility for ensuring that their children could read the basic religious texts. Luther urged the establishment of 'compulsory education arguing that a neglect of learning would result in "divine wrath, inflation, the plague and syphilis, bloodthirsty tyrants, wars and revolutions, the whole country laid to waste by Turks and tartars, even the pope restored to power"'.[22]

The Reformation, with its emphasis on the religious obligation to read the Bible, made a tremendous contribution to the spread of literacy. As the Swedish historian Egil Johansson states, the Reformation 'stimulated the popularization of reading' in the vernacular since the 'individual was now expected to acquaint himself with the words of the Scriptures in his own native language'.[23] Harvey Graff argues that the Reformation 'represented the first great literacy campaign'.[24] In many cases the results of these campaigns were truly impressive. Sweden succeeded in attaining near-universal levels of literacy within a century of launching a drive to educate people to read the Scriptures. In the seventeenth century, the campaign promoted by the Lutheran Church resulted in a law that required everyone to learn how to read.

What may strike the contemporary observer as remarkable is that a near-universal level of literacy was achieved without the contribution of formal schooling. This literacy campaign relied on the vigilant supervision and enforcement of the law, which 'included regular personal examination by parish clergy' and support for home education.[25]

Studies of the literacy campaigns promoted by the Protestant Churches have pointed to the conservative and instrumental motives behind them.

Writing in this vein, Graff stated that the rationale for the Swedish literacy campaign begun by King Charles XI was 'conservative; piety, orderliness, and military preparedness were the major goals'.[26] But whatever the political and ideological forces that motivated the promotion of literacy, its consequence was radically to transform European culture. Through the encouragement of literacy, an ever-growing constituency of readers could directly participate in the great doctrinal controversies that engulfed early modern Europe.

No doubt Church-led literacy campaigns were inspired by the impulse of deepening the influence of doctrine on members of the religious community: hence the emphasis was on the teaching of reading, and writing was seen as not a skill that needed to be taught. But despite their limitations, the Reformation-inspired literacy campaigns represent a significant development in the education of what came to be known as the 'Western world'.

In effect the Reformation posited reading as a serious religious obligation for everyone. As François Furet and Mona Ozouf indicate, during the Middle Ages disputes over doctrine 'did not filter down' to the masses. In contrast, the Reformation:

> confronted everyone, even the ignorant, with the problem of doctrine. Everybody was henceforth obliged to turn to the Book in place of oral tradition; each individual's relationship with God ceased to be taken for granted … it now became a citizenship to which access was gained through reading, just at the very moment when the advent of printing was democratizing the book.[27]

Furet and Ozouf represent the synthesis of Gutenberg's printing press and Luther's celebration of the reading of the Scriptures as a transformative moment in European culture. They conclude that 'the modern world, which was the fruit of this meeting, henceforth belonged body and soul to the written word'.[28] This was an important moment of transition in the history of the reader. Until the sixteenth and early seventeenth centuries, reading was confined to a small minority of privileged and relatively privileged individuals. However, from this point onwards 'even popular culture was dominated by the written word'.[29]

The encouragement of mass reading raised questions about how to control the interpretation of the Bible. Luther argued that since the

'Scriptures are their own interpreters', readers could draw the correct interpretation on their own.[30] His opponents feared that if ordinary folk were
allowed to interpret the Scriptures and, worse still, were given access to
the vernacular Bible, the integrity of Christian doctrine would be compromised. Sir Thomas More (1478–1535), who was initially open to the idea
of translating the Bible into the vernacular, eventually became hostile to it
because he feared that it would 'stir up disputation rather than piety among
the common people'.[31]

More's premonition about the destabilizing potential of providing
people with access to the vernacular Bible proved prescient. Through
allowing lay readers direct access to the vernacular Bible, theological
interpretation and controversy gained a far wider public. The historian
Christopher Hill states that the reading of the Bible 'proved a time-bomb
which humbler Protestants used against their betters'.[32] The subversive
implications of individual readers interpreting the Scriptures in accordance
with their own inclinations became evident in the years leading up to the
outbreak of the English Civil War, where the difficulty in maintaining
theological and intellectual consensus was further complicated by the
growing availability of printed pamphlets and texts that passionately argued
a variety of sundry opinions. Hill claims that printing 'ruined Protestantism
as a single coherent creed, because the reading of books is even harder to
control than the reading of manuscripts'.[33]

From the outset of early modernity, the project of guiding or
controlling the activities of the reader was a regular topic of discussion.
Humanist and later religious thinkers regarded reading as a moral enterprise that required intellectual and spiritual guidance. Humanist thinkers
who associated reading with the cultivation of the mind and self were
nevertheless quite prescriptive in the advice they issued to readers. The
theologian and philosopher Desiderius Erasmus (1466–1536) warned
that since 'through reading mute letters are changed into *mores* (morals)
and state of mind, a naturally headstrong and violent boy might become
tyrannical if he should read about Achilles, Alexander the Great, Xerxes
or Julius Caesar without a preventative antidote'.[34] Some humanists offered
guidance that stressed the need to limit the number of books consulted,
whilst others insisted that readers, especially young ones, needed to
avoid the distracting influence of pamphlets and corrupting publications.

Attempts to control and guide the activities of the reader in the post-Reformation era could have only a limited impact on the growing numbers of individual consumers of the printed word. The era of a public of readers, whose reactions and interpretations of the printed text were guided by their individual conscience, had arrived. The sense of autonomy achieved through reading inevitably opened up the printed text to alternative interpretations. At its best 'Protestant humanism preached the need and fosters the skills for a new criticism – the capacity to hear and read, to compare and conflate, to discern and apply meaning'.[35]

The knowledge and insight attained through reading and guided by conscience was legitimized by the valuation of the authority of the self. This growing interest in the self was poignantly captured in John Bunyan's *The Pilgrim's Progress* (1678), which became one of the most widely read books, offering a powerful allegory that highlighted the theme of self-discovery and self-realization.

One of the unanticipated consequences of the growth of individualized reading was its contribution to the advent of the early modern sensibility of *self*. The connection between reading and an emerging sense of self-awareness was frequently echoed by major thinkers between the sixteenth and eighteenth centuries. The French philosopher Michel de Montaigne noted that reading and writing were a 'progress of self-knowledge' and invited his reader 'to constitute himself as a subject through the act of reading'.[36]

The consciousness of the self cultivated through reading was paralleled by a growing awareness of the conceptual distinction between subject and object and between the internal and external world. Elizabeth Eisenstein argues that the availability of printed books reinforced the consciousness of the private self: 'private life as well as public affairs underwent transformation', and 'indeed the new medium encouraged a sharper division between these two zones'.[37]

One individual who was intensely sensitive to the potentially disruptive consequences of autonomous readers was the English philosopher Thomas Hobbes. Hobbes denounced the celebration of individual conscience as a dangerous folly that helped precipitate the political crisis resulting in the outbreak of the English Civil War. In a chapter of *Leviathan* titled 'Of Those Things that Weaken or Tend to the Dissolution of a Commonwealth',

Hobbes pointed the finger of blame at those who claim that 'whatsoever a man does against his conscience is sin'.[38] In his list of the 'diseases of a Commonwealth' that he regarded as 'of the greatest and most present danger', Hobbes included the perils of reading the wrong sort of texts. Hobbes had no doubt that the reading of ancient classics led many readers towards republicanism, and blamed the reading of such books for the upheavals of the Civil War.

Hobbes regarded readers who formed their opinions in line with their individual conscience as a threat to the integrity of the social order; and the anxiety that he demonstrated towards the exercise of individual judgement through reading constitutes a recurring theme in the history of readers. Hobbes understood that the authorization of the individual conscience would have the effect of devaluing external authority. His fear – that once readers felt encouraged to cultivate their selves they were unlikely to acquiesce in the regulation of this activity – proved to be insightful. Despite the atmosphere of chaos and anarchy that surrounded the pamphlet wars before and during the Civil War, members of the reading public continued to construct their own, often dissenting, views and values.

THE CONSTITUTION OF A PUBLIC OF READERS

One of the most momentous outcomes of the printing revolution was the constitution of a public of readers. With the availability of large numbers of printed texts, the numbers of readers owning their own books expanded, and more and more readers consumed their books in silence and on their own. However, despite their physical isolation, these individuals were drawn together through their common experience of reading the influential texts of their era. Their responses to religious, political and literary texts really mattered.

The religious controversies conducted through printed texts between the proponents of the Reformation and their foes not only influenced, but also expanded, the public of readers. As Eisenstein points out, 'for the first time in human history a great reading public judged the validity of revolutionary ideas through a mass-medium which used the vernacular languages together with the arts of the journalist and the cartoonist'.[39]

The introduction of the printing press and the subsequent expansion of books, pamphlets and texts played a crucial role in the construction of a new, modernizing force that was characterized as public opinion.[40] The significance and power of opinion had been widely recognized since the sixteenth century: Shakespeare represented opinion as the 'mistress of success', and the French philosopher Blaise Pascal originated the often-cited aphorism that opinion was the 'queen of the world'. What would be described in the eighteenth century as an omnipotent force that no ruler could ignore evolved through the assimilation of printed publications into public life.

The American historical sociologist David Zaret offers a fascinating account of the transformative influence of printed text on public life in seventeenth-century England, arguing that the 'proliferation of printed political materials' was 'both a cause and consequence of the growing importance attached to appeals to public opinion'.[41] Printing extended the audience for political literature and in the process transformed the way in which public affairs were conducted. Zaret argues that prior to the English Revolution there was no space available for open public political debate outside Parliament, where debate was protected by secrecy norms whose violation was a punishable offence. Common people were excluded from political life, and even the procedures where grievances could be expressed through petitioning were subject to carefully regulated rules.

One of the dramatic, if unintended, consequences of the application of printing technology to petitioning was to alter the content and the meaning of this activity. The traditional norms of petitioning 'referred local grievances to central authority'. In contrast, printed petitions appealed to the authority of public opinion, and were as much directed at influencing the new public of readers as they were at addressing Parliament. Through the publicizing of a grievance, printed petitions challenged the prevailing secrecy norms and the usual restrictions on the conduct of public political life.[42]

The publishing of printed petitions was motivated by the presumption that there existed a body of readers who had at least the potential capability of evaluating reasoned arguments. As Zaret writes, the 'framers of petitions produced texts for an anonymous audience of readers, a public presumed not only to be capable of rational thought but also to possess moral competency for resolving rival political claims'.[43] The appeal to an anonymous audience of readers was also implicitly a call for this group to identify itself with the as yet unformed self-conscious public of readers. One reviewer of Zaret's work noted that 'the general, often unlearned, readership imagined for a printed pamphlet leads almost inevitably to appeals to a nominal "public opinion" in discourse'.[44]

In this way, printing assisted the transformation of a public of readers from an idea to an influential political force. As one historian of seventeenth-century England explained, 'printing could construct a cohesive body of readers who did not know each other personally, but who were linked by a common reforming mission'.[45]

A FIT READER?

As the experience of printed petitioning suggests, the identity of readers is not simply the accomplishment of an individual's interaction with the text. Attempts by authors to guide their audience's interpretation required that they imagined or visualized what their anonymous readers looked like and what made them tick. There were contrasting views about the capacity of readers and the influence that printed texts exercised on their outlook.

By the seventeenth century, reading was perceived as 'part of the solution or part of the problem, able either to promote understanding or to provoke sometimes dangerous passion'.[46] In England, Royalist polemicists and supporters of aristocratic privilege used the metaphor of Babel to denigrate the newly constituted public of readers. Their opponents provided a positive account of the moral status of the English public of readers. It was one that associated readership with moral virtues and the potential for playing an active democratizing role.

One of the most ambitious attempts to elevate the moral status of the reader and to promote that person's capacity for independent judgement was Milton's attempt to propagate his idealized concept of the Fit Reader. This radical supporter of the republican cause in the English Civil War 'deliberatively promoted the independence of the reader as the key to successful revolution'.[47] This theme was most famously captured in the epic poem *Paradise Lost* (1667), in which Milton expressed the hope that his poem will a 'fit audience find'. Written after the defeat of the 'Good Old Cause', Milton continued to invest his hope in the influence of the opinions and judgements expressed by his readers. He invited individual readers to become 'part of that "fit audience" by reading the poem'.[48]

Milton's attempt to cultivate the education of a nation of revolutionary readers was a prominent feature of his writing in the years leading up to and during the Civil War. The use of the term 'fit' to characterize his idealized version of readers suggested that Milton was challenging his audience to rise to the occasion and assert its capacity for judgement and independent thought. The hopes he invested in a select group of fit readers conveyed more than a hint of an elitist vision of those elected above the rest. In *Paradise Lost*, Milton is resigned to the fact that a fit audience for his poem will consist of a 'few'. But despite the defeat of his political views, Milton did not waver in his conviction that an independent-minded readership was both possible and necessary for underwriting a free and just society.

One of the most eloquent statements about the reader's capacity to exercise rational judgement is to be found in *Areopagitica*. Written in 1644 at the height of the Civil War, Milton's stirring pamphlet was directed at the Licensing Order of 1643, which was passed by Parliament in order to force authors to possess a licence issued by the government before their text could be published. *Areopagitica* took issue with the system of censorship on the grounds that it undermined the conduct of a free, open and rational debate that constituted the foundation of a just society.

For Milton, a public of readers who were prepared to exercise their independent judgement and weigh up the issues of the day formed the most reliable guardians of a just society. As one commentator notes, *Areopagitica* posits a public sphere in which political discussions need to be 'carried on before a broad reading public'. Milton's arguments about the critical role of the public of readers are grounded in 'his conception of virtue, which melds the religious notion of conscience with a classical sense of civic duty'.[49]

The argument for the freedom of the press advanced in *Areopagitica* indicts censorship as an insult to the intelligence of English readers. Milton maintained that English citizens possessed the moral and intellectual resources to resist the evils that might be propagated in bad books. His interpretation of the Scriptures led him to the conclusion: 'Read any books what ever come to thy hands, for thou art sufficient both to judge aright, and to examine each matter.'[50] Milton had great trust in his fit readers and their ability to withstand the corrupting influence of pernicious books.

The extraordinary confidence that Milton attached to the capacity of readers to make reasoned judgements was coupled with his conviction that what caused evil was not the content and arguments contained in the printed text, but the failure to challenge and discredit misguided and corrupt arguments. He criticized the impulse to censor on the grounds that 'knowledge cannot defile, nor consequently the books, if the will and conscience be not defiled'. Readers of virtue would not be corrupted by what they read. Indeed, Milton went so far as to argue that independent readers could actually learn from having to engage with misguided ideas:

> Bad meats will scarce breed good nourishment in the healthiest concoction; but herein the difference is of bad books, that they to a discreet and judicious Reader serve in many respects to discover, to confute, to forewarn and to illustrate.[51]

Even a bad book could serve the purpose of assisting judicious readers to clarify their ideas. From this perspective, censorship not only belittled the capacity of readers but also prevented society from learning valuable lessons through its reaction to 'bad' books.

Milton's critique of censorship should be interpreted as an attack on the widely held sentiment that regarded readers as dull, gullible and incapable of exercising judicious judgement. He castigated supporters of censorship for regarding the readers of England as 'not thought fit to be turn'd loose to three sheets of paper without a licencer'.[52] Milton's association of good reading with the development of the habit of exercising the liberty of conscience, and educating the public to make the kind of judgements that underpin the free exercise of choice, represent an early formulation of modern ideals associated with critical Enlightenment thinking.

Milton perceived reading as an active and challenging process through which individuals are put to the test and forced to think for themselves. Fit readers are those who are trained by 'trial of books' – 'books that try him, and he that tries books'.[53] For Milton the act of reading was directly associated with that of reasoning, which in turn was intimately intermeshed with that of judging. In one of the most memorable passages of *Areopagitica*, Milton reminds his audience that when God gave Adam reason, 'he gave him freedom to choose, for reason is but choosing'.[54] His insistence that 'reason is but choosing' provided a powerful argument for the freedom of the press and also offered a moral case for uncensored reading, where the opinion of a public of readers is posited as the source of moral authority. As Achinstein notes, 'in his arguments for a free press, Milton turned authority from external officials and state monitors to the consciences of judging readers, whom he deemed responsible enough to decide matters themselves'.[55]

It is worth noting that Milton was writing at a time when reading was often associated with radical values. John Lilburne (1614–1657), a radical leader of Levellers, could draw on his own experience to vindicate the idealization of readers as the nation's jury. Lilburne, who was tried for treason in 1649, appealed to the conscience of the jurors sitting in the courtroom, and to the consternation of his judges he was found not guilty. He was tried again in 1653, and turned this event into a campaign to mobilize public opinion. In his pamphlet *A Jury-man's Judgment*, Lilburne cast his readership into the role of a national jury that possessed the moral authority to determine his fate and sought to mobilize support for his radical stance. Once again he was acquitted. According to one account, 'with the trial of John Lilburne, the metaphor of trial and judgment by readers had become a political reality, and conscience was the ground on which citizens were to render judgment.'[56]

Milton's wholehearted faith in the reader's power of conscience emerged at a dramatic historical moment when it seemed that the cumulative influence of the technology of printing, radical political and religious movements, and the ascendancy of the new power of public opinion, could lead to a more enlightened and freer society. The emergence of a reading public had a significant influence on strengthening hopes in a radical future. Seventeenth-century England experienced a massive increase in the quantity of printed material, with the number of pamphlets published increasing from 22 in 1640 to 1,966 in 1642. An influential section of the wider public became involved in political life and the authority of the old order came under severe criticism.

The growth of literacy itself had a dramatically radicalizing impact on public affairs. The support that Puritanism gave readers to exercise their individual conscience was perceived by those in authority at the time as a threat to order. This was a dangerous development, writes Lawrence Stone, because 'it aroused expectations of political and religious participation and exposed large numbers of humble people to the heady egalitarian wine of the New Testament'.[57] One account of this historical moment describes the 'extraordinary period of freedom as authority withered away'.[58] A study of the politics of reading in this era states: 'The Civil War, as we know was preceded by a print war, a war of words – and one that the king lost.'[59] The aggregate effect of the widening of debate among the new constituency of readers was the entry of common people into the public life of the nation.[60]

What proved to be significant about Milton's conceptualization of the role of reading was that his model of an independent-minded rational reader stirred the imagination of successive generations of enlightened thinkers and educators. The ideal of a public sphere informed by the discussion and judgement of fit readers – though rarely realized in practice – inspired many of the individuals associated with the eighteenth-century Enlightenment. The German philosopher Immanuel Kant's famous statement '*sapere aude*' – dare to know – extolled the virtues of the Miltonian ideal of having the courage to think for oneself. At least in principle, the Enlightenment asserted that the spread of knowledge through reading would assist the progressive reform of the world. Despite periodic setbacks to Enlightenment thinking, the Miltonian association of an independent-thinking reading public with the moral virtues and values of freedom continues to influence the outlook of democratic educators to this day.

Milton was lucky to escape the death penalty after the restoration of the monarchy and the defeat of his cause in 1660. However, his books were condemned to death – burned in bonfires throughout that summer and autumn.[61] Thus the seventeenth-century book-burners demonstrated Milton's point: that it was the fear of allowing readers to read freely that underpinned intolerance towards free speech.

APPREHENSIONS ABOUT THE REVOLUTION IN PRINTING

Milton and Hobbes personify the two poles of the continuum of reaction to the consequences of the printing revolution. Although much of the philosophical and official discourse on the impact of reading in the early modern era was focused on concerns about religious dissidence and political subversion, apprehensions were also frequently raised about the potentially corrosive influence of reading on the intellectual, moral and psychological life of society.

So while Hobbes took exception to wayward readers extracting radical ideas from the classics, religious polemicists were preoccupied with the corrupting influence of popular literature on the morals of the public. From a Protestant perspective, reading constituted a religious duty, not a medium for distraction and entertainment. Puritans in particular regarded such literature as an object of moral condemnation, and from the sixteenth century onwards 'ceaselessly denounced the reading of books which offered no more than idle entertainment'.[62]

While many welcomed the contribution that printing made to the quality of intellectual and cultural life, there were also frequent allusions to a multiplicity of fears about the unanticipated consequences of this new technology. The printing press had established the technological infrastructure for the first mass medium – the mass production of printed texts.

From the outset, anxieties were raised about what would in the twentieth century be labelled as the *media effect* of printing. The invention of the printing press was criticized for a bewildering variety of distressing conditions, and reading – especially the uncontrolled consumption of mass-produced printed texts – was regularly associated with a variety of personal, social and cultural threats. The narrative of pathology, which has attached itself to every new media – novels, newspapers, radio, cinema, television, computer games, the internet – had already surfaced in the sixteenth century and evolved into an influential discourse in the seventeenth and eighteenth centuries.

Apprehensions about the impact of printing, like subsequent expressions of unease about new media, were shaped by the disquiet that accompanies a sense of uncertainty about the consequences of a new medium of communication. In the seventeenth century the scepticism, disbelief and mistrust that the public expressed towards official statements and versions of events were frequently coupled with the excesses of the pamphleteering press. The inevitable sense of disorientation that prevailed in a dramatically changing world was often attributed to the conflicting and exaggerated information fed to readers by periodicals and pamphlets.[63]

Competing claims and arguments promoted in diverse publications were held responsible for inflating differences between competing views.

One study of the concerns provoked by news-related publications argues that in the seventeenth century many 'blamed the invention of the printing press, or of the movable type, for the dissemination of news and pamphlets that threatened to promote sedition and to corrupt morals and good understanding'.[64] The blaming of the messenger for unwelcome news – which is an enduring theme in criticisms of technologies of mass communication – was often an unconscious response to the premonition that the effect of such news on readers was both unpredictable and potentially corrupting.

The Catholic Church most vividly expressed hostility towards the printed text and a mood of disquiet towards its deleterious impact on readers. Church censors referred to the printed book as 'the silent heretic'.[65] However, unease about mass access to unprocessed information and conflicting views and opinions was not confined to the Church. Secular authority and elite opinion varied from ambiguity to outright alarm about the unpredictable outcome of mass reading. In England the widening of access to printed news publications was a constant source of alarm. As one study noted, 'news was the object of a series of anxieties' about 'popular access to privileged matters of state'.[66]

Almost every theme that recurs in the panic-like reactions surrounding a new medium can already be detected in the reactions provoked by the invention of printing. As we note in the next chapter, an assortment of physical and psychological harms were associated with reading in the early modern era. Printing was attacked for making reading far too easy and for undermining people's capacity to read challenging texts, and pamphlets were criticized for distracting people from reading longer and more rewarding texts. In 1647 a pamphleteer described his times as 'this lazy age, wherein no man will take paines to read a Pamphlet that containes above a sheet'. Another writer and Catholic theologian, Thomas Wright, wrote of 'these lightweight and ungodly books' that were an 'impediment to virtue'.[67]

The oft-repeated refrain, 'too much information', directed at digital technology today has a history that goes back to ancient times. However, the powerful forces of communication unleashed through the application of the technology of printing fostered a climate in which the proliferation of new publications would be perceived as a new era of information overload. This was the first, and arguably the most significant, media revolution.

Anxieties about the effects of new media are historically specific and mediated through the cultural norms of the times. In the sixteenth and seventeenth centuries, the moral corruption of readers through consuming heretical vernacular texts was a common complaint. The growth in the number and diversity of publications raised questions about readers' capacity to discriminate between authoritative and valuable books and those that had little intellectual or moral worth. Educators were at a loss as to how to guide the reading of their students. The educator Juan Luis Vives lamented, 'if all knowledge is from books', the 'number of books is now grown so immense' that 'not a few are seized by terror, and a hatred of study, when they confront in every discipline the volumes requiring inexhaustible labour to read'.[68] Educators and their pupils had become conscious of the fact that it was not possible to read everything. With so many books to choose from, directing or guiding the choices and activities of readers became a major enterprise.

Ann Blair's study *Too Much to Know: Managing Scholarly Information before the Modern Age* finds that 'by the mid-sixteenth century comments on the impact of printing often focused on the vast and cumulative increase in the numbers of books being written and printed'.[69] Complaints about an abundance of books or information were often sublimated expressions of the unease associated with the contestation of the intellectual authority of texts. With authors offering competing versions and interpretations of the 'truth', readers were confronted with the constant challenge to decide what was and was not worth reading. Blair explains that the 'problem of overabundance involved not only too many books, but books ferrying too many different, new and conflicting authorities, opinions, and experiences'. For European societies, which were 'founded on the mastery of long-lived textual traditions' in both philosophy and religion, the 'printing of new and newly recovered opinions posed with renewed intensity the difficult problem of reconciling conflicting authorities'.[70]

Concern about information overload assumed that readers were likely to be overwhelmed by the sheer scale of the challenge of dealing with the vast number of publications confronting them. The presumption that readers would struggle with the excessive number of books, and the concomitant explosion of knowledge, provided the justification for the production of reading guides. Indeed, it seemed that very few authors could resist the temptation of offering reading guidance to their public. The frustration expressed by authors about the abundance of useless publications sometimes served as a prelude to justifying their own books; and a whole industry of guidebooks for readers, catalogues and works of reference evolved to help readers make the right choices about their reading material. In the seventeenth century, 'warnings about overabundance became more alarmist than ever, typically in service of a solution offered by their author', writes Blair.[71] Warnings about information overload often served the objective of publicity: gaining the attention of potential customers and readers.

Apprehensions about the deleterious consequences of the mushrooming of new publications were not simply a direct response to the effects of this technology. Complaints about the overabundance of books pre-dated printing – in a different guise they had recurred in response to other media. In the early modern era, scaremongering about the overabundance of books served to justify a variety of initiatives designed to control, regulate or at least guide the activity of a new public of readers.

Most important thinkers of the seventeenth and eighteenth centuries had something to say about what constituted a model of good reading. The advice offered by well-known philosophical figures such as Erasmus or Kant was to tell readers to read with discrimination and to avoid the temptation of reading too much. The aim of such advice was to insulate readers from the temptations offered by the mass media of printed publishing and to cultivate an identity for readers that was harmonious with the outlook of their authors. In a roundabout way, warnings about the media effects of printing also constituted an invitation to adopt a distinct reader-identity.

DEBATE ON THE PRINTING REVOLUTION

Since the publication in 1979 of Elizabeth Eisenstein's magisterial study, *The Printing Revolution as an Agent of Change*, there has been a strong reaction against the historic significance that she and others attached to the positive transformative consequences of this technology. Many historians and commentators have argued that the invention of printing does not represent a qualitative revolutionary break with the past, and that its consequences have been overrated. Criticisms of the idea of a printing revolution are often coupled with a pessimistic assessment of the cultural significance of literacy and the tendency to devalue its positive and progressive contribution to human progress and development. As we argue in Chapter 8, since the 1960s there has been a discernible tendency to devalue literacy, and this sentiment influences the attitudes towards its progressive historical significance.

Arguments directed at the notion of a printing revolution are often influenced by a wider current tendency to downgrade the civilizing force of the intellectual movements associated with the Renaissance, Reformation and Enlightenment. Scepticism about the achievements of these momentous events extends to criticisms of positive and progressive accounts of the modernizing and democratizing legacy of literacy and reading.

Martyn Lyons's account of what he calls 'The Gutenberg myth' argues that 'the modern ideology of the print revolution is chiefly a construction of the French Revolution and the nineteenth century'.[72] He argues that for French revolutionaries, 'print production separated modern thinking from the barbaric, "Gothic" and irrational Middle Ages'. According to this idea, the celebration of printing is indissolubly linked to a self-serving ideology that attaches printing to the spread of reading, the diffusion of the philosophy of the Enlightenment, the French Revolution, and civilization and progress.

The main argument put forward by critics of the so-called Gutenberg myth is to dismiss it as a fallacy of 'The Eureka Factor'; to argue that the speed of dissemination of the printed text has been overestimated and to call into question its impact on the lives of people, society and culture.[73] Critics of the notion of a printing revolution transform Gutenberg from a humanist hero into an unremarkable artisan. According to Lyons, Gutenberg was a 'jobbing printer for the ecclesiastical authorities', whose main customer was the Catholic Church.[74]

However, as we noted earlier in this chapter, the printing revolution was not a stand-alone event. It represented, at least in part, a response to the epistemological and intellectual demands of the era. The potential power of printing was realized through the rise of the Reformation and the flourishing of this media was linked to the growth in economic activity and prosperity in parts of western Europe. Critics of the 'Eureka Factor' are tilting at windmills, since most serious historical accounts acknowledge that the complex dynamic that followed the application of printing cannot be reduced to the role of a heroic genius.

The notion of a printing revolution does not rely on the claim that it transformed the world overnight. Historical change is always realized through competing and countervailing trends of development, and the transformative impact on reading is no exception to this rule. No doubt the impact of printing, the spread of literacy, and their influence on everyday life was uneven. The reaction to printing was highly variable, and the responses of Hobbes and Milton represented the two opposite poles.

Lyons represents the culture surrounding printing as one dominated by elite privilege. So while printing helped transform 'the life of the scholar', it 'did not touch the lives of ordinary people who remained part of a rich oral culture', and 'it barely touched the mass of the people of Europe who remained for the most part illiterate'.[75] The claim that printing did not 'touch' the mass of Europeans overlooks the powerful indirect influence that new opportunities for reading texts had on society. Universal literacy lay in the future, but the growing public of readers played a powerful role in cultural and political life. That publications were now written for the common people indicated that reading had transcended the confines of a privileged audience of scholars, aristocrats and prosperous merchants. By the sixteenth century, 'people knew that they lived in a "printing age"'.[76]

It is not surprising that the legacy of the printing revolution was only comprehended after the event. People who directly experience technological innovation and change do not always grasp its significance; only a small minority possessing unusual sensitivity and foresight tend to intuit its impact. As Richard Abel notes, 'the blind Milton, in his defense of the freedom of the press at the time of the English Revolution, was one of the few to recognize the crucial importance of the immense and powerful knowledge engine of cultural generation that Gutenberg brought into being'.[77]

More recently, criticism of the notion of a printing revolution has referred to the experience of subsequent innovations in media communication. Often advances in electronic communication and digital technology are used as a vantage point to belittle the significance and legacy of printing. Adrian Johns has criticized Eisenstein's work by arguing that the experience of the twentieth and twenty-first centuries sheds new light on the rise of earlier technologies of communication. Reading history backwards, Johns claims that the 'advent of electronic communications is inevitably casting the era of print in a new light'.[78] The recurrence of technological innovation in media technology is used as an argument for casting doubt on the singular achievements claimed by printing. Eisenstein has responded by asserting that Johns's assessment of the past is influenced by the values of his time: his version of the 'printing revolution' is 'infected by a (postmodern?) sensibility that seems to be tone deaf to the music of the time'.[79]

The current fashion for diminishing the historical significance of the printing revolution echoes a wider cultural reaction against the ideals of the European Enlightenment. Optimistic accounts of the achievements of the humanist Renaissance and the Enlightenment today tend to be belittled as naive and ideological, and the faith that was once invested in the power of reading often gives way to the association of literacy with elite ideologies of control and discrimination.[80] Yet as the example of Milton indicates, the printing revolution brought the Word down from heaven to earth.

The desacralization of the printed word should be seen as a symptom of the normalization and, by implication, the democratization of reading. But as we discuss in the next chapter, no sooner was the printed word desacralized than the act of reading became an object of secular reverence.

4

THE ENLIGHTENMENT: A READER'S REVOLUTION

Paradoxically, reading was culturally consecrated by the very same secular imagination that shaped the Enlightenment. During the eighteenth century the ideal of 'love of reading' gained cultural validation to the point that some commentators and officials began to worry about the potential consequences of what they described as a reading mania. Reading was still mainly perceived as a means to an end – principally the attainment of knowledge – but it was also frequently depicted as an activity that was valuable, even pleasurable, in its own right. The Enlightenment and its core constituency of an active and influential public sphere of readers attached an unprecedented positive significance to reading, and the democratization of reading gained significant momentum.

The eighteenth century has been frequently characterized as an Age of Improvement.[1] A sermon by the Scottish author and theologian Hugh Blair (1718–1800), 'On the Improvement of Time', identified improvement as the distinguishing feature of the age.[2] Reading was regarded as one of the principal media through which the ideal of self-improvement ought to be pursued:[3] reading was now directly associated with enlightenment and emancipation, and a growing section of society was committed to gaining access to the knowledge and the cultural capital associated with it. Although the era of universal education was still far off, new schools were founded to service the growing demand for reading and knowledge. However, with such a high value attached to reading, it was inevitable that this activity invited scrutiny, regulation and even censorship.

THE READING REVOLUTION

During the eighteenth century it appeared to many European commentators that everyone was engaged in reading. They pointed to a veritable media explosion of new innovative publications such as novels and newspapers. Between 1789 and 1799 more than 2,000 new newspapers were published in Paris, and newspaper circulation in England increased eightfold between 1712 and 1757. The commercialization of publishing, which first took off in England, created a literary market that serviced the expanding number of readers. Stimulating a demand for books, 'advertising also fostered a taste for novelty', notes an account of the newly constituted reading public.[4] This media revolution was facilitated during the second half of the century with the rise of lending libraries and reading clubs.

The spread of literacy in eighteenth-century Europe meant that the habit of reading was gradually integrated into popular culture. The aspiration by members of the urban masses to master the art of reading was widely recognized. In London, one publisher – Charles Ackers – 'printed and sold 27,500 copies of one English grammar alone between 1730 and 1758'.[5] A new European reading public consisting of artisans, tradespeople, yeomen and women provided a market for a range of popular publications such chapbooks, almanacs and news periodicals. Attitudes characterized by the phrase a 'culture of improvement' inter-twined with the celebration of knowledge and encouraged a disposition towards reading.[6] The emergence of a new constituency of plebeian readers indicated that the cultural veneration of reading had succeeded in tempting a wider public to embrace literacy.

In recent decades, the question of what the public read has become a focus of debate for historians interested in the relationship between literacy and the French Revolution and the Enlightenment. How much did the essays and books written by Enlightenment philosophers such as Diderot, Montesquieu and Voltaire shape the mentality of the public on the eve of the French Revolution? Scholars inspired by the work of the historian Robert Darnton often make a distinction between the serious publications associated with the 'High Enlightenment' and 'low-life literature'. It is frequently suggested that publications conveying gossip and salacious accounts of the scandalous behaviour of leading members of the *ancien régime* were far more influential than those authored by leading figures associated with the Enlightenment.[7] The ongoing debate around what members of the French public read, which publications influenced them the most, and what the relationship was between the ideas they gained from their reading and the French Revolution, is unlikely to be resolved because of the difficulty of retrospectively capturing the internal thoughts of a heterogeneous group of French readers.

Often the contrast that historians draw between 'high' and 'low' literature is far too unmediated, since it is unlikely that these different genres of publications inhabited a parallel universe. Despite their differences, dissimilar genres of literature appealing to a diverse group of readers were still subject to the influence of the cultural climate associated with an era described as the Age of Reason or the Age of Improvement. Indeed the very proliferation of so-called low-life literature was made possible by the spirit of criticism that was endorsed and communicated by the thinkers of the Enlightenment.

The literary public sphere was dominated by the rising middle class, which gained confidence from its intellectual and cultural accomplishments. The Irish writer and co-founder of *The Spectator*, Richard Steele (1671–1729), echoed the spirit of the times when he stated that 'Reading is to the mind what exercise is to the body.' The ability to read was now deemed to be an essential skill for the modern individual, and the acquisition of a facility for literate reflection was perceived as a precious form of cultural capital.

For the new middle classes the acquisition of this type of cultural capital provided a resource for contesting the moral authority of the old order. As Peter Hohendahl remarks: 'Literature served the emancipation movement of the middle class as an instrument to gain self-esteem and to articulate its human demands against the absolutist state and hierarchical society.'[8] Other groups, too, looked upon reading as a key that opened the door to new opportunities, knowledge and adventure.

The eighteenth-century literary public played a significant role in the constitution of European public opinion. How people read, the conclusions they drew from the written text, and the judgements they made about the affairs of the day were perceived as increasingly decisive in the forging of public opinion. Recognition of the power of this new force overlapped with the decline in moral and intellectual authority of the absolutist monarchical order. The new media of printed books and pamphlets circulated ideas and values that questioned the old order – and sometimes explicitly, when an author such as Thomas Paine raised issues that were direct challenges.

More importantly, reading provided an opportunity for the reader to react, assimilate and engage with ideas that occasionally led towards unexpected conclusions. Reading allowed individuals to develop thoughts in accordance with their own personal circumstances and inclinations, which sometimes did not conform to official sentiment – creating tension between the authority of the self and the prevailing moral order.

In this Age of Reason the exercise of the power of rationality was connected to the exercise of judgement gained through reading. As Eagleton notes, 'every judgement is designed to be directed toward a public; communication with the reader is an integral part of the system.' He adds that 'Through its relationship with the reading public, critical reflection loses its private character'.[9] The emergence of a literary public and the crystallization of the new ideal of the authority of public opinion were the products of the intellectual temper of the time, which insisted that people must be 'taught to rely on evidence provided by nature or reason, not by arguments supplied by tradition'.[10]

The spirit of criticism and openness to new ideas strengthened the conviction that the opinion of the reading public counted for far more than the wisdom of the past. The quest for new knowledge promoted the publication of new philosophical, political and scientific ideas, and writers appealed to 'public opinion' for affirmation. At times it seemed as if every writer was speaking on behalf of the public of readers. As one study of public opinion in pre-revolutionary France observes, 'suddenly it designated a new source of authority, the supreme tribunal to which the absolute monarchy, no less than its critics was compelled to appeal'.[11] The legitimation of public opinion directly boosted the cultural status of readers, particularly those who were part of the literary public. Jürgen Habermas's seminal study *The Structural Transformation of the Public Sphere* advanced the compelling argument that bourgeois public opinion developed through literature. It was through literary culture that the middle class sought to construct its distinct independent identity.[12]

Authors and public figures adopted the tactic of claiming to speak on behalf of public opinion in order to assert their literary or political authority. Such claims implicitly questioned the foundations on which traditional authority rested. Thus the appeal to public opinion meant 'going over the heads of duly constituted authorities and appealing to the good sense of a reading public at large'.[13]

Historians and literary theorists are often at odds about how to capture the relationship between different groups of readers and the idea of a literary public and public opinion. From a sociological perspective, it is useful to perceive the eighteenth-century reading revolution as manifesting both a tendency towards the creation of a unified literary public and a propensity for constructing different classes of readers. On the one hand, one study suggests that 'by the end of the eighteenth century, not only professionals from the middle classes, but merchants, tradesmen, women from the aristocracy to the peasantry, urban servants, and even laborers, were reading'. But the reading public was subject to important socio-economic and cultural distinctions: not all readers could afford books, and 'being able to read meant more than mere capability'. It required access to books, the availability of resources and leisure time, and ties to a 'social context in which what you read mattered'.[14]

Many recent studies emphasize the restricted and exclusive manner in which leading Enlightenment critics of the old order conceived the ideal of the literary public. They 'held that only those with sufficient level of culture and education could make reliable aesthetic judgments', and the 'public invoked by Enlightenment critics was in the end a relatively restricted stratum of educated propertied, principally bourgeois and noble readers'.[15] By all accounts the polarization of this part of society increased in the late eighteenth century, when sections of the middle-class literary public began to feel uneasy with the growing influence of a reading culture that appealed to the masses. Indeed it is at this point that the moral contrast between high and mass, or popular, culture also took hold.

Although the public invoked by leading figures of the Enlightenment was a restricted one, these figures expressed their views in a language that appealed to wider universal norms, such as rationality and progress. Joseph Addison (1672–1719), the essayist and co-founder of *The Spectator*, claimed that if the great philosophers of antiquity had had access to the printing press, they would have used it to 'diffuse good sense through the Bulk of People'. Addison was proud of *The Spectator*'s role in diffusing knowledge to the wider public, writing in 1711 that 'it was said of Socrates, that he brought philosophy down from heaven to inhabit among men: and I shall be ambitious to have it said of me, that I brought philosophy out of closets, libraries, schools and colleges to dwell in clubs and assemblies, at tea tables and in coffee houses'.[16]

The clientele of clubs and coffee-houses were members of the rising middle class, who represented a relatively small minority of England's population. But once the project of promoting knowledge to a wider public was recognized as a route for improving society, it became an ambition that would transcend the barriers of class and create a demand for education amongst an ever-widening section of society.

At times, the ideal of a 'nation of readers' corresponded to powerful cultural trends. Certainly in the early decades of the eighteenth century, reading provided a medium through which a relatively consensual public sphere was constructed in England. Alexandre Beljame's study of English public life in that century stresses the integrative function of reading, positing a culture of reading that was allied to a critical but rational and polite exchange of opinions amongst the literate public. He observes that 'readers were no longer segregated into watertight compartments of Puritan and Cavalier, Court and City, the metropolis and province: *all the English were now readers*'.[17] This is an extravagant assessment of the size and homogeneity of the public of readers: Terry Eagleton points out that at this point in time the influential *Spectator* sold about 3,000 copies in a population of five and a half million, and that the book-buying public could be 'measured in tens of thousands, and a great many of the English were illiterate or barely literate'.[18]

Not every literate individual was integrated into the public sphere of educated critical and rational readers. Those who were could participate in a network that was distinguished by its 'consensual character'. During the early decades of the eighteenth century, the 'body of opinions concerning things cultural was relatively homogeneous. This was due to the cohesiveness of the English educated classes that produced and circulated those opinions.'[19] For a variety of reasons, this cohesive literary public disintegrated towards the end of the century. The fragmentation of the literary public did not simply develop along lines of class; it was also influenced by the aesthetic or practical interests that motivated readers. Different attitudes towards reading encouraged the development of distinctive reading publics as well as the moral psychological distancing of 'high' and 'low' literary culture.

How people read and what they read became increasingly intertwined with the construction of an individual's identity. Not all forms of reading were equally valued and certainly not everyone who could decode written texts was considered a literate reader. 'There were naturally many degrees of literacy in eighteenth-century England, but there was an obvious distinction between those who could "read" in a sense of the term inseparable from the ideological notions of gentility and those who could not,' notes Eagleton.[20]

Distinction between different types of readers played a significant role in how individuals presented themselves and served to discriminate between different types of identities. The prestige and status attached to literacy meant that differences between types of readers had weighty social consequences, blending in with social and class attitudes. The construction of the identity of an accomplished reader was often accompanied by the impulse to aesthetically delegitimize the literacy skills of others. The German poet and philosopher Friedrich Schiller (1759–1805) personified the trend towards perceiving the mass culture of reading as a threat. He had previously declared that the 'public is everything to me, my school, my school, my sovereign, my trusted friend'. Towards the end of his life, however, Schiller insisted that the 'only reasonable relationship with the public that one cannot regret is war'.[21]

The fragmentation of the eighteenth-century public sphere, which coincided 'with the disintegration of the reading public into the educated minority and the masses', provided the foundation for the subsequent debate about the role and influence of publishing and the capacity of readers. Once the fragmentation of the reading public became consolidated, it was easy to overlook or forget that previously considerable hopes had been invested in the positive and progressive role of the nation of readers. Such hopes in the power of reason, education and reading were integral to the Enlightenment mentality, and important gains were made, especially in England and in America, in the spread of education and literacy.

Samuel Johnson wrote of the year 1748 as a 'time when so many schemes of education have been projected' and 'so many schools opened for general knowledge, and so many lectures in particular sciences attended'. He also pointed to a significant development: knowledge was now circulating in 'common talk'.[22] The diffusion of reading had reached the point where by 1775 there was an 'abundance of good literature for children'. Women played a growing role in the literary public and Johnson exclaimed in 1778 that 'all our ladies read now; which is a great extension'.[23] The falling cost of printed publications also helped to widen the reading public. The growth of relatively cheap commercial libraries provided the lower orders access to books and 'made possible the penetration of ideas expressed in print to both genders and to social strata well outside the elites'.[24]

EXTENSIVE READING

The enthusiasm for reading was already evident in the early part of the eighteenth century in England. France soon followed suit, and Germany after that. By the turn of the nineteenth century, reading had become a popular pastime to the point that frequent concerns were raised about what was initially diagnosed as the 'reading bug' but which 'quickly escalated into a collective "reading epidemic"'.[25]

The German historian Rolf Engelsing has characterized the popularization of reading and the expanding influence of the literary public in the eighteenth century as a Reading Revolution.[26] Engelsing concludes from his study of middle-class readers in the city of Bremen that between the middle and the end of the century, the way people read and experienced this activity underwent a qualitative change: from *intensive* to *extensive* reading.

Engelsing argues that until the second half of the eighteenth century, most literate people read intensively: reading and re-reading a small number of books. Most people owned or had access to a relatively limited number of texts, which were read over and over again often in silence but also aloud to members of a household or to friends. The classic book of the era of intensive reading was the Bible, which, as Engelsing points out, was read by some people as many as fifty times. Intensive reading had a devotional and reflective quality: 'As a devotional tool, moreover, reading was often a household and not a solitary activity', and it often involved the head of household reading out loud to its members.[27] Oral reading tended to be slow and deliberate, which reinforced its intensive character. This type of reading is often portrayed as the moral opposite to the subsequent tendency to consume books and hurry from one text to the next.

The availability of a large number of relatively affordable publications created the foundation for the adoption of reading practices that changed people's intensive focus on a small number of texts. Readers began to consult a range of different books on the same topic and sometimes compared and evaluated the merits of the arguments they contained. According to one account, 'in the course of the eighteenth century, the act of reading became more mobile and variegated'.[28]

Attitudes towards reading were also shaped by important developments in the cultural attitudes of the eighteenth century. The literate public was still engaged in the reading of religious books, but increasingly they were drawn to secular books. Readers who were interested in gaining new knowledge, improving themselves, or searching for escapism or entertainment could now have access to a great range of different texts. The availability of mass-produced texts coincided with the production of new literary genres and of publications that were written for the moment and not for intensive study.

Engelsing has singled out newspapers and other types of periodical literature as literary innovations that fostered a turn away from intensive towards extensive reading. Newspapers were not published to be intensively studied but to provide information that would soon be outdated, and invited the public to engage with its topical diversity through extensive reading.[29] The attitude of an individual who is hungry for new information and the latest news, and jumps from one text to another, is characteristic of the extensive reader.

Extensive reading is associated with a shift away from contemplative reading to a more pragmatic and selective dipping in and out of different texts in a quest for information and knowledge – a move towards a distinct secular approach to the consumption of texts. Critics of extensive reading were concerned about the unpredictable and potentially disturbing effects that unrestrained and uncontrolled reading would have on impressionable members of the public, especially on those who indulged in novels.

The adoption of extensive reading practices was in part influenced by the changing perception of time. Greater access to printed publications coincided with the increased availability of clocks and watches. A heightened sense of temporality and of historical consciousness promoted the feeling that time was a precious commodity. One manifestation of this sentiment was that as readers became more conscious of time, they did not feel compelled to read books from beginning to end. Dr Johnson expressed this sentiment when he asked 'a book may be good for nothing; or there may be only one thing in it worth knowing; are we to read it all through?' In short, Johnson, whose *Dictionary* made a major contribution to defining elements of the English language, personified the extensive reader.[30]

The findings of a study by the American historian David Hall support the arguments advanced by Engelsing. Hall notes that by the eighteenth century, the New England communities that he studied appeared to have abandoned their dependence on a small number of devotional texts and began to consume the new genres of publications – newspapers, periodicals, novels – that were available through a flourishing literary market. Hall argues that the transformation of the practice of reading from intensive to extensive was bound up with important wider cultural changes that were enveloping Western societies. Some of these changes involved the 'transition from the religious to the secular' and from 'self-sufficiency to the "commercial", or from scarcity to abundance in material goods'.[31]

Although there is an ongoing debate about the significance of the shift from intensive to extensive reading, there is little doubt that one consequence of the mechanization of printing was that it provided readers with a greater choice of publications, and that in response to this opportunity people often altered their reading habits.[32] Of course, people did not entirely stop reading intensively in the eighteenth century. Engelsing warns against dramatizing the scale and speed of the reading revolution: by all accounts there was a coexistence between different reading practices, and even oral reading survived until well into the nineteenth century.

But important elements of continuity with the reading habits of the past should not be allowed to obscure the qualitative change in attitudes that occurred over this time. As Jane Curran remarks in her study of the

German Enlightenment, 'a revolution in reading habits certainly occurred during the course of the seventeenth and eighteenth centuries'. She points out that this revolution was not simply an outcome of the greater availability of published texts: it was also a consequence of cultural change, which expressed itself through the 'spread of the love of reading'.[33]

The spread of the 'love of reading' and its idealization is testimony to an important development in the history of the reader. In previous centuries, reading was associated with powerful moral, spiritual and passionate qualities; but as Ilkka Mäkinen explains, the discourse of Love of Reading fully crystallized in the eighteenth century, and was perceptible in many societies of Europe:

> Reading behaviour and motivation is described in the major European languages with phrases and terms that refer to crystallised concepts. The most frequently used terms that refer to a spontaneous motivation for reading are in French, *goût de la lecture*; in English, the love of reading, the habit of reading, the desire to read; and in German, *Leselust*.[34]

The intensification of the discourse of love of reading can be misunderstood as simply a new version of the old form of intensive reading. But the very fact that reading was now also intimately associated with pleasure and emotion indicated that the moral restraints that were integral to devotional reading had lost much of their force. As Mäkinen indicates, the reading revolution can 'also be called a revolution of the love of reading'.[35]

From the standpoint of long-term historical development, one of the most notable features of the transformation in the habits of eighteenth-century readers was the appearance of a variety of different reading practices. Readers could now choose between different practices, and they often opted to adopt different approaches to different types of texts. The availability of various genres of publications and the pluralization of reading practices altered both the meaning and activity of reading. The availability of a diverse narrative of reading invited debate about what constituted good and bad reading, raised apprehensions about the likely trajectory of the reading public, and led to the proliferation of initiatives that were designed to guide or regulate this activity.

As we observed in our discussion of the cultural contradictions of reading, fear and suspicion of this activity tend to coexist with more positive accounts. The alarmist discourse on reading was influential in the eighteenth century, but it was not the dominant discourse. Mäkinen offers a balanced assessment of the competing accounts of the likely impact made by books on readers:

> Discourses not only reflect reality, but also mould it. How reading is talked about does make a difference. If the discourse employs terms with negative connotations, such as reading rage (*rage de lire*, *Lesewut*), the picture that is produced of reading is more negative than when neutral or positive terms, such as the love of reading, *goût de la lecture*, *Leselust*, are used. Even though in the history of reading it is the agitated and dramatic testimonies that are often used to illustrate the situation, the picture that my research presents is more balanced and positive.[36]

The alarmist terms that were used to warn about the risks of reading are founded on the premise that reading constituted a very attractive, powerful and transformative experience. Many moralists interpreted the evident demand for more and more reading material – especially novels – as a threat, whereas others regarded this need as proof that the hunger for education meant human progress was possible.

In one sense, the moralists were right. The effect and trajectory of the love of reading is unpredictable. As a motivating factor, the love of reading is expressed through personal desire and does not require institutional approval or any prior external form of legitimation. Socrates was by no means the last person to worry about the random effects of the written text on readers: establishing rules for reading and guiding readers became an integral feature of the literary culture of the Enlightenment.

RULES OF READING

Eighteenth-century writers and commentators were constantly attempting to influence the taste and practices of the reading public. The novelist Samuel Richardson (1689–1761) frequently revised his novels to guide his readers with the right moral message. He even published an abbreviated digest of his 18 volumes of collected fiction, titled 'Moral and Instructive Sentiments, Maxims, Cautions, and Reflexions', which provided a summary of his statements for those who did not have time to read his novels.[37] Writers and publishers assumed the position of moral arbiters, charged with the responsibility of directing the tastes and reading habits of their public. 'To enliven morality with wit – to temper wit with morality' was how Addison characterized the mission of his publications.[38]

The moral guidance offered by writers and publishers sought to socialize readers into literary practices favoured by the Establishment. It had as its premise the belief that there were good and bad reading practices. Bad reading practices were often depicted as aimless, irresponsible, and involved the unrestrained consumption of easily digestible texts. The reading of novels was regularly singled out as a practice likely to tempt and disorient the misguided reader.

The contrast drawn between the serious reader of books and the practitioner of casual skimming always contained the implication of a moral judgement. The principal value advocated by the rules of reading upheld during the Enlightenment was to practise this activity purposefully and for instruction. One of the most influential guides to reading in the English language was John Locke's *New Method of a Common-Place Book*.[39] Originally published in French in 1676, *New Method* was released in English for the first time in 1706. Locke advocated the taking and careful organization of notes so that the reader could cultivate critical and orderly thinking. His approach proved to be extremely popular and the *New Method* underwent numerous editions and adaptations.

Locke's guidebook promoted values that were consistent with the norms of reading held by the literary establishment, and all readers, not just scholars and 'men of letters', were presumed to benefit from it. In an updated version of this guide released in 1770, the editor John Bell stated:

> It is not solely for the Divine, the Lawyer, the Poet, Philosopher, or Historian, that this publication is calculated: by these its uses are experimentally known and universally admitted. It is for the use and emolument of the man of business as well as of letters; for men of fashion and fortune as well as of study; for the Traveler, The Trader, and in short for all those who would form a system of useful and agreeable knowledge, in a manner peculiar to themselves, while they are following their accustomed pursuits, either of profit or pleasure.[40]

Locke's guide to reading proved to be so successful because it resonated with the spirit of self-improvement that prevailed at the time.

Samuel Johnson stood out as one of the leading representatives of the Lockean self-critical and orderly reader. Dr Johnson was a purposeful consumer of the printed text – he believed that 'true' reading was reading for instruction and not for entertainment. At the same time he was sufficiently pragmatic to realize that the commercialization of publishing had led to the rise of forms of reading that were different to his own. Johnson made a conceptual distinction between four different types of reading: study, perusal, mere reading, and curious reading.[41] Although he was concerned about the distracted and purposeless forms of curious reading invited by novels, he also understood that a balance had to be established between the different ways of engaging with publications, and recognized that people needed to read in accordance with their inclination if they were to benefit from the experience. Dr Johnson explained that what 'we read with inclination makes a much stronger impression' than what's read 'without inclination'.[42]

Dr Johnson, along with other writers, grasped that the public were not simply the passive recipients of authorial advice: they possessed influence and authority, and authors needed their support.[43] That was one reason why 'throughout the eighteenth century, authors battled to control literary values', and to 'control the contemporary passion for the new print by emphasising the necessity of discriminating between the good and the merely new'.[44] The emphasis on discrimination and guidelines about the publications to be avoided were informed by writers' version of the ideal cultured reader. Warnings about the 'unstable and morally feckless figure' served to consolidate the moral contrast with the 'worthy reading public'.[45]

The moralization of reading practices helped establish a literary hierarchy of standards – but what influence the different literary guidelines and warnings had on the behaviour and practice of the reading public is far from evident. People interpreted such guidelines in accordance with their inclinations, and could forget them when absorbed in the act of reading.

As Patrick Bratlinger wrote in a different context, 'no sociology of readers can fathom exactly how actual readers responded to texts'.[46] What went on in the minds of eighteenth-century individual readers cannot be accurately captured by the external observer. As Janice Radway noted, 'reading is not eating', and despite the claims of many early modern commentators, readers do not internalize what they consume in a way that is analogous to the digesting of food.[47] So the interpretative strategy and literary values advocated by the cultural elites do not directly influence the target of their advice. During the course of consuming texts, people react to, absorb, ignore or sometimes reject the rules of reading that prevail.

The rules of reading offered by the literary elite provided a narrative through which an idealized culture of reading was constructed. The distinctions drawn between good and bad reading tacitly distinguished between different types of readers. Reading the right way and the right literature represented a claim to cultural authority. In this way, its principal outcome was to consolidate a self-consciousness of what was expected of the superior reader. The problem that the rules of reading did not resolve was to anticipate how readers would react to different types of publication, and what would be the social and political outcome of mass reading.

A PRECARIOUS BALANCE

During the Enlightenment, views about the role and likely evolution of the reading public were mixed and often contradictory, and conflicting interpretations of the influence of reading on the mass of readers existed alongside one another. The Enlightenment fostered a climate that encouraged education and reading, where reading was represented as liberating and served as a medium for gaining cultural status and authority. Reinhard Wittmann argues:

> Reading acquired an emancipatory function and became a productive social force: it expanded one's moral and intellectual horizon. It made of the reader a useful member of society, allowed him to command his range of duties better, and was even an aid to his social career. The printed word became the vehicle of bourgeois culture.[48]

Today, when there is widespread intellectual scepticism towards the legacy of the Enlightenment, it is important to recall that one of the important achievements of this movement was to create an extraordinary appetite for reading and studying. This meant that there was a close interest in the activities of individuals and groups of readers. Reading subversive publications may have served the cause of the French Revolution, but after this event there were numerous attempts to regulate unruly readers – particularly those who read for themselves 'to the discomfort of the leading political and social classes, who were increasingly determined to oppose this intellectual emancipation'.[49]

Almost all the leading philosophers and commentators had contradictory attitudes towards the reader. They invariably acclaimed those who read to study or to improve themselves while decrying unruly or indiscriminate reading practices. Even the relatively liberal movement associated with Immanuel Kant in Germany opted to embrace a 'progressive' critique of reading for entertainment. Such critics justified their stance on the grounds that the unrestrained reading of escapist literature compromised the 'emancipatory promise of the Enlightenment'.[50] Samuel Johnson exemplified the mild schizophrenia that leading thinkers had towards the public of readers. In *A Dictionary of the English Language* (1755) he stated 'I rejoice to concur with the common reader'. At the same time he was on occasions quite dismissive of the 'multitude', who were allegedly possessed by 'passions or corrupted by prejudices'.[51]

On balance, Dr Johnson was an enthusiastic advocate of the virtues of reading and held up the 'man of letters' as his model reader. At a time when some cultural pessimists sought to revive or endorse the merits of oral dialogue and conversation, Johnson adopted a distinctly literary approach.[52] His essay 'On Studies' (1753) directly confronted the views of those who asserted that a life of reading obstructed 'the powers of nature, to cultivate memory at the expense of judgment, and to bury reason under the chaos of indigested learning'. Johnson's view was strikingly anti-Socratic – and not just in relation to the claim that reading weakened the power of memory.

Johnson argued that oral arguments often encourage participants to perform for effect and score cheap points at the expense of clarifying arguments. Against the confusion produced through rhetorical sophistry, Johnson upheld the superiority of conclusions reached through reading:

> To fix the thoughts by writing, and subject them to frequent examinations and reviews, is the best method of enabling the mind to detect its own sophisms, and keep it on guard against the fallacies which it practises on others: in conversation we naturally diffuse our thoughts, and in writing we contract them; method is the excellence of writing, and unconstraint the grace of conversation.[53]

Johnson was convinced that reading provided the medium through which the quest for the truth had to be conducted. His affirmation of the written word, and his lack of enthusiasm for the spoken word, was connected to a wider eighteenth-century debate about the respective merits of these two modes of communication.

Many of the Enlightenment's leading figures believed that the reasoned resolution of controversy was far more likely to be realized through the reading of written texts than through oral debate. In France the 'replacement of political oratory by printed discourse was welcomed by French Academicians, who associated demagoguery and religious "enthusiasm" with speech and thoughtful appraisal with reading'.[54] The French political philosopher the Marquis de Condorcet (1743–1794), who was arguably the most eloquent advocate of the Enlightenment and the idea of progress, believed that reading would lead to the triumph of reason and science. Condorcet identified the spoken word with 'passion and prejudice, the written word with science and progress'.[55]

At times, reflection about the respective merits of oral dialogue and the written text made explicit reference to the old debates on this issue in the ancient world. In his statement upon being admitted to the French Academy, the statesman Malesherbes (1721–1794) described his 'enlightened century' as a 'century when each citizen can speak to the entire nation by means of a printing press'. He added that 'men of letters' are 'in the midst of a dispersed public' not unlike the assemblies addressed by the 'orators of Rome and Athens'.[56] Speaking to the Academy in 1771, the philologist Abbé Arnaud (1721–1784) 'contrasted zealous Athenians, who were swayed by demagogues with tranquil French subject who were readers'. He asked 'what were the Athenians, a people of listeners and zealots' and 'what are we today, a people of tranquil and intelligent readers'.[57]

Supporters of the French Revolution in 1789 celebrated the power of reading. Many of France's leading radical thinkers assumed that the printing press was directly responsible for the outbreak of the Revolution. The reading and re-reading of thoughts fixed by writing around this seminal moment provided scope for the careful evaluation of arguments. The written text invited the exercise of rationality and encouraged readers to re-examine arguments rather than come to intemperate and hasty conclusions. In contrast, speech was associated with the provocation of an immediate, emotionally charged response to current events, leading to confusion and disorder. Optimism regarding the capacity of enlightened intellectuals to influence the reading public through a rational exchange of opinion was not confined to France. In his first major statement on the subject, the Scottish philosopher David Hume (1711–1776) indicated that he was far more concerned with the rhetorical power of the charismatic leader of the mob than with individuals indulging in the private act of reading. Hume's 1741 essay 'Of the Liberty of the Press' justified his liberal attitude towards the freedom to publish by drawing a contrast with ancient times, declaring that 'we need not dread from this liberty any such ill consequences as followed from the harangues of popular demagogues of ATHENS and tribunes of ROME'.[58]

It was the power of speech and ideas spread through rumour that Hume found disquieting. Although he had no more sympathy than Greek demagogues for the multitude, he assumed that their 'natural' deference to the authority of their rational intellectual superiors could exercise influence over the direction of their thinking, and that individuals reading in private would be well insulated from the influence of subversive political forces:

> A man reads a book or pamphlet alone and coolly. There is none present from whom he can catch passion by contagion ... The liberty of the press, therefore, however abused, can scarce ever excite popular tumults ... the *people* are no such dangerous monster as they have been represented, and in every respect better to guide them, like rational creatures, than to lead or drive them like brute beasts.[59]

This image of a solitary individual sitting at a desk, silently reflecting on passages from written manuscripts, is one that endures to this day. The private study filled with books has often served as a symbol of the endless possibilities opened up to the reader. It speaks to a sensibility that sometimes regards reading as an escape from the hurly-burly of everyday life, and one that invites the individual to embark on a very private journey.

Hume's essay, influenced by this image, expressed the hope that this solitary reader would turn out to be a much-needed counterweight to the arbitrary power of the monarch. According to one account, Hume at this point in time regarded 'the press as an alarm system' that could protect the nation against the exercise of arbitrary power.[60] He allowed himself to imagine that the readers of a free press would develop their capacity to deliberate on public issues, and therefore would 'be with greater difficulty seduced by every idle rumour and popular clamour'.[61]

Hume's advocacy of the virtues of press freedom did not endure for long. Serious urban unrest in England during the 1760s and 1770s, particularly the Wilkes riots in London, destroyed his confidence in the capacity of the reading public to respond with detachment and rationality to the intemperate ideas communicated by the press. When Hume republished his essay in 1770, he removed his positive endorsement of the free press that featured in his original concluding paragraph and added a final sentence that decried it as 'one of the evils' with which the nation had to live.[62] This radical change of attitude was motivated by the presentiment that the reading public could be easily manipulated by dangerous ideas.

Apprehension regarding the destabilizing power of the printed word on the 'uneducated', 'semi-educated' or 'unruly' reader gained momentum during the aftermath of the French Revolution. Whereas hostility towards 'unruly' reading had previously targeted its negative impact on the moral outlook and behaviour of the individual reader, after the Revolution concern was directed at the political threat posed by subversive literature. In England the apparent success of Thomas Paine's mass best-seller *The Rights of Man* (1791) provoked a sense of insecurity and fear among the ruling elites who feared the pamphlet's influence on readers. The religious propagandist Hannah More (1745–1833), who pioneered the production of cheap moral booklets to neutralize the effect of 'immoral' and subversive literature, warned that 'every new reader in the lower ranks of society meant another potential victim of radical contagion'.[63]

For many public figures of a conservative disposition, the French Revolution confirmed their pre-existing anxieties about the effects of the written word on the behaviour of readers from the lower order. In the conservative imagination of the late eighteenth and early nineteenth centuries, the Enlightenment's men of letters mutated into the demagogues of Athens and Rome. Reading was recast as a channel for the circulation of sedition. The old anxieties raised by Thomas Hobbes about subversive intellectuals reappeared in an alarmist form with the conservative political philosopher Edmund Burke (1729–1797), whose *Reflections on the*

Revolution in France denounced the conspiracy of the men of letters for discrediting the old order and for manipulating their readership. Burke had no doubt that writers possessed a formidable power of demagoguery. He noted that when they act as a group, writers have 'great influence on the public mind', and Burke criticized them for flattering the masses while vilifying the nobility and the Church. 'They became a sort of demagogues,' he asserted.[64]

Burke believed that far from promoting a considered and rational public culture, the printed text could silently manipulate the emotions of the individual reader. His analysis of events in France led him to the conclusion, as Eisenstein noted, that 'As silent medium, it was more subversive than oratory'.[65] In one respect, Burke's pathology of the mass media shared the conviction of many of his opponents, which was that one of the main causes of the French Revolution was the impact of the printed text on the public of readers. The radical critics of the old order in England attributed tremendous power to the capacity of printed publications to alter the world. William Godwin wrote in 1793 that 'few engines can be more powerful, and at the same time more salutary in their tendency than literature'.[66]

It was in the decades following the French Revolution that ideological polarization acquired the form of Left versus Right. These ideological differences were also reflected through antithetical views about the role of reading and education. The British reform movement of the late eighteenth century saw reading and literature as the 'single most effective means by which people could engage each other in rational debate'.[67] Their conservative opponents regarded the spread of reading as a potential threat to the stability of society.

But by the turn of the nineteenth century, reading had become so widespread that even the opponents of mass reading and education knew that they had to live with this uncomfortable fact of life. The question confronting supporters of the old order was, 'How could the people's reading be made safe?' Evangelical Christians sought to 'substitute good reading for bad' and 'conducted an endless war against "dangerous" publications which the common reader not only considered harmless but, more importantly, truly enjoyed'.[68] That even those who were uncomfortable with the outlook of the Enlightenment and the rise of mass publishing were forced to accommodate to these developments is testimony to the cultural authority of the reading public. From both a political and a cultural point of view, the question was now how to live with the reader.

FROM POLITICS TO MORALITY

Changing attitudes towards the role of the new medium of printing and its impact on readers were informed by the new social and political landscape of the late eighteenth century. The perceptible shift from a relatively optimistic to a more pessimistic sensibility regarding the role of publishing was correlated to growing social and political polarization and the eruption of a mood of political crisis.

One reason why concerns of the elites about the new media were relatively restrained up to that point was because the press tended not to question the normative foundation of moral authority that prevailed. It was only when publications became more heterogeneous and society more polarized that anxieties about the moral effects crystallized. The commercialization of publishing alongside the growth of the reading public raised queries about the likely impact of the new media. Inevitably religious campaigners were most sensitive to the risks posed to the moral order by a more diverse and commercially driven media. By the end of the eighteenth century, religious groups began both to fear the press but also look to it as a potential instrument for containing immorality.

Religious activists, particularly those of an evangelical disposition, were at the forefront of those challenging the supposedly morally corrupting influence of cheap, mass-produced, popular publications. Hannah More's well-known campaign to produce Cheap Repository Tracts sought to combat 'vulgar and licentious publications'. These were the Chapbooks, cheap publications produced for the mass market,[69] which More and her colleagues perceived as a direct threat to the Christian middle-class moral order. One study draws the following contrast between the rival publications: 'chapbooks presented a fictional world where the sexual and social order was fluid and changeable; the evangelicals countered by calling for strict domestic hierarchies and the grateful acceptance of one's social place'.[70]

Mass literacy was now interpreted as a problem inviting moral regulation. Moreover, in the context of the American and French

Revolutions the popular press was often depicted as 'both poisoned and poisonous'.[71] It was at this point in time that panics about the media began to acquire the characteristics that in the twentieth century would come to be labelled as moral panics.

The conservative reaction to the upheavals of the late eighteenth century could not undermine the optimistic message of the Enlightenment regarding the dramatic transformative power of literacy. Throughout the Western world, reading had become closely coupled with enlightenment and knowledge. The democratizing potential of literacy was widely recognized and reading was the medium through which intellectual emancipation and social progress could be realized. Those who felt uncomfortable with the democratization of literacy knew that the age of mass reading had arrived and that all that could be done was to carefully police and minimize its disruptive effects. Illiteracy was now equated with ignorance and super-stition: not even those who were suspicious of the reading of the masses could advocate a return to the pre-literate epoch.

These attitudes clearly influenced the manner in which people were socialized and encouraged to adopt sound reading practices. Exhortations about reading had considerable force, but they had to compete with the gradual privatization of moral life, which was guided by individual disposi-tions rather than duty to an outside authority. So although official concerns about the dangers of reading were continually circulated through different publications, an ever-increasing number of people opted to ignore their advice, and carried on reading.

The coexistence of the reading revolution and the narrative of the love of reading with moral anxieties about reading only serves to highlight the contradictory cultural narrative that surrounds the role of literacy. In the next chapter we explore some of the forms in which reading has become subject to the imperative of moralization, and we will discuss in detail the first mass media-focused moral panic. This surrounded the publication of *The Sorrows of Young Werther* – an epistolary novel written by Johann Wolfgang von Goethe.

5

THE WERTHER EFFECT: THE READER AT RISK

The sublimation of moral anxieties through concerns about the impact of reading served as the foundation for the first mass media-led moral panics. This chapter explores the moral disquiet provoked by the publication of Goethe's novel *The Sorrows of Young Werther* in 1774. The intensity of the reaction against this novel on both sides of the Atlantic was influenced by a growing tendency to perceive reading as one of the principal sources of threats to the moral order.

Historically, moral anxiety about reading had been directed at religious heresy. From the eighteenth century onwards, there was a perceptible shift towards targeting subversion, followed later by an intense focus on the corrupting influence of obscenity. This shift in concerns was in part a reaction to the perception that traditional moral authority had lost its influence over the emerging modern world, leading to a belief that reading would 'have a profound impact on the mental and moral character of the individual and by extension of his society'.[1] The question of the long-term consequences of reading on an ever expanding public of readers was continually debated during deliberations on the cultural and political life of the nineteenth century.

Although the meaning of subversion today conveys the idea of a threat to political institutions and order, historically it also alluded to moral perils to the soul. From the fifteenth century onwards, subversion was also associated with 'spiritual corruption or downfall' and 'moral destruction'.[2] Edmund Burke's hostility to writers and the democratization of reading was animated by his fear for the traditional moral order. Burke regarded the growth of the mass media and the expansion of the reading public as a problem because 'learning' was no longer situated in its 'proper place', and warned that the refusal of readers to defer to their traditional superiors would have a corrupting effect on society, as the 'natural protectors and guardians' of the community 'will be cast into the mire, and trodden down under the hoofs of a swinish multitude'.[3]

Burke's censure of the 'swinish multitude' expressed in a vivid form the hierarchical attitudes of defenders of the traditional order. The influence of reading on the moral order was an issue of serious interest not only to Burkean traditionalists but to all sections of the cultural, economic and political elites. General unease with the direction of a changing world was expressed through a language of suspicion and foreboding about the influence of the mass media – particularly the press and popular literature – on its readership. These anxieties intensified with the growing commercialization of publishing and the availability of cheaply produced texts in the nineteenth century.

CHANNELLING MORAL ANXIETIES THROUGH THE READER

When, in 1750, Lord Chesterfield warned his son to 'Beware of Biblomane', he knew that he would understand the reference to this dangerous reading practice. Terms like 'Bibliomania', 'book madness' and 'reading mania' signified the concern that, if conducted in the wrong manner, reading could become a risk both to individual readers and to the communities they inhabited. As the size of the reading public increased, so too did the warnings about the dangers of indiscriminate reading. The ideal of the love of reading attracted the popular imagination and drew new groups of readers towards the consumption of novels and other publications produced in the recently commercialized literary marketplace.

Reading was no longer regarded simply as a medium of self-improvement: it had become a source of entertainment, escapism and gratification. Consequently, it was no longer merely the exposure of readers to seditious thoughts that worried authorities, but also the effect on prevailing moral and cultural standards of popular literature that appealed to 'base instincts'.

The censure of popular reading habits appeared to have the backing of the cultural and political elites. Conservative and religious critics of readers of popular literature believed that these publications exposed an impressionable group of poorly educated people to subversive and immoral views and sentiments. In France, public figures associated with the Revolution condemned popular novels for 'corrupting republican virtue by encouraging an immoral taste for pleasure and leisure'.[4] In Germany, supporters of the Enlightenment and progressive causes turned on popular literature for distracting the public from reading serious and elevating texts, drawing a sharp contrast between reading to educate oneself and reading to seek pleasure and escape.

The condemnation of popular taste at the turn of the nineteenth century represented an important moment in the development of the contrast between high culture and a market-driven mass culture. In his *Art of Reading* (1799), the German Kantian philosopher Johann Adam Bergk denounced readers of popular novels because they 'stupefy themselves with mindless and tasteless novels and cannot grasp how someone could have any desire higher than physical sustenance and pleasure'.[5] Bergk was not simply making an aesthetic judgement about the bad taste of readers of popular literature. He was also accusing these readers of possessing base motives and instincts, of lacking taste and indulging in stupefaction.

Martha Woodmansee's study of the German Reading Debate of the 1790s uncovered a 'veritable war on reading' that mobilized numerous commentators to challenge the 'reading epidemic' that was apparently 'sweeping their country'.[6] While commentators of all shades of opinion tended to disapprove of what they considered to be the unrestrained reading habits of the public, they 'diverged sharply' over their long-term consequences.[7] For the conservative commentators, 'extensive reading represented a threat to the established moral and social order', leading these readers to abandon their responsibilities to their families, home and place of work.[8] Liberal and pro-Enlightenment critics of the reading 'mania' objected to readers who sought pleasure and entertainment because they turned an activity that should be an instrument of instruction and emancipation into a means of dependence and acquiescence.

The detractors of passionate reading were convinced that what they characterized as *Lesewut* (reading rage), *Lesesucht* (reading lust) or *Leserei* (reading mania) represented a significant moral danger – especially as it affected women, juvenile readers and those from the lower classes. The narrative constructed around the pathology of the sensation-seeking reader of dubious escapist literature served as the focus for recurring debates around mass and popular culture and the role of education well into the twentieth century. The epidemic of reading, which was remarked on in Germany around the turn of the nineteenth century, continued to fascinate literary moralists during the century to follow. The Scottish journalist and critic Alexander Innes Shand (1832–1907) wrote in 1879 that this epidemic identified in Germany had now spread all over the Western world:

> With printing and the promiscuous circulation of books the mischief that had broken out in Germany was spread everywhere by insidious contagion, like the Black Death of the fourteenth century. But unlike that subtle and deadly plague, it has gone on running its course ever since, and diffusing itself gradually through all classes of the community.[9]

The use of the term 'insidious contagion' to describe the expansion of the reading public required neither justification nor explanation. Shand could assume that his middle-class readers would know what was so insidious about the literary ecology of late nineteenth-century Britain. The use of an alarmist and dramatic analogy that coupled mass reading with the Black Death featured regularly in narratives decrying the perils of popular culture.

At first, Revolutionary America appeared to provide an alternative to the suspicious manner with which European elite culture responded to the novel. Founding Fathers such as Thomas Jefferson and Benjamin Rush regarded the popular appeal of sentimental fiction as an opportunity for the promotion of virtue and positive moral ideals. According to one study:

> [W]ith rates of premarital pregnancy at record levels, these early supporters of the rise of the novel had once voiced hopes that fiction might smuggle lessons about female chastity and male self-discipline into the hearts and minds of adolescent readers by illustrating with riveting power the consequences of seduction.[10]

Some advocates of the novel sought to use this medium to promote civic virtues of responsibility and patriotism; and indeed the positive belief in the 'social utility of fiction' had become widespread by the mid-1780s. Yet within a few years, such upbeat sentiments gave way to disappointment and hostility. It was feared that the reading of novels served as a stimulus for such highly charged passions and emotions that its outcome would be the loss of moral clarity and the adoption of self-destructive behaviour.

The shift in the American political elite's attitude towards reading literature was clearly elucidated by Jefferson, previously one of its enthusiastic advocates. In a letter to the prominent Virginian public figure Nathaniel Burwell in 1818, Jefferson warned that 'a great obstacle to a good education is the inordinate passion prevalent for novels, and the time lost in that reading which should be instructively employed'. He was not merely worried about readers who wasted their time; he characterized novels as the moral equivalent of a poison 'that infects the mind, destroys its tone and revolts against wholesome reading'. Jefferson concluded that 'the result is a bloated imagination, sickly judgment and disgust towards all the real business of life'.[11]

For Jefferson the act of reading involved a moral choice between 'trash' and 'wholesome reading'. Given that the moral outlook of the public was at stake, what people read could not be left to chance – it required careful guidance. It was in this vein that he informed his correspondent that 'Pope, Dryden, Thomson, Shakespeare, and of the French, Moliere, Racine, the Corneilles may be read with pleasure and improvement'.[12]

Reading has always served as a subject of concern and regulation. With the emergence of commercial publishing in the eighteenth century and the constitution of an ever-widening audience of readers, such apprehensions gained intensity. The question of how a mass readership would react to the publications they consumed became a perennial subject of debate. In nineteenth-century Europe the fear that 'you become what you read' was constantly voiced by cultural and political elites.[13] It was as if insecurities and unease towards the working of mass society were transferred onto the reading public; and a bewildering variety of social and moral concerns were causally linked to reading. As Jacqueline Pearson, author of a study about the unease surrounding female reading, outlined:

> It seems there was hardly a crime, sin or personal catastrophe that injudicious reading was not held to cause directly or indirectly – from murder, suicide, rape, and violent revolution, through prostitution, adultery and divorce, to pride, vanity, and slapdash housewifery.[14]

Pearson's list by no means exhausts the number of immoral activities that were connected to reading. Women, the young and readers from the lower classes were diagnosed as particularly at risk of moral corruption. It seemed that no one was immune from the corrosive influence of novels, popular literature and the press.

The sublimation of moral anxieties through the reader implicitly cast doubt on people's capacity to engage with the published text – novels and periodicals – in a dispassionate, reflective and rational manner. The very term 'reading mania', with its implication of unrestrained lust for fiction, indicated that the consumers of literature could easily lose control over their lives. Such an interpretation of the power of the printed text assumed that by appealing to sensations and gratifying readers' base instincts, the capacity for agency and self-control would be diminished. Ideas about the corrosive imperative of literacy had in effect called into question the humanist ideal of the individual capable of self-reflection, critical thought and the exercise of autonomy.

The disassociation of the exercise of autonomy from reading did not only apply to groups such as women and young or uneducated people. It was feared that potentially anyone, even educated middle-class men, could lose grasp of their moral compass through reading. Critics claimed that excessive reading made young men 'too mentally stimulated', which led to a 'debilitating state of being in thrall of fiction', a state that one critic in 1867 termed 'mental debauch'.[15]

There are numerous nineteenth-century accounts of educated young men who draw on their disturbing personal experiences to warn about the dangers of being misled and stripped of their morals through reading the wrong texts. The Catholic poet Coventry Patmore (1823–1896) acknowledged that he was driven to despair and nearly committed suicide as a result of reading the works of the Spanish-born English writer and poet Joseph Blanco White (1775–1841). At the age of 25, Patmore wrote to a friend: 'Take my advice and recommend that book to no young man. I was nearly lost by it. I wonder I did not commit suicide during the three months of despairing atheism induced by it.'[16]

Such melodramatic accounts of the ill effects of reading emphasize readers' powerlessness to resist the ability of the printed text to capture and enslave their imagination. 'I was born of respectable parentage,' wrote the anonymous American author of the essay 'Confessions of a Novel Reader' (1839), as if to underline the risks that reading posed even to members of the comfortable business classes. Unlike the *Confessions* of St Augustine, this is not a story of redemption: reading leads not to conversion but to a state of moral dissolution. In this cautionary tale, reading is represented as a risky enterprise and immoderate reading is depicted as the road to moral annihilation. Not even his privileged Virginia family and social background could save the author from being reduced 'to the condition of a miserable drone, unfit for any steady occupation'.[17]

Literary theories that promoted the idea of the diminished subjectivity of the reader often drew attention to the ease with which literature could excite emotions and passions, leading to an inability to distinguish fact from fiction. This claim, which is a recurring motif in discussions of the effects of reading fiction, was already vividly expressed in the early seventeenth century through the story of *Don Quixote* (1605). This powerful tale of a knight whose addiction to reading led him to lose touch with reality offers a paradigmatic account of the spell cast by fiction. In this novel, Cervantes communicated the widely cited belief in Golden Age Spain which held that fiction 'induces an almost hypnotic state of rapture on its readers'.[18]

The thesis that too much exposure to fiction leads the reader to lose touch with reality was rarely contested during the eighteenth and nineteenth centuries. Paradoxically, it was the realism of the novel form that was most heavily blamed. As Karin Littau explains in her study of *The Theories of Reading*, '[t]he fear that readers would over-identify with what they read', as 'Don Quixote famously did', and 'form false expectations about life is a widespread concern during the period of the rise of the novel'.[19] Anticipating a theme that regularly features in discussions of the media effect, Samuel Johnson was acutely worried about the impact of realistic literature on young people. From his perspective, the 'accurate observation of the familiar world' was more dangerous than the previous 'heroic romances'. Why? Because since it directly engages with the experience of readers it has the power to influence them.[20] What perturbed Johnson was that literature would provide impressionable youths with a form of moral guidance that could contradict and undermine the dominant norms.

Johnson's apprehension was directed at the media's ability to provide an alternative guide to behaviour, rather than at the threat it posed to a specific value. The very possibility that a section of a community could fall under the influence of an alternative set of values exacerbates insecurity about the preservation of the prevailing moral order. That is why historically, the influence of the media is frequently represented as a challenge to authority and discussed through an alarmist discourse.[21] By the nineteenth century the negative sentiments expressed by Johnson about the power of the novel had become widespread amongst the middle-class cultural elites. From this point onwards, popular literature – in its different forms – would often be treated in a manner not dissimilar to the moral devaluation of the tabloid press in the late twentieth and early twenty-first century.

The novel served as the medium through which the transference of moral anxieties was most frequently expressed. Literary critics and historians often explore novels with a view to deepening their understanding of the conditions that prevailed during the eighteenth and nineteenth centuries. However, useful insights can be gained through exploring the way in which commentators and public figures at the time reacted to the influence of the novel on readers. Such reactions reveal much about how readers and reading were conceptualized, and it was often through questions raised about the risks of reading that the underlying anxieties about the moral order gained clarity and definition. These anxieties acquired their most dramatic form in the discussion on suicide.

SUICIDE – READERS AT RISK

In 1790 the theologian Charles Moore published a massive two-volume study, *A Full Inquiry into the Subject of Suicide*. The study, which was dedicated to the Archbishop of Canterbury, set out to provide a comprehensive overview of a problem that preoccupied individuals concerned with the moral order in England. Opinion on the issue of suicide had become divided, and Moore was troubled about the ascendant influence of 'free thinking' and 'liberal principles' that he blamed for England's tolerant attitude towards suicide, which previously had been regarded as an unpardonable sin. David Hume's essay 'Of Suicide', published seven years before Moore's treatise, offered a utilitarian argument which asserted that suicide need not violate rational moral norms, and concluded that this act 'may be free of imputation of guilt and blame'.[22] For Moore, Hume's essay represented an irresponsible appeal for 'freedom from restraint of virtue and religion'.[23]

Although his focus was on the phenomenon of suicide, Moore situated his discussion within a wider assessment of the erosion of traditional moral values and the emergence of a competing system of liberal values. Writers whose publications allegedly encouraged their readers to adopt immoral sentiments particularly perturbed him. Moore cited with approval an anonymous writer, who warned that 'one of the most important symptoms' of the 'degeneracy of morals in the present day' is that the distinction between 'right and wrong' is 'almost swept away in polite conversation'.[24] As proof of this thesis, Moore declared that tolerance of suicide gained ground in proportion to the progress of 'infidelity and free-thinking'.[25]

In a section titled 'Containing A Review of Certain Publications On This Subject In Which Our Compassion Is Attempted To Be Excited In Opposition To Our Judgment', Moore outlined what was at once a critique of the novel and a media theory which linked the effect that novels had on their readers to the risk of suicide. Moore explicitly warned all potential readers to 'Take heinous offence' at the behaviour of Werther,[26] maintaining that Goethe's powerful and intensely passionate story of thwarted love, which led to the suicide of its protagonist, represented a far greater danger to the well-being of the reader and society than that posed by Hume's sceptical philosophical tracts.

Like most of the well-known eighteenth-century epistolary novels, *The Sorrows of Young Werther* recounted the sufferings of its protagonist through the medium of letters. Moore maintained that such 'familiar letters', appealing to the 'emotions of the heart', posed a greater menace to the state of mind of the reader than those based on the 'cool deductions of reason'. Hume aimed at reasoning, 'which is too laborious a task for many a class of readers'; whereas Werther's letters 'apply immediately and solely to the passions; and therefore they gain a ready admission into every heart'.[27] Moore warned:

[R]eader take offence at the general scope and design of these infuri-
ating letters, which are calculated to snare innocence, under the idea of
extraordinary purity in love, to endanger virtue and conjugal fidelity,
under the plausibility of friendly attachment.[28]

Implicit in Moore's observation regarding the appeal of Goethe's novel
to the heart was the conviction that readers, especially women, are often
unable to retain psychic distance from the stories that appeal to their
emotions. Moore believed that they internalize as their own the passions
articulated by the characters of the story and so end up losing touch with
reality. Thus, it was precisely the aesthetic power of *Werther* and its ability
to forge a relation of intimacy with the reader that made this novel such a
threat to its readers' mental state. Moore commented that the 'sorrows are
described with so much warmth and passion, as to have caused an almost
universal tear of pity to be shed over his untimely fate'. His use of the term
'caused' is noteworthy, for Moore held Goethe responsible for the 'unlawful
and uncontrolled' behaviour of some of his readers.[29]

The 'unlawful and uncontrolled' behaviour that agitated Moore the
most was the apparent outbreak of copycat suicides throughout Europe
by young readers, who were caught up with the dramatic intensity of
Werther's predicament. By all accounts the publication of *The Sorrows
of Young Werther* turned into an almost instant media event, becoming
the first documented literary sensation of modern Europe. The novel
was translated into French (1775), English (1779), Italian (1781) and
Russian (1788), and repeatedly republished in different editions. There
were more that 20 pirated editions published within 12 years of the novel's
appearance in Germany. *Werther* also enjoyed a remarkable success in the
United States, becoming one of the best-selling novels before the War of
1812 and exerting a powerful influence on the early American literary
public.

Werther provided the focus for a very early example of a phenomenon
that would be labelled in the twentieth century as a youth subculture. A
generation of idealistic and romantic youths adopted Werther as their hero,
many memorizing excerpts from his letters and imitating the affectations
associated with their tragic idol. It was widely reported that young men and
women were weeping for days, even weeks, over his tragic demise. Groups of
young men adopted the fashion of wearing yellow trousers in combination

with blue tailcoat and high boots in imitation of their hero's appearance, and the novel spawned a cottage industry devoted to the merchandising of *Werther*-related souvenirs.

What was frequently described as 'Werther Fever' was reflected through the mass marketing of drawings, engravings and everyday objects decorated with scenes from the novel.[30] This commercialization of 'fan products' included cups and plates by the manufacturer of the well-known Meissen china; one entrepreneur even came up with the brand 'Eau de Werther' to market his perfume. The appeal of *Werther* was not an overnight temporary phenomenon: it lasted until the early 1800s, and decades after its publication Napoleon declared his admiration for *Werther* and asserted that he had read the novel seven times.

Authorities throughout Europe were perturbed by the scale of the enthusiastic and passionate reaction to *Werther*. Many officials and critics perceived the vivid and sympathetic manner with which Goethe described Werther's descent into self-destruction as legitimating the act of suicide, and depicted the novel as a danger to the public because of its disorienting influence on young readers. The numerous initiatives taken to ban this novel indicated that the authorities took these claims very seriously. In 1775 the Theological Faculty of the University of Leipzig petitioned officials to ban *Werther* on the grounds that its circulation would lead to the promotion of suicide; the City Council of Leipzig concurred and cited the increased frequency of suicides as justification for banning both the novel and the wearing of the Werther costume. The ban was introduced in 1775 and not lifted until 1825. The novel was also banned in Italy and Denmark.

The Hamburg Protestant pastor Johann Goeze denounced the novel as a 'heinous book': 'Consider for God's sake how many of our youth could end in circumstances similar to those of Werther,' he asked in his call to ban the book in order to protect public morals.[31] The Catholic Bishop of Milan shared the apprehensions of his German Protestant colleague, and was so disturbed by the peril that *Werther* represented to public morality that he bought up all available copies of the novel to protect Milanese readers from its influence.[32] Unease was not confined to theologians and public moralists. During the course of a debate on this novel in Sweden, the poet Johan Kellgren (1751–1795) indicated that he was worried that the 'Werther suicide might become contagious by suggestion and warned of literature where emotions played a dominating role'.[33]

Even one of the most prominent representatives of the Enlightenment era, the German writer and philosopher Gotthold Ephraim Lessing (1729–1781), was uncomfortable about *Werther*'s influence on its impressionable readers. Lessing acknowledged that he enjoyed reading *Werther* but he nevertheless wrote to a friend that the 'novel could cause more harm than good'; he was unsettled by the novel's sympathetic treatment of the protagonist and of the manner of his demise, and feared that 'a young man of similar disposition' might adopt a similar course of action.[34] Although Lessing possessed an intellectual and moral outlook very different from *Werther*'s religious critics, they all shared an instinctive mistrust of readers' ability to resist the influence of Goethe's apparent condoning of romantic suicide.

The claim that readers of *Werther* were at risk of committing an act of self-destruction continued well into the nineteenth century. In 1865 the German author J. W. Appel outlined two cases of suicide by readers of the novel. In one instance, a young man who killed himself by jumping off a tall building had a copy in his possession; in the other, a mother whose son committed suicide had 'underlined several parts in *Werther*'.[35]

THE ENGLISH 'MALADY' AND THE NOVEL EFFECT

Paradoxically, public concern about suicide and its connection to the printed media was shaped in part by the way that the press, novels and other forms of publications portrayed the problem. The notion of an English 'malady', which suggested that the English were unusually prone to the affliction of melancholy and therefore had a per-capita suicide rate much higher than elsewhere, was itself a tale that was spread through the printed media.

The growth of newspapers and periodicals during the eighteenth century 'transformed the social context within which suicide was understood', and the 'press made suicide a much more public event than it had been before'.[36] The fear that suicide was contagious was frequently communicated in the press through its reports of copycat incidents throughout England; it is likely that the sensationalized coverage of suicides offered an opportunity to gain new readers. The coverage of this disturbing malady went as far as titillating readers by publishing suicide notes.[37] Today, the media would justify this sensationalization of suicide as providing the service of 'raising awareness'; in the eighteenth century, the new mass media were rarely called upon to validate their dramatic claims.

At the time, observers frequently interpreted the press interest in the English malady as evidence of the extent of this malaise. The *Monthly Mirror* in 1796 pointed to the 'frequency of suicides which fill the daily journals', and concluded that this development 'must shock the mind of every reflecting reader'.[38] Pre-existing media interest in the problem of suicide provided the cultural setting for the publication of *Werther* in English in 1779. The reading public was already familiar with the press interest in suicide, and the editor of the first English edition assumed that readers would share his assumption that suicide was a widespread occurrence when he stated that the 'design of the book was to "exhibit a picture of that disordered mind too common in our own country"'.[39] Predictably, the publication of *Werther* gave the impetus for further discussion of suicide, and inevitably the novel continued to be attacked by some for encouraging this act.

In November 1784, five years after the publication of the first English translation of *Werther*, *The Gentleman's Magazine* published the following notice under its obituaries:

> Suddenly at the Chaceside, Southgate, Miss Glover, daughter of the late Mr. G., formerly an eminent dancing master. The *Sorrows of Werther* were found under her pillow; a circumstance which deserves to be known in order, if possible to defeat the evil tendency of that pernicious work.[40]

The condemnation of this 'pernicious work' and the assertion that it bore responsibility for the demise of Miss Glover provided the foundation for the construction of a legend about the novel's destructive influence on its English readers. In informing the public about a 'circumstance which deserves to be known', the author of this notice helped construct a story that would be integral to the folklore of suicide. The notice of Miss Glover's demise immediately roused a correspondent named Theophilius to write a letter denouncing 'the gloomy and violent passions that agitate and torment the mind of a *Werther*.[41] Soon the display of moral outrage at the novel served as proof of a person's moral respectability.

In February and April 1785 *The European Magazine* published two letters from angry correspondents, who condemned *Werther* for corrupting the morals of the youth of England.[42] Writing on the same theme, a contributor to *The Analytical Review* for 1788 stated 'I am sorry to see a taste prevail for novels which exhibit unnatural pictures of misery, and diffuse a kind of taste for the woeful.' The novel that he used to highlight his case was *Werther*, which 'cannot have failed to have given the falsely delicate, the overrefined, the idolizers of themselves, additional encouragement in the affectation of misery'.[43] By the time Charles Moore published his treatise on suicide in 1790, the sad demise of Miss Glover had been transformed into an urban legend that there was an epidemic of suicide amongst young readers of *Werther*, and this served as a cautionary tale to would-be readers of novels.

In fact the only evidence offered by Moore of a *Werther*-induced suicide was the now frequently cited obituary of Miss Glover in the *Gentleman's Magazine*. Moore inserted this reference to lend credibility to his claim that there was 'many a wretched self-victim' of Goethe's novel. Moore confidently asserted that 'many a deluded female has been discovered in the hour of her self-destruction, to have reclined her aching head[s] on this poisonous tale'.[44] The absence of factual evidence notwithstanding, the image of the corpses of helpless female readers lying in bed near a copy of *Werther* resonated with the public imagination. As Kelly McGuire points out in her study of the discourse of suicide contagion: '[N]ewspapers ran accounts of British men and women casting themselves from windows and overdosing on laudanum, all the while clutching the book that was seen as an accessory to their deaths.' However, 'these cases were fairly few in number, but this reality either did not register or did not signify with those who subscribed to a belief that suicide could be spread through social contagion'.[45]

Back in 1777, it was reported that a 'young Swede' named Karstens shot himself with a pistol, a copy of *Werther* by his side.[46] It is likely that this story provided the dramatic plot through which the association between self-destruction and the reading of the novel was framed in the decades to follow. The tragic image of a dead woman or man clasping a copy of *Werther* was probably constructed around the story of the suicide of Christel von Lassberg, who on 16 January 1778 drowned herself in the River Ilm in Weimar; she had reportedly been abandoned by the man she loved, and was found with a copy of the novel in her pocket. From this point onwards, stories of suicides staged to highlight the 'Sorrows' of the anguished reader acquired the status of a compelling cultural myth.

Time and again, allusions to the staged version of a *Werther*-induced suicide were accompanied by the repetition of a remark allegedly made by the famous French woman of letters, Madame de Staël (1766–1817), to the effect that *Werther* 'had caused more suicides than the most beautiful woman in the world'. Did Byron really state that *Werther* was 'responsible for more deaths than Napoleon himself'?[47] In a sense it does not matter because, like so many of the allegations made about the effects of this novel, they were effortlessly integrated into the urban legend surrounding it.

In the United States, the campaign of moral outrage against *Werther* was far less restrained than in Europe. During the final decade of the eighteenth century, American publications regularly reported on the devastating effects of *Werther* on their readership. One contributor to the Philadelphia-based *Weekly Magazine* in 1798 sought to convince booksellers 'to remove the book from their shelves, by alleging that it had already proved "the bane of more than one family" in the state'.[48] Yet as the novel continued to be a best-seller well into the 1800s, its critics became more and more hysterical in their attacks on its author. Goethe was charged with producing a novel 'that seemed to condone and even valorize self-murder'.[49] America's moral anxieties seemed to be sublimated through its reaction to this novel. As Richard Bell wrote, 'parents of adolescent children displaced their growing disillusionment about the atomizing changes reshaping early national society onto Werther's slender shoulders'.[50]

Whatever the veracity of the rumours surrounding the deadly consequences of *Werther* on its readers, the controversy surrounding this novel exposes a slippage between reality and fiction. Critics used their imagination to construct a fictitious urban legend, and communicated it in the language of facts. Charles Moore explicitly acknowledged his indifference to the question of whether Goethe's character Werther was a real person or a fictitious character, informing his readers that he intended to 'fall in with common opinion, that Werther is not a fictitious, but a real character;

which opinion, whether it be true or false, is of no consequence to the point at hand; only that its being read as a true story more engages the attention and increases the mischief.'[51]

Moore's decision to treat Werther as a real person and the novel as a work of non-fiction has paradoxical consequences. One of the frequent criticisms levelled at novels during the eighteenth and nineteenth centuries was that because they were so realistic in the presentation of their story, their readers were easily transposed into a world of fantasy and lost touch with their own reality. Novels were perceived as the seducers of women and the corrupters of easily impressionable young men. In effect Moore himself adopted the behaviour of a reader who has lost sight of the boundary that separates fiction from reality. He devoted 43 pages of his treatise on suicide to conducting a conversation with the main character of a work of fiction, thereby converting *Werther* into an empirical case study used to prove a scientific thesis.

In passing, it should be noted that Moore's integration of *Werther* into the 'scientific' literature on suicide served as a legacy that others would draw on. The massive six-volume study *A System of Complete Medical Police* by the German physician Johann Peter Frank (1745–1821) outlined a comprehensive review of the problem of suicide. Among the numerous causes of suicides, Frank listed 'irreligiousness, debauchery, and idleness, lavishness and its attendant unaccustomed misery, but especially the reading of poisonous novels' – which presented suicide as a 'heroic display of contempt for earthly affairs.'[52]

One of the most intriguing features of the controversy surrounding *Werther* is the almost imperceptible manner in which the print media itself became preoccupied with the task of warning readers about the so-called media effect, which in the eighteenth century was framed through the narrative of the effect of the novel. With the time and energy that authors of novels and of articles in the periodical press devoted to the policing of reading and literature, it was as if the print media was warning its readership about itself.

Moore himself cited fictional literature criticizing *Werther* to document his argument. In his study on suicide, he favourably contrasts Herbert Croft's epistolary novel *Love and Madness; or A Story Too True* (1780), which 'seems anxious through the whole to show a pointed abhorrence of suicide in every shape', to the 'pernicious example of *Werther*.[53] For his part, Croft denounced the character of Werther as a 'very bad man' and its author Goethe as 'not a much better man'. Croft's criticism anticipated that of Moore, who treated Goethe as the author, not of a novel, but of an autobiography.[54]

There is little evidence that suicide rates in England were notably higher than in other European societies. However, the media appeared to become wedded to the myth of the English malady to the point that the association of novel-reading with the peril of suicide and moral corruption became one of its unquestioned tropes. Alarmist accounts about suicidal acts stimulated by reading became a recurrent theme in fiction, and the depiction of *Werther* as the personification of moral corruption was widely adopted by English writers. For example, in Charlotte Turner Smith's novel *Emmeline: The Orphan of the Castle* (1788), Lord Delamere attempts to use *Werther* to 'emotionally blackmail the heroine' – who is fortunately virtuous enough to withstand this corrupting influence.[55] In *Thoughts on the Frequency of Divorces* (1800) by Adam Sibbit, novels like *Werther* are blamed for the disintegration of family life.[56]

Nineteenth-century British literature is littered with characters reading *Werther*, 'in the works of Herbert Croft, Maria Edgeworth, Charlotte Smith, Jane Austen, Lady Morgan (Sydney Owenson), and Mary Shelley, as well as in lesser-known works by William Godwin, Elizabeth Tomlins, Jane Porter, Lord Byron, George Crabbe, Helen Maria Williams, Susannah Rowson, Clara Reeve, William Hill Brown, Charles Maturin, Catherine Hutton, and Thomas Love Peacock'.[57]

The moral panic surrounding *Werther* in the United States adapted the themes that circulated in Europe and recycled them in an American form. According to Richard Bell's study of literary anxiety about suicide in the newly constituted United States, '*Werther* could not be stopped'. Bell cites a writer in the *Weekly Magazine* asserting that Goethe's book 'has already proved "the bane of more than one family" in Pennsylvania'.[58] In his lecture 'Thoughts upon Female Education', given at the Young Ladies Academy in Philadelphia in July 1787, Benjamin Rush, professor of chemistry and signatory of the Declaration of Independence, warned his female audience to avoid reading novels because of the threat they posed to the moral order of America, and singled out *Werther* as the focus of his moral outrage.[59]

During the decade before and after the turn of the nineteenth century, 'the conviction that reading Goethe's novel could lead to copycat deaths had become gospel in certain circles'. Bell refers to an anti-*Werther* diatribe that was circulated in numerous newspapers, which claimed that the novel's 'mortal effects had been felt in "hundreds of families" over the past few years'. The author of the article intimated that he personally knew of two acquaintances 'who rushed unbidden into eternity, deluded by the sophisticated arguments of *Werther* in favour or in vindication of suicide'.[60] Both cases were examples of 'textbook cases of Wertherism' – their bodies were found with the novel next to their hearts.

Early American literature was fascinated with the Werther myth and frequently alluded to its devastating consequences. Moreover, '[b]etween 1780–1810, suicide spread through the pages of fashionable fiction like yellow fever'. According to Bell's calculations, 15 of the first 45 novels written by Americans and published before 1810 depict a character 'dying by his or her hands',[61] several of which depicted suicidal characters immersed in reading *Werther*.

The Power of Sympathy (1789), by William Hill Brown, is usually cited as the first American novel. This epistolary novel about virtue and love was, according to one critic, 'one of the earliest attempts at the moral regeneration of American youth'.[62] In the preface, Brown boasts that he had succeeded in exposing the 'dangerous Consequences of Seduction' and to set forth the 'Advantages of Female Education'.[63] The novel sought to expose the disastrous consequences of allowing oneself to be overwhelmed by passion. Predictably, the excess of sympathetic sentiments leads to the suicide of one of the main characters, Harrington. When the main rational character, Worthy, describes the scene of Harrington's death, he notes: 'A Letter that he had written for me laid unsealed upon the table, and *The Sorrows of Werther* was found lying by its side.'[64] As Bell indicates, no reader of this novel 'needed any explanation to understand the significance of the presence of Goethe's novel' at the suicide scene.[65]

The customary performance of a *Werther*-induced suicide scene was re-enacted in *The Hapless Orphan* (1793), a novel written by the anonymous 'An American Lady'. Following the well-established literary pattern, during the weeks preceding the climactic murder of Fanny by Ashley, the latter had been absorbed in reading *Werther*. Enacting the now-familiar ritual, Ashley leaves behind a suicide note testifying that 'The *Sorrows of Werther* is now open upon my table: It animates my heart: it cheers my soul; it will sustain me through the scene which I am about to act.'[66] Richard Bell notes that 'several English novels that circulated in America at this time offered similar tableaux: *Werther*, it seems, was more than an instruction manual – it had become the ultimate literary accessory.'[67]

WHAT WAS THE IMPACT ON READERS?

The highly charged moral reaction that surrounded the publication of *Werther* made constant references to the necessity of protecting the novel's readers from themselves. But how did its readership react to the novel? Answering this question is fraught with difficulty, since just about everything that has been written about the reaction and behaviour of novel readers is filtered through the comments of second- and usually third-hand observers, which are invariably speculative and reflect their own preconceived prejudices. The narrative of outrage surrounding *Werther* exemplifies a disposition to perceive the worst about the novel, rather than an objective evaluation of readers' responses to it.

Our exploration of the narrative of 'Werther fever' suggests that it acquired a life of its own, to the point that it mutated into a taken-for-granted rhetorical idiom that accounted for the moral problems facing society.[68] The continual allusions to Miss Glover, to nameless victims and to similarly framed death scenes, indicate that these reports had very little factual content to draw on. Stories about an epidemic of suicide were as fictional as the demise of Werther in Goethe's novel.

It is likely that readers of *Werther* were influenced by the controversy surrounding the novel. In his autobiography, Goethe lamented that so many of his readers felt called upon to 're-enact the novel, and possibly shoot themselves'.[69] Yet despite the sanctimonious scaremongering, the novel continued to attract a large readership. While there is no evidence that *Werther* was responsible for the promotion of a wave of copycat suicides, the emergence of what today would be described as a cult of fans with some of the trappings of a youth subculture is testimony to the novel's powerful appeal.

Insofar as it refers to the outburst of sudden popularity and the self-conscious adoption of imitative attitudes and lifestyles, the term 'Werther fever' captured an important media event. The rapid diffusion of interest in reading *Werther* and other novels demonstrated that this genre possessed an appeal to ideals and sentiments that made the establishment apprehensive. The literary theorist Georg Lukacs has argued that the enduring appeal of *Werther* was the protagonist's heroic refusal to compromise his principles, and that it was this unswerving devotion to his 'humanistic-revolutionary ideals' that was perceived as so subversive to the moral order.[70]

Werther appealed directly to a sensibility that experienced the prevailing social and moral order as a barrier to the cultivation and development of the individual self. Werther himself struggled to transcend the forces contending between the realization of individual personality and the conventions of society. The tragic consequences of his struggle served to highlight his heroic quality and reinforce his appeal to the novel's readers. In this regard, readers' responses were influenced by the emergence of a new individual-oriented romantic fashion that valorized their intense emotional experience and self-discovery. This was a sensibility that was readily attracted to the reading of novels, since it provided scope for emotional identification with characters and resonated with the existential uncertainties faced by readers.

Werther fever was not the only 'malady' afflicting the reading public. Prior to the publication of *Werther*, books like Samuel Richardson's *Pamela, or Virtue Rewarded* (1740) and Jean-Jacques Rousseau's *Julie, or the New Heloise* (1761) became literary sensations that gripped their readers' imaginations. The very enthusiasm that greeted the appearance of these novels created a sense of unease amongst members of the Establishment. 'Pamela fever' in England alerted authorities to the realization that 'reading is not without its dangers, for it affects, it was felt at the time, precisely those readers with a more delicate disposition, such as the man of feeling or those with a rather gullible disposition, such as children and women'.[71]

The appeal of novels like *Pamela* and *Werther* to sentiment, and the nervousness of the establishment about the consequences of a public outburst of emotionalism, are often interpreted by literary theorists as a reflection of the tension between eighteenth-century romanticism and the rationality of the Enlightenment. One study of this debate describes it as a conflict about 'privileging the head over the heart'.[72] It is true that the discussion surrounding reading was often expressed through a language that set reason and sentiment in sharp opposition, but it would be far too simplistic to draw a polarized contrast between rationally motivated critics of the novel and its passionate, emotionally driven supporters. The moral outrage directed against *Werther* was anything but detached and rational. Its indictment of sentiment was underpinned by a lack of belief in the appeal of rationality, and its solution was to mobilize the emotion of fear to uphold the moral order.

What made critics nervous was their sense that it was precisely the most idealistic individuals, those possessed of virtuous sensibilities and sensitivity to the plight of others, who were likely to be drawn towards views that questioned the moral order. Time and again, critics of the novel accused authors of manipulating the lofty sentiments of their readers towards malevolent ends. 'Those generous sentiments, those liberal opinions, those tender tales abounding with fine feeling, soft ideas, fascinating gentleness, and warm descriptions have been the ruin of us', complained an anonymous correspondent in *The New England Quarterly Magazine* in 1802.[73] The ease with which virtue gave way to moral corruption signified a sense of insecurity regarding the ability of the traditional moral order to hold the line against the sentiments celebrated by subversive novelists.

What all the stories about novel 'fevers' stressed was the ascendancy of a potentially risky phenomenon: the forging of an intense and intimate interaction between the reader and literary character. Moralists were also concerned that the excessive identification of readers with literary characters could lead people, particularly women, to adopt dramatic changes to their behaviour.

That novels could have a profound aesthetic and psychological impact on their readers is not in doubt – for example, there is evidence that readers of Rousseau's *Julie* followed the author's encouragement to abandon themselves to reading.[74] In the eighteenth and nineteenth centuries, critics were 'preoccupied with the imaginative exercise novel reading might inspire in readers'.[75] But these contemporary observers were uncertain how a novel affected its readers, and '[t]he question of what goes on in a novel reader's mind presented a source of anxiety to early critics of the genre'.[76]

Speculation about the impact of novel reading rarely rose above guess-work. The 1858 essay on 'The Unknown Public' by the novelist Wilkie Collins described the millions of new readers as 'a mystery which the sharpest man among us may not find it easy to solve'.[77] This mystery remains unsolved to this day, since, as the literary scholar Richard Altick acknowledges in *The English Common Reader*, the retrospective attempt to capture the reader's subjective experience is fraught with difficulty.[78]

But while it is impossible to recover the internal emotional reactions of past readers, it is possible to assess the claims made about the diverse forms of immoral and antisocial behaviour allegedly caused by reading. More than two centuries of scaremongering about the effects of novels, newspapers, the cinema, television, video-nasties, video-games and the internet serve as testimony to the never-ending compulsion to interpret moral and social problems through the prism of the media. Indirectly, panics about the media also express a statement about the foolishness of readers and audiences. Yet the case study of the reaction to *Werther* indicates more foolishness on the part of commentators, who detected an epidemic of suicide where none existed.

Novelists themselves were obsessively drawn towards the exploration of this question. Sometimes within novels the readers of novels were depicted in a positive light, as agents in pursuit of self-improvement – for example, Jane Eyre learns from books to gain knowledge about herself. Other novelists wrote about characters who could not help but be misled by their reading material. In such novels, readers like Flaubert's Madame Bovary are led astray or, like Catherine from Jane Austen's *Northanger Abbey*, they lose touch with reality. It is unclear whether these depictions of fictional readers reflected the wider climate of moral anxiety or whether they helped frame the way in which the problem of reading was conceptualized. That the medium of the novel should be warning its readers about the dangers associated with the very activity of reading had become an enduring theme in the cultural landscape of modernity.

Deliberations on the effects of reading recognized that here was a question of fundamental importance to the future of society. A correspondent wrote in the January 1887 issue of the *Edinburgh Review* that education and reading 'are mighty factors in the progress of every nation, and both have to be well weighed, guided and guarded', and warned that 'it would be difficult to overestimate the future harvest of good or evil to which they may give rise'.[79] In the nineteenth century it was evident that the association of reading with progress had become widespread in Western societies. That did not stop the outbreaks of anguish about the moral risks of reading; rather, the cultural contradictions of reading continued to be played out in new forms.

PANIC ABOUT THE MEDIA

Kirsten Drotner has used the term *media panic* – in the sense of a panic about the media – to highlight the recurrent tendency for change and innovation of the media to incite anxiety and fear.[80] Such reactions were a response to the growth of both publishing and the reading public in the eighteenth century. The expansion and commercialization of newspapers, journals and novels created an environment in which competing views and opinions helped foster a climate where moral authority could be questioned. A new medium of communication, particularly when it assumes the form of a mass medium, represents an implicit challenge to moral authority. By providing a public forum a new mass medium offers fresh opportunities for discussion, which in turn may raise questions about the legitimacy of the moral order. The inevitable uncertainties in elite circles about a new medium are also based on the perception that it has the potential to question that order.

The experience of the eighteenth and nineteenth centuries suggests that apprehensions provoked by the mass media and the growing reading public began *prior* to any specific effects attributed to the appearance of newspapers, journals and novels. Those who questioned the prevailing conventions were not only criticized for their mistaken views, but they were also condemned as immoral. Since the consumption of newspapers, journals and novels was likely to lead readers in undesirable directions, these media were held ultimately responsible for the decline in moral standards.

The association of the press and literature with a decline in the moral order led to newspapers, journals and novels being attributed with formidable powers of persuasion in the eighteenth and nineteenth centuries. This in turn provided the cultural resources on which the much later reactions to the cinema, television and the internet would draw. It is worth noting that the anxieties surrounding the effects of all the new media were not confined to their content. Indeed, the most threatening effect was the creation of a vast new mass audience who might decide to reject the habits and conventions of the prevailing moral order. From the late eighteenth century onwards, political and cultural commentators often displayed their insecurities by inflated assessments of the power and size of the reading public.[81] There was a parallel tendency to endow the media with fantastical powers. It was sometimes claimed that novels and newspapers possessed a power of suggestion that literally seduced and morally disarmed readers. For example, the Reverend Robert Clarke told the Literary and Philosophical Society of Newcastle upon Tyne in a lecture in February 1815 that 'by seizing upon those features which captivate the eye', an author ensured that 'the seduction of our heart is accomplished before we are aware'.[82]

An examination of the highly charged climate surrounding the emergence of mass literacy and popular culture suggests that what was at issue was the capacity of the moral order to retain some authority over public attitudes and behaviour. In the nineteenth century, as the size of the reading public increased, this defensive reaction acquired great force. The response to the popular press and to the so-called sensationalist novels was 'related directly to the strength of its appeal to the masses'. Such concerns were intensified by the size of this constituency of mass readership. 'The greater the audience, the greater the presumed threat to individual health and to social order' concludes a study on the 'Fear of Fiction'.[83]

The nineteenth-century novelist Anthony Trollope represented the novel as a compelling source of alternative moral knowledge that overshadowed the influence of the family and community, writing that the 'bulk of the young people in the upper and middle classes receive their moral teachings chiefly from the novels they read'. According to Trollope's diagnosis, the traditional institutions of moral education and socialization were no match for the omnipotent novel:

> [T]he novelist creeps in closer than the schoolmaster, closer than the father, closer almost than the mother. He is the chosen guide, the tutor whom the young pupil chooses for herself. She retires with him, suspecting no lesson, safe against rebuke, throwing herself head and heart into the narration as she can hardly do into her task-work; and there she is taught,—how she shall learn to love; how she shall receive the lover when he comes; how far she should advance to meet the joy;

why she should be reticent, and not throw herself at once into this new delight. It is the same with the young man, though he would be more prone even than she to reject the suspicion of such tutorship.[84]

Trollope had no doubt that a traditional instrument for moral communication, such as the sermon, could not compete with the appeal of the novel. In his view, the novel was a medium that had an intoxicating effect of inciting the reader to throw 'herself head and heart into the narration'.

In his 1879 overview of cultural and political developments in Britain, the historian Spencer Walpole drew attention to a new almighty power:

> It might be said of the present age that the power of controlling thought is passing ... to the novel-writer. Political speeches are studied by some; sermons are avoided by many; history has only a few students; but every one reads novels. The novel influences for good or for evil the thoughts of its readers: the thoughts of its readers may ultimately determine the government of the world.[85]

Walpole's extravagant claim about the novel writer's 'power of controlling thought' was paralleled by the recognition that the influence of religion had waned –'sermons are avoided' – and the vitality of traditional moral influences had become exhausted. Uncertainties about religion, values, and the durability of the Victorian social order heightened elite sensitivities towards potential competitors to its moral authority.

By the late nineteenth century, the anxieties associated with the novel had shifted to the mass-produced newspaper. In Britain the so-called New Journalism, which catered to a mass readership, became a target of those worried about the corrupting effects of popular culture. After the Third Reform Act of 1884 and the extension of the franchise, there was an escalation of disquiet regarding the influence of the New Journalism. According to one account, a 'new moral panic was triggered by the possibility that a "mass" press could shape a "mass culture" that could now wield actual power through the ballot box'.[86]

Thus in retrospect the nineteenth century can be seen as an age in which insecurities and fears about the status of morality tended to be refracted through debates about the role of the press and other forms of popular publication. What was referred to as *public opinion* was often depicted as the creation of the press and of popular literature. It followed that the influence that these media exercised on the reading public would have far-reaching implications for the moral order.

THE 'WERTHER EFFECT'

In the present day, when literary commentators frequently complain that people are far too distracted to read novels, it is difficult to imagine that readers could become so immersed in the text that they would kill themselves. Yet when the influential English Romantic poet and critic Samuel Taylor Coleridge (1772–1834) lectured his audience on this topic, he warned 'where the reading of novels prevails as a habit, it occasions in time the entire destruction of the powers of the mind; it is such an utter loss to the reader, that it is not so much to be called pass time as kill-time'.[87]

The attribution of a deathly power to the novel intuitively made sense to those looking for an explanation for what they perceived as a loss of traditional values and of moral restraint. According to Richard Bell, the extraordinary impact of *Werther* on the American moral imagination was in part a reaction to the erosion of the coherence of the traditional moral order:

> [N]ervous witnesses to the disintegration of customary social restraint in early national society intuitively linked every portrayal of suicide in popular literature to *Werther* and thus to their larger concerns about community integrity and the preservation of their status.[88]

Curiously, the passage of time has not entirely undermined the association of Werther fever with an epidemic of suicide. In 1974 the American sociologist Dave Phillips coined the term 'the Werther Effect' to describe media-stimulated imitation of suicidal behaviour. Phillips has argued that the 'number of suicides increases after a story of a suicide is publicized in the newspapers'.[89] Thirty years after the discovery of the Werther Effect, a book devoted to exposing the copycat effect of the media recycled the urban legend surrounding Goethe's novel for the benefit of the twenty-first-century reader, recalling that in the years following its publication 'so many young men shot themselves while dressed as Werther and seated at their writing desks with an open copy of *The Sorrows of Werther* in front of them that the book was banned'.[90]

The durability of the *Werther* myth notwithstanding, media panics have changed their form, shifting from the novel to electronic and digital media. Nevertheless claims about the risks of the media effect have endured, and the belief that consumers of the media imitate and internalize what they hear, see or read continues to appeal to common sense. In the twenty-first century, the simplistic cause-and-effect model of the Werther Effect is most strikingly expressed through moral anxieties that focus on the danger of 'cybersuicide' – copycat suicides allegedly provoked online.[91]

The Werther Effect and the epidemic of suicides that it induced was understood as a form of moral contagion. The original version of this thesis was based on the belief that sentiment and emotional attitudes could be caught like a physical disease. 'One could "catch" sentiment, which was everywhere on the page and on the stage, and reading provided the best medium to facilitate this transfer', notes an interesting review of *Werther*'s reception.[92] That is why literary characters who describe their experience of reading novels often use terms like 'infection' and 'contagion' to account for their response.[93] The tendency to shift from the moral to the physical or medical indicates that the afflictions caused by reading have often been interpreted through the model of diseases. The fascinating interplay of the medicalization of morality and the moralization of the health of the reader serves as the subject of the next chapter.

6

Reading and Health: An Enduring Dilemma

The controversy surrounding Goethe's *The Sorrows of Young Werther* illustrates the ease with which the rhetoric used to depict the impact and experience of reading leaps from the sphere of the moral to that of physical and mental health. It was frequently reported that readers were *infected* by the sentiments that they absorbed through the reading of the novel. From this perspective, sentiment could be *caught* like a common cold and, in the case of *Werther*, lead to a moral disease or even a condition that terminated with the physical act of self-destruction. Reviews of the reception of best-selling novels in the eighteenth century propose the 'idea of literary contagion' as a 'useful descriptive model' to account for their popularity.[1]

More than two centuries later, the language of toxicity, physical harm and contagion continues to be used to portray the risks accompanying the consumption of different forms of media. Moral and physical categories have frequently been combined or used interchangeably to express the risks of reading. The description of romantic fiction in the nineteenth century as 'moral poison' is paradigmatic in this respect. Although the poison contaminating the reader is used as a metaphor, the illness inflicted on the person is no less serious than that of a physical disease:[2] moral contamination is experienced as a physical condition expressed through medical symptoms.

Throughout history, the relationship between morality and health has been ambiguous. Moral virtue is frequently expressed through physical attributes that radiate its qualities, and moral corruption is signified through physically repulsive symptoms. In the Old Testament leprosy was diagnosed as a disease inflicted by the Almighty against those who deserved such punishment. Health warnings about the dangers of reading have historically highlighted such conditions as mental gluttony, insanity, going mad, hysteria, addictive behaviour, moral corruption and self-destruction.

The diseasing of media consumption continues to the present day. Online addiction, psychological trauma, a proclivity for antisocial and violent behaviour, and damage inflicted on the cognitive functioning of the brain are some of the conditions connected with the media in the twenty-first century. Medicalization – the process through which everyday life has come under the purview of medical authority – has gained unprecedented influence in the modern era, when an expanding range of human experiences have become redefined as issues requiring medical intervention.

Since the rise of secularism and science, moral and cultural concerns have been increasingly depicted through the narrative of mental or physical illness. For example, in recent decades, objections to excessive use of media or undisciplined reading have often been framed through warnings about their effects on cognition. This was the intention of the Cambridge literary critic I. A. Richards, the father of New Criticism, when in 1929 he tried to establish a link between the problem of reading and 'the sudden diffusion of indigestible ideas', which 'are disturbing throughout the world the whole order of human mentality, that our minds are, as it were, becoming of an inferior shape – thin, brittle and patchy, rather than controllable and coherent'.[3] Richards' concern with the capacity of the reader to digest 'indigestible ideas' was not simply directed at the old problem of information overload but also at its cognitive effects.

Of course, reading can generate psychological and physical reactions. The power of the written text on the imagination is one of its special and indeed wonderful qualities. The literary critic George Steiner has claimed that 'to read well is to take great risks', since 'it is to make vulnerable our identity'.[4] Steiner's reference to the psychological and physical upheavals caused by reading describe a spiritual or aesthetic reaction – a process that others perceive almost entirely through the prism of health. The aim of this chapter is to examine the interweaving of the medical and the moral in narratives about what reading does to the reader.

MORALITY AND PHYSICALITY

Precisely how the world enters the mind through reading and its influence on the reader is difficult to anticipate. Debates about specific books and the practice of reading have often focused on physical and moral themes such as whether they enlighten and strengthen, or corrupt and weaken, the mind and body. As we discussed previously, Socrates' representation of writing as a 'drug' conveyed the proposition that reading could be either a cure or a poison.

The reaction of readers to sacred texts was of great concern to religious authorities. It was recognized that the practice of reading could lead to spiritual conversion, but could also result in the adoption of heretical conclusions. Throughout the medieval and early modern eras, there were contradictory reports on this subject. Numerous readers of the Scriptures claimed to have had visions – some with positive consequences, others with negative ones.[5] The belief that the reading of the Scriptures possessed transformative qualities meant that religious authorities could not leave the outcome of this activity to chance.

In early modern times, the effects of reading were interpreted through the physiological discourse of passions, which emphasized the link between emotional reactions to the text and physical and mental health. Passions had specific meaning – 'they were motions of the sensitive (or sometimes the rational) soul, excited by and in response to impressions generated by the senses and other stimuli'[6] – and were represented as possessing the influence to direct human behaviour towards specific forms of action and behaviour.

The aetiology of the passions was of great importance to both theologians and philosophical thinkers. The question that preoccupied them was the relationship between the influence of reading on the passions, and their subsequent effect on behaviour. Michael Schoenfeldt argues that the capacity of literature to move readers was both 'prized and feared'; the 'bodies and minds of individual readers were imagined as battlegrounds between the corollary forces of good and evil, and of health and illness'. Readers had to be wary and careful to ensure that they remained immune to the influence of the work of devil.[7] Warnings about the intoxicating effects of reading pointed to its disturbing and corrupting influence on emotions and well-being. Yet at times reading could 'inspire conversion, or even true novelty'. The German mathematician Johannes Kepler (1571–1630) reported that when he finished reading Euclid's *Elements* he was 'seized by an unbelievable rapture' as he 'perceived the role of the regular polyhedral in the cosmos'. Thomas Hobbes also claimed to have undergone a conversion after reading Euclid.[8]

Numerous well-known figures drew on their personal experiences to warn about the emotional and physical upheavals that reading inflicted on them. Their accounts often blamed the excitement and disturbance incited by reading for undermining their capacity to retain mastery and direction over their emotional life. The philosopher and chemist Robert Boyle (1627–1691) believed that he was never able to recover from the effects of reading the 'adventures of *Amadis de Gaule* and other fabulous stories' while a schoolboy. Boyle stated that these romances 'prejudiced him, by unsettling his thoughts', since they 'accustomed his thoughts to such a habitude of roving, that he [had] scarce ever been their master since'.[9]

Although the narrative of the passions gave way to newer ideas in medical science about the relationship between the body and the mind, its common-sense meaning retained influence in discussions about the impact of literature and other publications on the reader. Since Boyle's time, the loss of focus and concentration has been frequently represented as the legacy of morally dubious reading practices. Until recently, one of the riskiest literary practices diagnosed was that of 'over-reading'. The physician and astrologer Richard Napier (1559–1634) identified 'excessive reading' with a variety of mental health problems, claiming to have found numerous women readers whose brains were 'overheated from the effort': they 'complained of insomnia, breathlessness, trembling, upset stomachs, vertigo, headaches, ringing ears, "rising" sensations, swooning and general weakness'.[10]

The act of reading and the internalization of the text were frequently conveyed through an analogy with the physical act of eating and digestion. The metaphor of eating was regularly used in discussions about reading until the turn of the twentieth century. Francis Bacon advised that 'some books are to be tasted, others to be swallowed and some few to be chewed and digested'[11] – and his distinction between tasting, swallowing, chewing and digesting corresponded to different types of reading practices. He counselled that only a very few books deserved to be read with 'diligence and attention', and therefore entirely digested. As one commentary on Bacon explained, 'digestion, the necessary separation of that which is useful from that which is harmful, becomes a very literal metaphor for the proper act of reading'.[12]

The careful digestion of books was promoted as the healthy way to read the printed text in the nineteenth century. The German philosopher Friedrich Nietzsche (1844–1900) proposed that one should eat like a 'cow' to ensure that ideas were slowly mulled over, 'ruminated, consumed twice'.[13] However, the analogy between reading and the metabolic process of digestion frequently contained the implication that the consumption of books may be carried to excess – particularly by the newly emergent mass public of readers. The philosopher John Stuart Mill (1806–1873), who was unsettled by the extraordinary expansion of publishing in his time, observed that the public now 'gorges itself with intellectual food, and in order to swallow the more, *bolts* it'.[14] For many critics of the indiscriminate gluttony of the plebeian reader, the cheap Penny Dreadfuls were the moral equivalent of today's fast food.

Twentieth-century commentators worried about the indiscriminate literary practices of mass culture regularly echoed Mill's sentiments. The Anglican commentator A. L. Maycock stated in 1929 that he had 'little doubt that we all read too much nowadays and place far too heavy a tax on the assimilative powers of the mind; for just as gluttony defeats the end of healthy nourishment, so inordinate reading will simply clog the mind and induce a condition of mental torpor and inactivity'. Maycock could not think of a 'more efficacious method of intellectual suicide' than such gluttony, and predicted that unless something was done to contain its effects, 'the mighty tide of contemporary printed matter will overwhelm us and whirl us into chattering insanity'.[15]

The use of the physical analogy of digestion for the depiction of reading conveyed a moral critique of this practice. Consequently those who read more than the recommended healthy amount were accused of 'devouring books'; these gluttons of literature were indicted as far more 'guilty of abusing nature' than those who merely 'overcharge their stomachs' with food.[16] This sentiment was argued at length by the art critic John Ruskin (1819–1900), whose warnings about 'gluttonous reading' constituted a moral critique of the undigested consumption of books. With Ruskin, the transformation of the aesthetic and intellectual dimension of reading into an uneasy tension between the physical and the moral representation of this experience acquired an exaggerated moralistic tone: 'You must read, for the nourishment of your mind, precisely under the same moral laws which regulate your eating for the nourishment of the body.'[17] For Ruskin, the moral laws that regulated both eating and reading discouraged any hedonistic or sensual aspiration for gaining pleasure from these activities. He explained that 'you must not eat for the pleasure of eating, nor read for the pleasure of reading', but acknowledged that under the right conditions both 'your dinner and your book' can be enjoyed.[18]

As far as Ruskin was concerned, 'filthy and foul reading' was a 'much more loathsome habit than filthy eating', because the former represented a threat to the soul while the latter only inflicted damage on the body. He concluded that 'all acting for pleasure before use, or instead of use, is in one word, Fornication'.[19] Ruskin used the word 'fornication' in its biblical sense, which connotes the forsaking of God for idols: his denunciation of gluttonous reading is entirely directed at the moral hazards of reading for pleasure.

Ruskin's views were widely held amongst literary critics of popular culture and mass reading in the nineteenth century. As Kelly Mays writes, 'even in eating, ideally, the higher powers of the mind –will, reason and judgment – were in full control', whereas the hedonism and pleasure-seeking that led to the devouring of books overwhelmed the imagination of the reader. Mays explains that 'driven by sensual attraction rather than a rational calculation of nutritional value, such reading confused the proper hierarchical relation between body and mind'.[20]

The constant shift from the physical to the moral effects of reading was and remains a recurring theme of the moral censure of the misuse of literary and media consumption. The arguments used to justify such censure tended to be pragmatic and opportunistic, and often shifted from warnings about risks to the reader's physical or mental health to alarmist accounts about the dire effects of moral contamination. In her review of the different approaches adopted by critics of the novel in the nineteenth century, Ana Vogrinčič indicates that:

> [B]roadly, one could divide the reproaches into those ascribing to novels the dangerous psychological affects, triggering imitation and inoculating wrong ideas of love and life; and into those referring to the mere habit of novel-reading as a physically harmful waste of time, damaging not only the mind and the morale of readers, but also their eyesight and posture.[21]

Such accounts of the moral and physical risks of reading often presumed that the reader was literally helpless against the irresistible attraction, seductive power and temptation of the printed text. The power of books to subvert the virtuous meant that they had to be regulated; and censorship served as the moral equivalent of protecting the physically healthy through quarantining the victims of an infectious disease. One American critic of 'printed poison' argued that an 'impure man' who is 'poisoning society' with 'smutty stories' was a 'moral ulcer, a plague spot, a leper,' who should be 'banished from society' as 'were lepers of old'.[22] A review of Oscar Wilde's novel *The Picture of Dorian Gray* (1890) adopted a similar tone, denouncing it as a 'tale spawned from the leprous literature of the French Décadents – a poisonous book, the atmosphere of which is heavy with the mephitic odours of moral and spiritual putrefaction – a gloating study of the mental and physical corruption of a fresh, fair and golden youth'.[23]

INSATIABLE APPETITES

Since the beginning of modernity, one of the main risks connected with reading and the other media has been their power to turn consumers into addicts with insatiable appetites. The Socratic characterization of writing as a drug mutated into the representation of reading as addictive. According to the model of literary addiction adopted in most descriptions of this ailment, not all books were equally risky. The literature that was regarded as most analogous to a dangerous drug were the sensationalist and cheap publications that excited the emotions and whose consumption required very little effort. In the nineteenth century, the so-called 'sensation novel' was regularly described as an addictive drug like opium.[24] The English philosopher Henry Mansel (1820–1871) asserted that 'the readers of sensational novels resembled "dram drinkers" in the grip of "perpetual cravings"'.[25]

Such assertions were rarely supported by evidence, and their authors did not make an attempt to explain the origins of the perpetual cravings or the insatiable appetites of sections of the reading public. Were these addictions caused by the literature these people read, or was it the way they read that triggered their unhappy mental state?

Often the metaphors of gluttonous eating and ingesting drugs were used alongside one another to draw attention to the pathology of excessive reading. At the turn of the twentieth century, President Gilman of Johns Hopkins University stated that 'the present excess of reading is something in the nature of a craze, a vice; and people may be really eating literature as they eat opium'.[26] Over a century earlier the German philosopher Johann Gottlieb Fichte (1762–1814) had explained the narcotic effects of reading for its own sake in the following terms:

> This custom of reading for its own sake is specifically different from every other habit of mind; and, having something about it in the highest degree agreeable, it soon becomes an indispensable want to those who once indulge in it. Like other narcotic remedies, it places those who use it in the pleasant condition betwixt sleeping and waking, and lulls them into sweet self-forgetfulness, without calling for the slightest exertion on their part. It has always appeared to me to have the greatest resemblance to tobacco-smoking, and to be best illustrated by that habit. He who has once tasted the delights of this condition will desire continually to enjoy them, and will devote himself to nothing else: he now reads even without regard to the knowledge of Literature, or to advancing with his Age, but with this view only – that he may read, and reading live; and so represents in his person the character of the pure Reader.[27]

Fichte's musing on the custom of reading for 'its own sake' recognized that unlike other vices which had no redeeming qualities, this activity was a source of aesthetic pleasure. The danger of this highly 'agreeable' activity was that it could turn into an 'indispensable want' with highly addictive consequences.

The metamorphosis of an agreeable activity into a deadly vice parallels the transformation of virtue into a sin, and sin into a medical condition. Fichte's target is what he describes as the 'pure Reader'. These are readers who have adopted the 'custom of reading for its own sake' and have detached themselves from the responsibilities of everyday life. Fichte's rebuke to the 'pure Reader' made no distinction between the genres of literature used to satisfy the cravings of the addict. The transformation of the love of reading into the pathology of addiction by a philosopher devoted to the exploration of the problem of self-consciousness and subjectivity speaks to the influence of the medical model of reading in his time.

In contrast to Fichte, most exposés of the dangers of addiction tended specifically to blame mass-produced publications that appealed to base instincts for intensifying the public's appetite for literary narcotics. An essay titled 'The Literature of the Streets', which reviewed ten popular publications directed at schoolchildren and was published by the *Edinburgh Review* in 1887, warned that sensationalist periodicals such as *Police News* and *Newgate Calendar* were far too easily available to young people. The essayist portrayed this literature, which sought to appeal to young people's desire for gratification, thus:

> The feast spread for them is ready and abundant; but every dish is poisoned, unclean and shameful. Every flavour is a false one, every condiment vile. Every morsel of food is doctored, every draught of wine is drugged; no true hunger is satisfied and no true thirst is quenched.[28]

This interweaving of food, alcohol and drugs illustrated a tendency to search for a compelling metaphor for capturing the pathology of reading.

The analogy of gluttony stressed the self-destructive character of the hunger for reading, claiming that it was not true hunger or a true thirst for knowledge that drove the passion for unrestrained reading. This was influenced by the emergence of what in the current era would be characterized as an anti-consumerist sensibility. This ethos through which distinctions between the refined and the coarse sensibility was drawn, and its denunciation of readers addicted to the quick fix of a cheap literary buzz, anticipates the twentieth-century anti-consumerist critique of false needs.[29] In 1874, Alfred Austin (1835–1913) – soon to be appointed Poet Laureate – sought to throw light on the 'vice of reading' by claiming that the 'habit of novel reading, novel upon novel for reading's sake' was relatively inexpensive compared to other vices. Austin claimed that 'novel drinking is not so expensive, so outwardly repulsive, as dram drinking, nor can it be said that it brings the same ruin and disgrace upon families – but the individual is as surely enfeebled by it, taste corrupted, will unstrung, understanding saddened'.[30]

Austin's model of addiction offered a synthesis through which the risk to health and moral well-being could be expressed. The characteristics of human weakness, irresponsibility and loss of moral virtue were communicated through the idiom of a vice, and his association of the vice of habitual novel reading with alcohol became part of an elitist cultural narrative directed at mass culture. Writing in 1932, the prominent literary critic Q. D. Leavis recalled that the 'effect of an inordinate addiction to light reading was known (mainly by repute) to the nineteenth century: it came under the head of "dissipation", and to read novels, as to drink wine, in the morning was far into the century a sign of vice'.[31] For her part, Leavis had little doubt that the continuing prevalence of this addiction in the twentieth century was symptomatic of a wider trend towards cultural decline.

The representation of publications targeting the market of mass readers as comparable to the selling of addictive substances continued to be widely promoted in criticisms of popular culture. For example, J. B. Priestley's 1942 novel *Blackout in Gretley* indicts shopkeepers selling romantic fiction for peddling 'dreams and dope'. Such books offer 'opium without a hangover at about a farthing an hour'.[32] This sentiment was echoed in 1950 by the novelist Lucille Iremonger who stated that women's weeklies were essentially 'mental drugs' that caused suburban neuroses and 'squalid divorces'.[33]

MORAL POISON

Lucille Iremonger's use of the term 'mental drug' to devalue the publications she held in contempt drew on a centuries-old tradition of demonizing literary texts. The representation of books as forms of poison was widespread within theological disputes about heresy. Sir Thomas More reacted to the literature of the Reformation by castigating these books as 'deadly poisons that threatened to infect readers with "contagious pestilence"';[34] others used terms like 'moral poison' or 'literary poison' to draw attention to the capacity of a written text to contaminate the body.[35] The German philosopher Arthur Schopenhauer (1778–1860) described 'bad books' as 'intellectual poison' that 'destroy the mind'.[36] For the author Sidney Dark (1874–1947), it was regrettable that for most of the new reading public the consumption of the text was regarded as a mere narcotic, and 'books that are nothing but narcotics are, in the long run, as destructive of real life and real living as cocaine'.[37]

The danger posed by moral poison to a gratification-seeking public was most frequently linked to publications that were deemed to be obscene. However, moral crusaders in the nineteenth and twentieth centuries tended to have an expansive definition of obscenity and were very liberal in their characterization of the 'toxic' effects of publications. Josiah Leeds, author of the pamphlet *Concerning Printed Poison* (1885), distinguished between the 'obscene' and the 'pernicious influence of cheap novels', which were not 'necessarily filthy' but nevertheless had a poisonous effect on society.[38]

From the late nineteenth century onwards, the medicalization and moralization of reading acquired a new momentum in response to a growing preoccupation with obscene publications and the dramatic expansion of sensation-provoking newspapers. In 1880 the New York Society for the Suppression of Vice stated: 'The result of this literary poison, cast into the very foundations of social life, is found everywhere. It is infecting the pure life and heart of our youth.' Its 1875 Report, written by the American Victorian moralist Anthony Comstock, warned of 'shrewd and wily' dealers of obscene material who had 'succeeded in inject[ing] a virus more destructive to innocence and purity of youth, if not counteracted, than can be most deadly disease in the body':

> If we had the ear of all the teachers, parents, and guardians, in our land
> we would plead with them, 'Guard with ceaseless vigilance your libraries,
> your closets, your children's and wards' correspondence and companion-
> ships, lest the contagion reach and blight the sweetness and purity of
> your homes.[39]

Comstock's call for parents to read their children's letters and police their reading materials was not simply an expression of Victorian obsession with moral pollution. Cautionary advice to parents highlighted anxieties about the capacity of the older generation to socialize and educate children and young people to adopt the values of the moral order. The teaching of reading, and children's literary habits, were perceived as subjects of moral concern because their impressionable minds made them prey to corrupting influences.

Just as Ruskin believed that gluttonous reading was more dangerous than over-eating food, the moral poison transmitted through reading was often considered to have far more perilous consequences than physical poison. James Douglas, the editor of the *Sunday Express* and self-declared campaigner against the 'contamination and corruption of English fiction', attacked *The Well of Loneliness* (1928), a novel by Radclyffe Hall about the isolation faced by lesbians, for its promotion of 'degeneracy'. He hoped that the outrage provoked by this novel would force society to undertake the 'task of cleansing itself from the leprosy of these lepers'. 'I would rather give a healthy boy or a healthy girl a phial of prussic acid than this novel,' declared Douglas, because 'poison kills the body, but moral poison kills the soul'.[40]

Readers who did not show refinement and the requisite amount of discrimination and taste were assumed to be bad readers. The Victorians 'were the first bad readers in Western history,' argues Nicholas Dames.[41] They didn't lack the skills to decode the text but rather the moral attributes necessary for reading well. The University of the State of New York drew attention to the absence of the 'higher' and 'purer' forms of thought required for good reading, distinguishing between people who read and those who were literary: 'The novel reading mania of the day, the trash and worse than trash that pours from the press, fills the bookstores and is found in nine parlours out of ten, proves that people read. But for all that they are not literary.'[42] For the authors of this report, the fact that people just 'read' was the marker of a failing.

THE CONSTRUCTION OF ATTENTION DEFICIT DISORDER

Through the medicalization of the impact of reading on the reader, a bewildering variety of moral deficits, illnesses and physical defects were attributed to it. Alfred Austin's essay 'The Vice of Reading' offered a veritable manual of disorders caused by the curse of misreading, warning that reading is far too often a 'vulgar, detrimental habit, like dram-drinking; an excuse for idleness; not only not an education in itself, but a stumbling-block in the way of education; a cloak thrown over ignorance; a softening, demoralising, relaxing practice, which if persisted in, will end by enfeebling the minds of men and women, making flabby the fibre of their bodies, and undermining the vigour of nations'. Austin indicted reading as 'rapidly destroying all thinking and all powers of thought'.[43]

Aside from undermining thinking, Austin saw the reading of books and newspapers as leading to the loss of conversation, and the physical decline of the reader. He asserted that 'books are used as an excuse for coddling and laziness', announcing that:

> [S]uch reading as at present prevails has, by reason both of its quality
> and quantity, led to a deterioration of the human species, physically,
> mentally, and morally, we entertain no doubt; nor do we see how, unless
> the vicious habit be somehow corrected, the race can escape from being
> ultimately divided into two sections, the members of one of which will
> be little removed from invalids, and the members of the other scarcely
> distinguishable from cretins.[44]

Today, Austin's reference to readers who become 'flabby' and turn into 'cretins' comes across as bizarre; and many of the distressing symptoms that he has connected with reading are the artefacts of the Victorian imagination. However, one affliction that has been consistently identified as one of the principal risks of media consumption is that of distraction. Austin's fear that reading served to divert attention from performing 'some duty which is distasteful' alluded to the loss of a sense of responsibility. When combined with a loss of the 'powers of thought', the distracted reader also risks a weakening of the normal functioning of cognition.

One of the first recorded attempts to warn readers about the distracting effects of books came in Seneca's letter to Lucilius, which was written between AD 63 and 65. Here Seneca counterposed the restless and disordered spirit to the ordered mind, and warned that the reading of too many books 'tends to make you discursive and unsteady'. Drawing a parallel with the consumption of food that is not properly digested, Seneca warned that in 'reading of many books is distraction'.[45]

Concern with the distracting effects of reading escalated with the print revolution, the growth of the mass market in publications, and the availability of relatively cheaply produced books and periodicals. At this point in time, the traditional concerns about the emotional upheavals caused by reading were reinforced by a growing sense of unease with the disorienting consequence of modernization and technological change. Karin Littau argues that the experience of modernity's assault on the senses was perceived as undermining many readers' capacity to reflect, contemplate and truly digest their books. In such circumstances, technological change and modernization created the conditions for 'the kind of "unsettled reading" which Richard Steele of *The Guardian* criticized as far back as 1713 because it "naturally seduces us into an undetermined manner of thinking".[46]

During the nineteenth century, the most important negative health impact of the novel was thought to be its toxic consequence for the exercise of cognition.[47] Nicholas Dames's study on *The Physiology of the Novel* notes that this preoccupation with cognition led to the elaboration of a theory that represented distracted inattentive reading as a major cultural problem. In this regard, the modern-day condition of Attention Deficit Disorder gained cultural legitimacy over a century ago. During the century that followed, what Dames has characterized as the 'morality of attention' played an important role in cultural and intellectual criticisms of distracted readers and inattentive audiences. Dames described the morality of attention as a 'social morality – concerned with the ability to act knowingly and responsibly'.[48] What Dames characterized as the morality of attention can also be interpreted as the *moralization* of attention, with distraction as its moral opposite.

In the present day, the pathology of distraction is expressed in the language of brain science. Through the narrative of neuroscience the old problem of cognition is recast in a language that is apparently free of moral judgement. 'Multitasking has been found to increase the production of the stress hormone cortisol as well as the fight-or-flight hormone adrenaline, which can overstimulate your brain and cause mental fog or scrambled thinking', claims one writer on the problem of information overload.[49] It appears that the reading mania of the nineteenth century has been displaced by the twenty-first-century condition of 'info-mania',[50] with distracted multitaskers as the contemporary equivalents of careless and irresponsible novel readers. David Mikics describes this condition as that of Continuous Partial Attention, which apparently occurs 'when we try to do too much at once'.[51]

In the nineteenth and early twentieth centuries, the construction of a causal connection between reading and a temporal shortening of attention was integral to a critique of adult reading habits of popular fiction. Accounts about the loss of attention and concentration sought to illustrate their concern by pointing to the reduction in the size of the British novel towards the end of nineteenth century. With the demise of the three-volume novel in 1894, 'observers of the phenomenon of literary shrinking began to wonder if the decline was caused by a reading public less interested in prolonged texts, or was instead gradually creating a public without the cognitive equipment necessary for their consumption.'[52]

References to poor or short attention spans first appeared around the middle of the nineteenth century,[53] and the shortening of the general reader's attention span emerged as a theme for discussion at the turn of the twentieth century. Attention span was defined as the length of time a person could attend continuously to one type of stimulus, and one of the concerns discussed in medical and psychological journals was its relation to poor reading habits. By the first decades of the twentieth century, psychologists actively pursued the testing and measuring of people's attention span.

The connection between poor reading practices and loss of the capacity for attention was rarely elaborated. In a tautological manner, it was sometimes assumed that the lack of effort required to absorb light reading material was proof of a failure to concentrate on a text for a prolonged period of time. Critics of bad reading habits also argued that it was precisely because readers became far too absorbed in novels that they lost the capacity to reflect and think. Lord Eustace Percy, a former Minister of Education, adopted this approach in his speech in 1927 to the Joint Session of Associated Booksellers and the National Book Council, noting that 'nearly everyone in this country' has the habit of reading but 'has it very badly.' Percy claimed that 'one of the great evils of present-day reading is that it discourages thought.'[54]

Today, when questions are raised about the difficulty of cultivating the habit of reading, Lord Eustace Percy's reservations about the value of such a habit comes across as positively perverse. So too does the claim that the Victorian novel offers casual readers the kind of distraction that will only diminish their attentiveness to the printed text. While apprehension about the distracted mind is a persistent feature of the modern era, the way the problem is perceived has undergone significant historical variations: as Dames points out, 'cognitive categories like attention or duration' do not have 'stable ethical and political meanings over time'.[55]

In the present day, distraction is rarely linked to reading. Indeed it is frequently claimed that people suffer from a deficit of the kind of attention required to read a book; and this is usually blamed on the digital media. The imperative of moralization and medicalization is often expressed through the idiom of neuroscience, via warnings about what the promiscuous consumption of digital technology is doing to the human brain. Apparently, digital addiction hits the part of the brain that some neuroscientists characterize as the 'pleasure centre', which 'regulates dopamine production and is the region that "lights up" when gamblers bet, drug addicts take cocaine, or people have orgasms'.[56]

In this way, the symptoms and diagnosis offered by eighteenth- and nineteenth-century critics of risky reading have been rediscovered by twenty-first-century neuroscientists. Cautionary tales are no longer focused on the demise of young maidens who read *Werther*; instead, digitally induced distraction is held responsible for acts of self-destruction. Thus the neuroscientist Daniel Levitin warns about the dangers of addictive behaviour on social media by evoking the spectacle of a 30-year-old man who died in Guangzhou, China, after playing videogames non-stop for three days, and a Korean man who suffered a fatal heart attack after 50 hours of gaming.[57]

'Even devotees of the Internet often confess to being frustrated by what happens when they are online: they waste hours of time everyday with distractions, and learn little beyond some handful of facts that are soon forgotten,' asserts a self-help book titled *Slow Reading in a Hurried Age*.[58] Outwardly, this diagnosis appears as an updated version of the nineteenth-century lament about the distracted reading habits of those engaged with sensationalist novels. But the problem is no longer seen as that of an individual's reading habits: rather it is the problem of a 'hurried age', in which the entire media landscape appears as a land of distraction. Books with titles like *Distracted: The Erosion of Attention and the Coming Dark Age* or *The Lost Art of Reading: Why Books Matter in a Distracted Time* draw attention to a problem that transcends the individual reader. The (in)capacity for attention has been naturalized to the point that reading implicitly conveys the idea of a problem.

THE ANALOGY CONTESTED

Despite all the scaremongering about the moral and health effects of risky reading habits, the market for literature, newspapers and popular publications continued to expand during most of the nineteenth and twentieth centuries. One study of the nineteenth-century reading public in England notes that working-class people often read books that they were warned against;[59] and although the literary establishment of Europe and America tended to adopt a medicalized language to describe the reading habits of the public, there was also a substantial group of writers and commentators whose love of reading led them to draw very different conclusion. They, too, connected intoxicating and even addictive properties with the practice, but attributed positive qualities to the unrestrained joy of reading.

Positive accounts of the powerful drug-like effects of reading pointed to its therapeutic properties. The older religious theme of gaining conversion and salvation through reading were reworked into a secular language that emphasized 'consolation and escape', a 'solace for loneliness, boredom, homesickness, worry, grief, even physical pain'.[60] For many readers it was this therapeutic effect that served as an invitation to pick up a book. Others regarded its drug-like properties as useful for gaining insight, inspiration and meaning. For some readers, books served as essential medicine. The Scottish publisher and author Robert Chambers (1802–1871) described books as the 'blessed chloroform of the mind', and wondered 'how folks in trouble did without them in old time'.[61] In his essay *The Hygienic Chemistry of Books* the novelist Edward Bulwer-Lytton (1803–1873) light-heartedly wrote that human psychological ailments can be cured by the right kind of reading. To some he prescribed books on geology; to others, the works of Fichte; and to an individual in deep sorrow he suggested the biography of 'good and great men'.[62]

The American essayist and poet Ralph Waldo Emerson (1803–1882) wrote in his diary that 'all the authors are enchanted men; intoxicated, plainly, with that stray drop of nectar or idealism they have imbibed'. The intoxication experienced by author or poet could lead to a 'sublime vision' when communicated through literature, which cannot but intoxicate the reader. Emerson wrote that 'if the imagination intoxicates the poet, it is not inactive in other men'; it was this experience of intoxication that helped the author to capture the truth.[63] Nietzsche made a similar point when he stated that 'for art to exist, for any sort of aesthetic activity or perception to exist, a certain physiological precondition is indispensable: *ecstasy*'. Nietzsche used the German word *Rausch* – a blend of the terms intoxication and elation – to signify the unleashing of unrestrained passions necessary for aesthetic creativity.[64]

That readers through the centuries have experienced the intoxicant of the books they consumed is a matter of record. Contrary to the medicalized health deficits assigned to imbibing this stimulant, most readers reported that the experience overwhelmed them in the positive sense of rousing their aesthetic, intellectual or psychological sensibilities. The novelist Hugh Walpole (1884–1941) made no concession to scaremongering about addiction in his 1926 essay *Reading*, when he stated that a 'true Reader' is 'one to whom books are like bottles of whisky to the inebriate, to whom anything that is between covers has a sort of intoxicating savour'.[65]

In a series of books written in the 1930s and 1940s the English writer and critic Holbrook Jackson (1874–1948) sought to expose the tendentious manner in which medical–moral categories were used in relation to reading. His approach was to question what he considered to be the one-sided characterization of reading as poisonous, and emphasize its therapeutic and curative effects: 'If we are to take sedatives books are better than drugs.'[66] Jackson recognized that books could be upsetting and overwhelming, but he argued that on balance the beneficial effects of reading far outweighed the risks, declaring that 'although one man's book is another's poison, the power of books in *generating virtue* is probably, as William Godwin speculated, much greater than in generating vice'.[67]

Jackson's studies did not reject the health-related analogies of reading; rather, he attempted to reprise and illuminate the traditional medical–moral narrative from the standpoint of the reader. He advocated dealing with the dangers of literary toxins through the application of common sense, writing that:

> Books are like food, every article of which has its poison: *the peach with its prussic acid, the pie-plant with oxalic acid, tea with its tannic acid, the tomato and even the potato, each with its own deleterious ingredient,* point

at dangers which we must conquer or starve; and just as we conquer the poisons by a judicious internal selection, an instructive cunning, so we must learn to digest what is good for us in books and eject what is bad.[68]

Jackson questioned what he interpreted as a one-sided emphasis on how books misguide and corrupt readers. He cited William Godwin's caution against the model of moral contagion through reading, namely that 'he that would extract poison from them, must for the most come to them with a mind already debauched'.[69]

Jackson was fully aware of the intoxicating power of reading, but he represented this physical and emotional effect as a positive experience. He believed that intoxication 'presumes a sensitised response to experience, a sense of power and a power of sense: the desire to receive and develop impressions, to produce that state of mind which encourages perception to express itself in immediate and gratifying sensation'. As far as he was concerned, this sensibility was related to a condition 'called inspiration'.[70]

One of the first attempts to offer a thoroughgoing critique of the medical–moral framing of reading was by the American free-speech advocate Theodore Schroeder (1864–1953). In a fascinating essay, *Freedom of the Press and 'Obscene' Literature* (1906), he directly called into question the project of legitimating the policing of reading through an appeal to the authority of medical science. Schroeder rejected the use of analogies with health and the metaphor of toxicity to interpret the experience of reading, intending to discredit intolerant calls for the censorship of immoral reading material. 'Much of the justification for intolerance derives its authority from false analogies, wrongfully carried over from physical relations into the realm of the psychic', wrote Schroeder, explaining that:

> [S]ome argue that because, by laws we protect the incompetent against being (unconsciously) infected with contagious disease, therefore the state should protect them (even though mature and able to protect themselves by mere inattention) against the literature of infectious morals. Here a figure of speech is mistaken for an analogy. 'Moral poison' exists only figuratively and not literally in any such sense as strychnine is a poison.[71]

Schroeder sought to elaborate his critique by arguing that the attempt to legitimate a moral standpoint on the basis of science was illegitimate, since ethics are subjective, historically specific and culturally relative: 'The morality of one country or age is viewed as the moral poison of another country or age'.[72]

Schroeder's argument about the historically variable character of moral perceptions and reactions is clearly validated by the shift in attitudes towards reading and specific genres of literature. Victorian readers of novels were often cast in the role of fickle and irresponsible individuals who were at risk of moral corruption; yet in the early twenty-first century the Victorian novel is still celebrated as a major cultural achievement. Even the most incorrigible present-day moralist is unlikely to be tempted to launch a crusade against the Victorian novel on the grounds that it poses medical and moral risks to the reader.

The shifting reaction to the moral status of the novel occurs because the act and the meaning of reading are both subject to historical variations. One reason why the reading of novels was denigrated in the nineteenth century was because almost anyone could gain access to and derive pleasure from this activity. Critics insisted that the reading of novels required little effort; reading was not associated with exertion, intellectual curiosity and determination, but rather with laziness and irresponsibility. Yet today we are continually informed that people lack the determination to read novels and literature, and it is engagement with electronic and digital media that is now condemned for being too easy.

THE IMPERATIVE OF MEDICALIZATION

The moral discourse that surrounded reading in the past has declined relative to the growing presence of the language of medicalization, where problems with any form of media are framed in terms of health effects. Take the example of E. L. James's semi-pornographic three-volume series *Fifty Shades of Grey*. *Fifty Shades* has topped the best-seller lists around the world since the publication of its first volume in 2011; the series has sold over 100 million copies and been translated into 52 languages.

In striking contrast to nineteenth- and twentieth-century reactions to novels whose narrative is dominated by sexual activity, there has been very little moral outrage expressed at the content of *Fifty Shades of Grey*. Numerous critics have questioned the poor quality of James's writing and its depiction of women but nevertheless treated it as just another routine novel to be reviewed. Mainstream Western society has been relaxed about its publication, to the point where *Publishers Weekly* named the author Publishing Person of the Year and millions of readers are prepared to be publicly identified with reading it. Indeed, by the time the film spin-off of this novel was released, *Fifty Shades of Grey* had become a topic of national conversation, with sections of the public indicating that they were curious about what they could learn from the sexual practices featured in the film.

From a historical perspective, what is fascinating about society's reception of *Fifty Shades* is that, insofar as any concerns were raised about its effects on readers, these were communicated through the language of mental and physical health deficits. Academic studies on the effects of the novel claimed to have discovered that reading it was linked to 'unhealthy behaviours' such as unsafe sex and binge drinking: apparently two-thirds of the novel's readers had had five or more sexual partners during their lifetime.

One study, published in *Journal of Women's Health,* claimed that reading *Fifty Shades* was a marker for being involved in an abusive relationship.[73] The study was justified on the grounds that there was no prior research on the association between 'health risks and reading popular fiction depicting violence against women'. Following the well-worn tracks of the Werther Effect, this study openly acknowledged that the absence of empirical evidence is not a barrier to drawing strong conclusions about the health effects of reading certain types of fiction: 'despite the lack of empirical studies on this topic, scholars suggest that individuals regularly alter their real-world beliefs and attitudes in response to fictional communication.'[74] Although the authors of this research implicitly believe that reading various types of fiction can have 'harmful effects on attitudes and beliefs', they are careful to refrain from offering an explicit moral critique.

The current tendency to articulate concerns about reading certain types of fiction in the language of risks to health, concerns that were previously framed through the grammar of morality, has important implications for the way in which reading is perceived. Literacy, which has often been perceived as a moral virtue, is today treated more as a cognitive skill. Being a cognitive skill, reading becomes denuded of any morally valued qualities and, as we discuss in the next chapter, faces the challenge of being culturally devalued.

7

The Complication of Reading

How people read and what they read is widely perceived as an important element of their identity, and the identities of readers are seen as a statement about their character. That is why observations about readers are so often both evaluative and prescriptive: such observations serve to enhance cultural distinctions between different types of readers. Statements on this subject are often designed to influence people's character through moral guidance of their reading. With the rise of mass schooling, such guidance became formalized and was communicated through educational psychology and pedagogy.

The use of authority figures to guide reading habits was justified on the grounds that expertise was necessary for undertaking this task. What followed was the transformation of reading into a complicated practice for which, it was claimed, many children were not naturally suited. With the expansion of education, the weight of society's apprehensions about certain types of reading matter moved from the adult to the child, blending with anxieties about socialization. This did not mean, however, that adult reading ceased to be an issue: from the 1940s onwards the shortcomings of the illiterate or semi-literate adult emerged as a topic for policy-makers, and society would frequently sublimate its unease through the narrative of a 'crisis of literacy'.

THE READING CLASS

By now it should be evident that comments made about readers or the effects of reading rarely have the character of a neutral observation. Such remarks, whether they criticize or eulogize readers, are based on the subjective experience of the commentator and are underpinned by a set of assumptions about the value of literacy. Statements about readers and reading, even when they are conveyed in the technical or scientific jargon of skills and cognition, are invariably prescriptive. The manner in which reading is discussed is informed by wider attitudes regarding values, taste, social order, views about human potential, and education.

Thus the guidance outlined by the American Bureau of National Literature in 1907 praised the 'love of reading' and stated that it was a 'chief means of mental growth'; but its acclaim of the love of reading had as its premise the capacity to choose 'what is clean and good'.[1] The making of choices about cleanliness and goodness transposes reading practices into the domain of morality and character formation. If indeed reading is the 'chief means of mental growth', its corollary is that, if this activity is misused, it can have grave consequences.

With so much energy devoted to finding solutions to the problems associated with reading, it is easy to overlook the fact that medicalized and moral condemnation tended to be directed at what other people, and other classes, read. Those who campaigned against the vice of reading were at the same time implicitly proclaiming themselves as the arbiters of good taste. Their narrative of condemnation had as its flipside the narrative of self-praise.

Reflections on reading often represent an argument about what makes a person an ideal reader, as well as a claim to the right to guide the reading of others. An essay titled 'What Books to Read, and How to Read Them', written by an anonymous reviewer in 1859, noted with disparagement that the 'vicarious way of reading through periodical literature, instead of valiantly mastering books themselves, utterly emasculates the mind'.[2] The connection of valiant mastery with reading suggests that this is a statement about image and character. Clearly the question of how to read was implicitly answered by the author with the precept 'Read the way I do'.

Sir John Lubbock, who in 1896 drew up a list of 100 books worth reading, emphasized the need to select reading material with care. He complained that 'many people read almost by hazard', and his criticism of people who do not use their library 'wisely' was integral to his unspoken claim to possess authority to guide the reader.[3] Lubbock, like most members of the Anglo-American literary establishment, represented good reading as bound up with the practice of discrimination. The philosopher and essayist Thomas Carlyle (1795–1881) regarded books as 'momentous, wonderful and worthy', demanding readers who would exercise care and attention. 'Learn to be good readers – which is perhaps a more difficult thing than you imagine,' lectured Carlyle, adding that one should 'learn to be discriminative in your reading'.[4] Similar sentiments were conveyed by the poet and critic Matthew Arnold (1822–1888), who asserted that 'culture is reading' – but only so long as it was reading 'with a purpose to guide it, and with a system'.[5]

A century later, Mao Zedong echoed Arnold's advocacy of purposeful reading. Mao, head of the Chinese Communist Party, came across as a Victorian moralist when he told his audience in February 1964 that 'it is evident that to read too many books is harmful'.[6] After dwelling on the state of the Chinese education system, he reiterated his dislike of 'reading so many books', offering a Stalinist variant of the Victorian narrative on the corrupting effect of indiscriminate reading. Mao proclaimed:

> We shouldn't read too many books. We should read Marxist books, but not too many of them either. It will be enough to read a dozen or so. If we read too many, we can move towards our opposites, become bookworms, dogmatists, revisionists. In the writings of Confucius, there is nothing about agriculture. Because of this, the limbs of his students were not accustomed to toil, and they could not distinguish between the five grains. We must do something about this.[7]

In this instance, the philistine outlook that underpinned Mao's warning about reading 'too many books' represented an alternative way of justifying discrimination in reading. The casual manner with which passionate readers are dismissed as 'bookworms' exposes the self-serving and selective way that guidance on reading is issued.

The term *discrimination* implies the making of distinctions, the drawing of differences and the use of judgement. The *Oxford English Dictionary* states that from the eighteenth century onwards this concept conveyed the implication of 'refined taste, good judgement, or knowledgeableness'.[8] Implicit in invoking the value of discrimination as an integral feature of good reading was the claim that only a relatively small minority of the public were likely to have the judgement to become a good reader. The American novelist Edith Wharton (1862–1937) was dismissive of what she labelled as 'mechanical reading' in her essay 'The Vice of Reading'. Wharton elevated the status of reading well to an 'art that only the born reader can acquire'. Wharton was far more explicit than most in spelling out a distinction between those who possessed the 'gift of reading' and the great mass of mechanical readers.[9]

The elevation of reading into an art form and its depiction as a gift conveys the assumption that not everyone who can read is a reader. In its most self-conscious form, the cultural depiction of reading as a gift was voiced through the contrast between the literary critic and the reading public. The novelist Virginia Woolf alluded to this contrast in her essay on the 'Common Reader', describing that person as someone who is 'worse educated' than a critic and who 'nature has not gifted' so 'generously' as his more elevated counterpart. According to Woolf, the common reader is 'hasty, inaccurate, and superficial', and of course 'his deficiencies as a critic are too obvious to be pointed out'.[10]

The unapologetically elitist contrast drawn between a small minority of gifted readers and the multitude of mechanical ones runs against the *Zeitgeist* of the present day. Nevertheless narratives that assign to reading the status of a unique art form and distinguish between a gifted few and the mediocre majority retain influence in literary circles. The literary critic Harold Bloom fears for the loss of the culture of great reading, and vigorously defends the tradition upheld by writers from Samuel Johnson to Virginia Woolf. Bloom insists that the revival of proper reading 'can only be performed by some version of elitism' and he laments 'that is now unacceptable, for reasons both good and bad'.[11] The distinction between those who possess literary taste and those who do not continues to permeate the culture of reading. One recent study of this subject articulated this attitude by making a distinction between 'readers' as opposed to 'people who read'.[12]

Historically, the imperative to provide moral guidance to the reader and to police literary practices was closely linked to the elitist project of drawing cultural distinctions and establishing literary authority. Although this stance was mainly adopted by those devoted to the preservation of a conservative literary tradition consistent with the maintenance of the moral order, it was also espoused by commentators with left-wing and radical leanings. Writing from such a viewpoint, Richard Hoggart's classic essay *The Uses of Literacy* (1957) was scathing about the effects of popular culture on its working-class readership. 'The strongest argument against modern mass entertainment is not that they debase taste,' wrote Hoggart, 'but that they over-excite it, eventually dull it, and finally kill it.'[13] Although Hoggart blamed the popular media for patronizing the working-class public, his pessimistic analysis of popular culture drove him to medicalize its effects.

When it comes to drawing distinctions between good and bad reading habits, the impulse of prescriptive moralizing transcends the political divide. In this respect at least, there is little to distinguish Hoggart from the sentiments voiced by the conservative critic Q. D. Leavis. This point is well made in Leah Price's review of the scholarly literature on reading. Price states that for commentators like Hoggart and Leavis 'the question of what people at some distant historical moment read rarely lies very far from the question of what people here and now should read'.[14]

Mortimer Adler's *How to Read a Book*, published in 1940, was one of the most ambitious and intelligent attempts during the mid-twentieth century to guide and cultivate the literary practices of the American public. In his preface to the 1972 edition, Adler explains that he decided to add a new subtitle – *A Guide to Reading the Great Books* – to underline the fact that the reading which really mattered was that directed at particular books.[15] Adler's manual made an explicit contrast between readers who could read and those who could not, explaining that his guide was for 'readers who cannot read'. According to Adler, this group was made up of 'average' readers, people who have not mastered the 'art of reading'. Unlike some of the more precious advocates of the unique aesthetic of the art of reading, Adler believed this was a gift that could be acquired by most people who were prepared to work hard to do so. However, he posits reading as an activity akin to a difficult art that requires great discipline and effort. He argues the reason that most readers do not know how to read is because:

> [M]ost of us do not regard reading as a complicated activity, involving many different steps in each of which we can acquire more and more skill through practice, as in the case of any other art. We may not even think there is an art of reading. We tend to think of reading almost as if it were

something as simple and natural to do as looking or walking. There is no
art of looking or walking.[16]

Adler's claim that reading is unnatural is coupled with a tendency to
complicate the practice of literacy. Despite his interest in converting the
average person into an accomplished reader, his representation of reading
as an art cements the distinction between different types of readers, helping
to reify a segmented world of literary practices. Judgements about how and
what to read are not simply based on aesthetic considerations, but involve
deeply held moral and intellectual convictions that are integral to the
identity of the literary guide. Adler prefixes the term 'Great Books' with
the definite article 'the' – not just any great books but a deeply moralized
concept, *the* Great Books.

The ongoing attempt to distinguish between different reading habits
and readers is integral to a wider process of constructing people's identity
through their literacy. Some sociologists argue that societies often construct
a *reading class* – a small minority of individuals who are involved in activities
that involve working with written texts. 'Every society that has writing has a
reading class, but not everyone who can read is a member' notes one study
on this subject.[17] In pre-modern societies the reading class consisted simply
of those who could read; but since the eighteenth century and especially
since the birth of mass reading in the mid-nineteenth century, the contrast
between the reading class and other readers was determined by distinctions
in cultural status, education, and by the publications consumed. Where
people are situated in the cultural hierarchy of literacy is mirrored by what
they read.

CONFERRING IDENTITY

Reading as a cultural achievement and as a skill plays an important role in
how people perceive themselves and how others see them. In the modern
world, people's capacity to express themselves and their understanding
of the world is realized principally through their literacy; 'our ability to
communicate and interact are at the heart of how we represent ourselves
to others'.[18] The importance of literacy as a component of self-identity has
increased with the development of a mass reading public, as the possession
of such skills is seen as necessary for social acceptance and cultural valuation.

Since the nineteenth century, how people read and what they read has become intertwined with their careers, social position and self-identity. 'We differ from one another more by what we have read than by what we have done, for what we have done is often determined by what we have read – or not read', observes Holbrook Jackson.[19] Reading influences both individual and social behaviour and action. In particular, it has an effect on interpersonal communication and engagement with public life.

The way people construct their sense of self and identity through reading is subject to a variety of historical, cultural and social variations. People do not simply read. Their approach towards reading is formed in the way this activity is practised in their community – especially family members and friends and by their social circumstances. Certain types of literary behaviour are associated with tastes and virtues, while other practices are depicted as inferior versions of cultured reading. Individuals quickly become sensitive to signals about what kind of reading enjoys prestige, and what kind of reading is regarded as a mechanical act. Illiteracy continues to be stigmatized and people who have difficulty reading texts are too often subject to derision. Numerous people are aware of 'the difference, therefore, between what one reads and what one should read'.[20]

In some contexts, literacy endowed individuals with an identity of social and cultural superiority. One scholar has argued that in eighteenth-century America reading was a defining feature of white identity – one that depended for its reproduction on the continuing illiteracy of black people.[21] As Pierre Bourdieu in his magisterial sociological essay, *Distinction*, noted, 'aesthetic intolerance can be terribly violent'. Bourdieu explained that 'struggles' over the 'art of living' serve to draw lines between behaviour and attitudes considered legitimate and those deserving moral condemnation.[22]

Richard Hoggart's study of the mass reading culture of the English working class of the 1950s attempted to give meaning to a condition that he perceived in the context of his time as akin to illiteracy. He accepted that illiteracy 'as it is normally measured has been largely removed'; but despite this development, society was confronted with 'the next and probably more difficult problem'. The problem that Hoggart identified was how to characterize the new form of non-literacy that coexisted with popular culture. He observed that a 'new word is needed', a 'word indicating a social change which takes advantage and thrives on basic literacy'.[23]

Hoggart did not use the word 'illiteracy' to describe the practices of the majority participating in the 'new mass culture', but it is evident that he was seeking a rhetorical equivalent. He pointed the finger of blame at the mass media and populist journalists, who glorified the 'common man' and sought to cultivate anti-intellectual and 'high-brow-hating attitudes' among working-class people.[24] For Hoggart, responsibility for non-literacy lay with the workings of mass culture rather than with the individuals who were influenced by it.

The concept of illiteracy embodies moral judgement and cultural taste far more than it denotes a technical assessment of the lack of capacity to decode texts. Like its counter-concept, literacy, illiteracy has become a free-floating moral attribute that attaches itself to a variety of human experiences. Terms like emotional illiteracy, cultural illiteracy, moral illiteracy and sexual illiteracy serve as explicit idioms of condemnation. Concepts like computer illiteracy, ecological illiteracy, financial illiteracy, health illiteracy or media illiteracy signal a similar attitude, albeit in a more implied form. Such terms are rarely applied by individuals to account for themselves: they are deployed to define and devalue others.

Despite centuries of cautionary advice about the effects of reading, this is an activity that enjoys a great deal of cultural validation. All sections of society, even people who lack formal education, acknowledge that reading is an important accomplishment and a useful skill. Social research shows that the public associates reading with being capable and intelligent. In many communities an individual who reads books as opposed to just magazines and newspapers can gain significant prestige.[25]

However people present themselves to others, their identity as readers is to a significant extent externally endowed. This identity is linked to the values attached to different types of reading, and is also a statement about the moral, intellectual and mental capacities of the reader. Nonetheless, individual readers make choices about the meaning they wish to give to their literary activities. Such choices do not simply pertain to the preferred genre and content of publications, but also to how a reader wants to be seen. Portraits of subjects with a book at hand or absorbed in reading fill the walls of European museums of classical or traditional art, testifying to the importance that painters and those who commissioned them attached to being seen as a reader. As the sociologist Ernest Goffman explained, 'there are very few situations in Western society in which one is called on to justify the presence of a book, and as an incidental result, this prop is useful to people who wish to avoid social scrutiny and interaction in public places'.[26]

More than a thousand years before the invention of printing, Seneca sarcastically drew attention to the fad for the ostentatious display of books. 'Many people without a school education use books not as tools for study but as decorations for the dining room,' he stated. Of the avid collector of scrolls, he wrote that 'you can see the complete works of orators and historians on shelves up to the ceiling, because like bathrooms, a library has become an essential ornament of a rich house'.[27] Nowadays, interior decorators promote this fashion and use shelves displaying books to create an impression of sophistication in a room. Television interviews and talk shows often use bookcases filled with-impressive looking texts as a background to endow their show with gravitas. Even in the age of the internet, digital technology and e-books, the bookcase reminds the audience that the interviewee is a serious person worth hearing.

People's orientation towards reading is in part an outcome of the influence – by values, tastes and cultural reference points – through which society gives meaning to literacy. What people read is connected to what other books and publications others recommend, criticize and discuss. Writing of the 'average man', Holbrook Jackson argues that 'apart from his own reading he is the product of the reading of others'. Jackson elaborates this point by noting that 'he sees what he has been taught to see at home and at school, and later by the popular press and the popular novelist'.[28] The wider social attitudes towards literacy do not simply bear down on the imagination of the 'average man' – they provide a cultural script through which all sections of public give meaning to their reading. Intellectual and cultured people are even more comprehensively influenced than ordinary people by the fashions and tastes celebrated by the literary establishment, claims Jackson.[29]

The cultural script of literacy signals ideas about how different literacy practices should be judged. Historically, one medium for transmitting this cultural script was the novel. In Jane Austen's *Northanger Abbey*, Catherine's misreading of gothic fiction disorients her to the point where she loses a sense of reality. In Flaubert's *Madame Bovary* the main protagonist becomes morally corrupted through the literature she reads. Authors convey ideas about how to distinguish between superior or inferior readers through direct or indirect asides and comments about their characters. The critic John Carey has provided an insightful analysis of the way in which the novelist George Gissing uses a character's bookcase to make a statement about his mental and moral constitution:

> Shelves which contain poetry, literature, history and no natural science belong to sensitive, imaginative, intelligent characters. Shelves which contain politics, social science, technology and modern thought of virtually any description brand their owner indelibly as at best semi-educated and at worst cruel, coarse and dishonest.[30]

The taken-for-granted manner with which people's reading habits are diagnosed as a marker of their personality indicates that judgements about literacy have wide-ranging consequences for identity.

Literary judgement can exert a powerful influence on the way people read and communicate, and according to the French sociologist Robert Escarpit, those who aspire to be thought of as cultured are particularly subject to the coercive power of judgement. The pressure to conform and act in line with what is expected of a literary connoisseur makes it difficult to deviate from the prevailing norm. 'How would a cultured man whose judgment enables him to appreciate the value of a play by Racine dare admit that his taste leads him to prefer reading the comic strip, *Tintin*?' asks Escarpit.[31]

Some scholars believe that the project of defining good readers and distinguishing them from bad ones served as a form of social control and as a way of sanctifying the role of literary authority.[32] It appears that literary figures have felt the need to make such pronouncements since ancient times. Cicero's writings offer one of the first attempts to draw a clear distinction between those with refined tastes who read for pleasure and undistinguished people who read instrumentally.[33] In medieval times the knowledge of Latin was essential for anyone with a pretence to literary authority, and those who did not know Latin were defined as illiterate. By the nineteenth century, literacy was represented as an extension of the moral character and aesthetic attributes of the reader. Goethe's threefold characterization of readers had as its focus the relationship between judgement and appreciation: 'There are three kinds of readers: one who enjoys without judgment; a third who judges without enjoyment; and, in between, a reader who judges while enjoying and enjoys while judging.'[34]

Goethe's categorization of different types of readers drew attention to the desirability of forging a harmonious relationship between the intellectual exercise of judgement and the aesthetic reaction of enjoyment. Others were more interested in reinforcing the divisions between readers of taste and distinction and those whose habits and behaviour threatened to lower cultural standards. Coleridge sought to acclaim the literary authority of a small minority of gifted people by emphasizing the psychic distance that separated them from the majority of base individuals, and he divided readers into four classes:

1. Sponges, who absorb all they read, and return it nearly in the same state, only a little dirtied
2. Sand-glasses, who retain nothing, and are content to get through a book for the sake of getting through the time
3. Strain-bags, who retain merely the dregs of what they read
4. Mogul diamonds, equally rare and valuable, who profit by what they read, and enable others to profit by it also.[35]

Coleridge's emphasis on the rare and exceptional attributes of those 'who profit by what they read' fed into a wider narrative about the unique innate qualities of those claiming literary authority. The terms through which a tiny minority of readers were 'authorized' ensured the 'de-authorization' of all those who failed to adopt the prescribed reading practices. The *Manual of Morals for Common Schools*, written for American educators and parents in 1849, draws on Coleridge's classification and asks, 'is it enough to have or to read books?' The presumed answer is clearly negative. The author advises that 'great care must be taken' to ensure that a love of reading is cultivated' through the careful choice of the 'very first order of books'.[36]

One widely debated question raised by Coleridge's hierarchy of readers was how stable the divisions were. The realization that the reading public was constantly increasing in size and would wield greater and greater power ensured that this question was of great interest not just to the literary and educational establishment but also to the political classes. Some looked to the expansion of education, while others hoped that through the democratization of society the growth of a literate public would lead to a more elevated and sophisticated culture of reading.

From the nineteenth century onwards, the question of how to educate the public to read in the right way became a recurrent topic of debate. In a fascinating essay on this question, the novelist Wilkie Collins wrote in 1858 of the 'unknown public of millions' whose reading habits were focused on 'quantity rather than quality'. The unknown public were consumers of publications, and yet Collins would not grant them the identity of being readers. This was a group who had not yet learned to read in the right way; thus 'the next thing to be done is, in a literary sense, to teach that public how to read'.[37]

Collins's depiction of the unknown public as a 'reading public of three millions which lies right out of the pale of literary civilization' mimics the Victorian rhetoric of a civilizational mission. This unknown reading public lies so far away from Collins's literary culture that he regards its very existence as a 'mystery', 'which the sharpest man among us may not find it easy to solve'.[38] That Collins can distance members of his community from his literary civilization to such an extent exemplifies the way that aesthetic judgements reinforce the project of cultural exclusion. Despite his condescending attitude, Collins was relatively optimistic about the future of the reading public. He wrote that 'it is probably a question of time' before the development of this audience learns to 'obey the universal law of progress' and 'sooner or later' learns 'to discriminate'.[39]

Wilkie Collins's civilizational discourse about morally inferior readers has, over the past century and a half, mutated into a discourse about the non-rational and uncritical reader. Throughout the twentieth century, critics pointed to the powerful influence that newspapers were able to exercise on the uncritical, passive and easily manipulated mass of readers.[40] The stigmatization of the emotionally illiterate reader persists to this day, as the consumer of tabloids is cast into the role of a moral inferior and culturally backward consumer of trash.

SOCIALIZATION AND READING

The civilizational reading discourse of the Victorian era was deeply concerned with ensuring that the expansion of public education contributed to the socialization of the younger generations. From this point onwards, the question of teaching children to read became an increasingly important focus for debates on literacy.

The issues associated with the teaching of reading are not simply reducible to pedagogic matters. Since the eighteenth century, manuals and commentaries on how children learn to read have also sought to guide their moral education. In the Anglo-American tradition, reading guides were not designed to be explicitly moral tracts – rather, they aimed to ensure that the stories children studied reinforced their virtuous character, and from the mid-nineteenth century onwards, reading aids and textbooks attempted to avoid coming across as directly preachy. *Aesop's Fables* replaced the Bible as the 'most common source of precept'.[41] In reviews, such texts were invariably assessed on the quality of their moral content. A review of a reading book for young children in *The Gentleman's Magazine* in 1856 praised the author, the Reverend Richard Dawes, for producing a book that 'leads his scholars into immediate contact with such people and scenes as they are likely to meet with in their daily walk, and without any intrusion of moral teaching, always manages to bring about a bias favourable to truth and goodness'.[42]

Ensuring that children were educated into the values of 'truth and goodness' raised questions about who would be held responsible for the moral guidance of the younger generation. Different approaches towards the domain of morality and politics also ensured that these pre-existing controversies would attach themselves to the way children were educated. As Cathy Davidson notes in relation to the nineteenth-century American experience, the debates on education and literacy were highly polarized.[43] The intimate connection between reading and the socialization of children ensured that the teaching of literacy became an intensely divisive issue, reflecting competing political and ideological approaches towards the fundamental questions of public life.

One study of the passionate conflicts over education in eighteenth- and nineteenth-century France argues that the divisions over the teaching of reading mirrored the differentiation between Left and Right. The study also notes that the 'history of literacy had aroused fierce passions in France' because 'it has been studied not for its own sake but rather in order to furnish ammunition in the political debate over education which until recently constituted one of the major lines of cleavage between left and right'.[44]

One of the curious features of history is that the recurring debates about the teaching of reading continue to reflect the pre-existing moral and political cleavages of society. If anything, the political and ideological commitments of protagonists in debates about the teaching of reading have become increasingly explicit and fierce. In the United States, some of the late twentieth-century advocates of whole-language teaching proudly refer to themselves as a movement that is not just interested in pedagogy but in promoting a political agenda.[45]

A similar pattern is evident in the United Kingdom. As one commentator observed in the early 1990s:

> Something irrevocably silly has happened in the educational world when wives of aspiring Labour prime ministers announce to the media that they are very left wing about teaching reading! What, on a common sense view, could possibly be political about teaching young children to read?[46]

Reflecting on the underlying motivation for what outwardly appeared as an incomprehensible tendency to politicize the teaching of reading, Martin Turner concludes that the 'political construction of different approaches to the initial teaching of reading is eye-opening'; indeed, 'it appears that there is, at bottom, a religious dispute about values, with opposing sides still fighting the English Civil War'.[47]

Heated debates about how to teach children to read serve as a proxy for competing perspectives on their moral education and socialization. That is why, by the early nineteenth century, all sides of the debate tended to conclude that the teaching of reading was perceived as far too important to be left to the charge of the parent. The main argument used to justify the professionalization of the teaching of reading was that the input of parents was unhelpful at best, and that at worst it led their youngsters astray. Whereas reading was previously seen as an activity integral to child-rearing, it became in this period an activity presumed to be best conducted by trained teachers, who possessed the requisite technical expertise.

However, in the eighteenth century, before the teaching of reading became equated with the possession of pedagogic skills, it was regarded as essentially a moral accomplishment. Both Locke and Hobbes argued that education required the channelling of children's passions in a healthy direction. Locke addressed his advice on reading to parents and suggested that they provide their children with works like *Aesop's Fables* because they combined moral lessons with entertainment.[48] His statements on the subject suggest that he did not assume that the teaching of reading was a particularly difficult skill so long as children's education was not too rigid and formal. Both the Greeks and the Romans had regarded the teaching of reading as 'something anybody could do'.[49] That the acquisition of literacy later in the nineteenth century did not in fact seem to require the input of sophisticated professionals is highlighted by the fact that in England almost 90 per cent of the population could read before the Education Act of 1870 – that is, before elementary schooling was widely available to children.[50] As one study points out, 'full' literacy was achieved 'before the creation of a full school system' in the Victorian era.[51]

Some have suggested that from the early modern era onwards, reading actually became more difficult because of the separation of spelling and sound.[52] It is also claimed that with the growing significance and application of literacy in the modern era, the consequences of poor reading practices became exposed; the writing and reading skills of the majority were far too mechanical to make effective connections between different bodies of knowledge.[53] But it is clear that whatever problems emerged or were discovered about the state of literacy, one of the key drivers of the professionalization of the teaching of reading was the imperative to assume charge of the socialization of young people. The by-product of this was the project of dispossessing the family of assuming responsibility for teaching their children how to read.

The corollary of the expansion of compulsory education was what one study describes as the 'sweeping rejection of the value of domestic instruction'. Condemnation of parental instruction in reading was particularly directed at the families of the labouring poor, who were often portrayed as incompetents guiding their children in the wrong directions. The pioneering English educator Samuel Wilderspin (1792–1866) wrote with affection about the 'judicious' manner with which his own parents educated him and taught him how to read,[54] and yet he regarded the involvement of other parents in the education of their children as a moral outrage: 'Shocking it is to think that the breath of a mother or a father should be the first to contaminate the minds of their children; yet such is the mournful truth.'[55] His concern was echoed by an English school inspector who wrote that 'it is indeed a sad and evil necessity, if the first lesson which they learn at school is to beware of their own parents and to look with disgust, if not horror at the filthinesss and abominations of their own homes'.[56]

Manuals and self-help books – particularly those directed at middle-class mothers – encouraged parents to converse with their children, but not to play the role of amateur teachers. One nineteenth-century manual urging parents not to neglect their children's education nevertheless warned that 'too often health, mental power, and even life' are 'sacrificed when children of docile, studious, or ambitious disposition' follow their parents' wishes.[57]

Over the twentieth century, blaming parents for the reading problems of their children became a frequent complaint of educators. Arthur Gates, a leading American expert on reading pedagogy, regularly held that the interference and anxieties of parents were responsible for their children's problems in learning how to read. 'When a mother storms to the school,' writes Gates, 'to protest delaying the starting of the child to read or what she imagines is the failure to teach good old phonics, it is likely that things have already happened in the home which are having a disadvantageous – indeed, sometimes a disastrous – influence on the pupil's efforts to learn.'[58] The threat of ignorant parents expecting far too much from their children was also internalized by British reading pedagogy. An editorial to a series of articles on *The Politics of Reading* in 1993 observed that 'many parents are understandably anxious, and in some schools, they express their feelings by demanding quick results from the teachers and early achievements from their children, often causing difficulties where there need be none.'[59]

The devaluation of parental competence was paralleled by the promotion of the authority of professional educators. This was the indirect outcome of a variety of trends associated with the consolidation of the modern nation state and the growth of modern industrial society. New political and technical developments created a constant demand for mass literacy. However, the emerging body of pedagogic knowledge on the teaching of reading was not simply a response to wider socio-economic developments; it was also influenced by the objective of legitimating the authority of educational expertise. One of the ways in which experts attempted to gain authority for themselves was by emphasizing the complexities and difficulties involved in teaching and learning how to read. Once reading was recast as a difficult skill to acquire, the problems associated with acquiring literacy acquired their own momentum.

The emerging pedagogic discourse on reading tended to represent it as unnatural and complicated. This perspective was vigorously advertised by the American educational psychologist Edmund Burke Huey, one of the most influential figures in reading pedagogy in the late nineteenth and early twentieth century. Huey's studies had as their premise the belief that reading is a habit both 'unnatural' and 'intensely artificial in many respects'. He claimed the authority of medical science to warn that the 'careless exercise' of this unnatural activity 'causes fatigue and, in very many cases, certain dangerous forms of degeneration' – which he characterized as 'race degeneration'. Huey's advice was to postpone the age at which children should be instructed in this unnatural enterprise.[60]

Stanley Hall played an important role in framing the teaching of reading as a challenging enterprise. In an essay published in 1901, he asserted that 'how to teach children to read, and what they should read, are two of the oldest and most complicated, as well as most important problems of pedagogy'.[61] Hall's framing of the teaching of reading as an unusually complicated task was coupled with a warning that children must read morally appropriate texts:

> When a child has acquired the power to read, a vast and before unknowable world opens up before him. On the one hand are means of culture in what is good and great, which impose new duties of unselfish living and excite high ideals through high examples; and on the other hand are degrees of degradation of many kinds, mental and moral, impossible before.[62]

Hall's interweaving of the need to provide guidance for the socialization of children with the need for a pedagogy that could deal with the difficult task of learning to read provided a compelling argument for assigning these tasks to the purview of professional authority.

In one sense Huey, Hall and their colleagues were right to depict reading as a technical accomplishment rather than a natural activity. Written texts do not grow in nature and learning to read, unlike learning to walk, is a historically determined and culturally mediated acquisition of a technical skill. But just because reading is not the product of nature does not mean that it is an unnatural practice. One of the consequences of the attribution of unnaturalness to reading was to legitimate the claim that the acquisition of the habit of reading threatens to compromise the health of readers. The leading role of educational psychology in the development of reading pedagogy ensured that problems to do with this unnatural practice would often be diagnosed through medical idioms.

By the 1920s and 1930s, complications experienced in learning how to read had become thoroughly medicalized. Researchers became preoccupied with eye movements and visual fatigue, and speculated on the possible damage to the health of an avid reader. A review of research in the United States on visual fatigue published in 1948 observed that 'some writers assert that the frequency with which ocular difficulties are today observed in men examined in schools or colleges or induction into the Army or navy is directly traceable to the prolonged activity imposed on the eyes by the educational and vocational demands of present-day life'; it warned that 'some physicians even go so far as to attribute what they characterize as the neurotic tendency of our times in part to the fact that continued eye fatigue imposes a cumulative strain upon modern man'.[63]

A review of the scientific research used to support new reading practices in the United States in the 1920s and 1930s underlines the trend towards accounting for reading problems in medical terms. It points out that one novel feature of the 1925 yearbook of the National Society for the Study of Education (NSSE) 'was the introduction of the concepts of diagnosis and remediation of reading failure'.[64] The diagnosis of reading failure led to the emergence of a new profession of remedial teachers. From the late 1940s onwards, the medical metaphor provided a medium through which problems relating to the learning of reading were explained. 'Good reading was regarded as a sign of health; poor reading was regarded as a kind of illness that needed the therapeutic intervention of specially trained personnel', observed this review.[65]

When nineteenth-century critics alluded to the people who were not reading well, they explained the problem as a consequence of the poverty of their moral and/or intellectual resources. From the 1920s onwards, such failures were much more likely to be attributed to a medical condition or a psychological deficit. Whereas critics in the previous century were disturbed by the unrestrained reading of an indiscriminate public, by the 1920s sections of the public were diagnosed as not reading enough.

The idea that reading is unnatural served to encourage its medicalization and establish the condition of a reading disability. The discourse of medicalization that prevailed between the medieval period and the twentieth century focused on the effects that reading had on the moral and physical health of the individual reader. From the early twentieth century, the focus of medicalization shifted towards the individual defects or disabilities of the problem reader.

Psychology spurred an interest in the problem, or 'backward', reader – implicitly shifting the discussion about the teaching of reading to the techniques that were best or most effective, to engaging children who were struggling. Huey's book *Backward and Feeble-Minded Children: Clinical Studies in the Psychology of Defectives, with a Syllabus for the Clinical Examination and Testing of Children* (1912) offered a paradigm for equating struggling readers with the state of feeble-mindedness. Discussions on the 'backward reader' coincided with a proliferation of diagnostic categories, such as 'brain damaged', 'learning disabled', 'world blindness', 'mind blindness', 'minimal brain dysfunction', 'brain crippled', 'cerebral disordered', 'neurologically impaired', 'dyslexic' and 'dysphasic'.[66]

The medicalization of reading problems accelerated in the 1960s with the construction of the generic diagnosis of *learning disabilities*. According to a study of the history of learning disability in the United States, since its introduction this new category 'developed at such a phenomenal rate that today it forms the largest focus of special education in many school districts'.[67] By this point in time the linkage between difficulties with reading and health deficits was a widely endorsed theme in pedagogy. The trend towards the representation of the problem of literacy as a health problem extended beyond the classroom to the wider world. Jack Morpurgo, head of the British National Book League, wrote in the monthly magazine of UNESCO in 1958 that 'the struggle to bring about the state of health which is literacy by ridding the world of the disease called illiteracy has been going on for centuries'.[68] Morpurgo's analogy of health with literacy and disease with illiteracy underlined an important turn in the medicalization of reading. It was not the reader but those who could not read who became the principal target of therapeutic intervention.

THE READING CRISIS

At the beginning of the twentieth century, the problems associated with literacy tended to focus on the individual. Concerns with individual pathology coexisted with a sense of optimism about the capacity of scientific pedagogy to eliminate illiteracy,[69] reinforced by the belief that the expansion of public schooling in industrial society would turn every child into a competent reader. Those disposed towards cultural pessimism about the effects of mass education still retained considerable influence in public life, but the importance that twentieth-century society attached to literacy ensured that the teaching of reading in schools was given a high priority.

Mass education did not guarantee that all pupils would turn into competent readers. That all was not well was revealed to the American military authorities during the First World War – in their discovery that many recruits were illiterate. The uncomfortable realization that a significant group of young men were illiterate despite the benefit of schooling initiated discussions about the problem adult reader. A similar discovery occurred during the 1940s, when both the American and British governments found that a significant proportion of their recruits were functionally illiterate. In 1942 the US army had to defer 433,000 of its potential recruits because they could not follow or grasp written instructions 'needed for carrying out basic military functions or tasks'.[70] Some estimates indicated that around a quarter of the British soldiers recruited to fight during the Second World War lacked functional literacy.

The exigencies of the war effort created both concern and interest in the ability of the adult population to read and write. It was at this point that policy-makers began to portray literacy as a skill that could be quantified. In 1947 the American Census Bureau opted to define those with fewer than five years of schooling as *functionally illiterate*. Across the Atlantic, the discovery of extensive functional illiteracy led the British government in 1947 to set up a parliamentary committee to explore and, if necessary, make recommendations to resolve this problem. The report, *Reading Ability: Some Suggestions for Helping the Backward*, published in 1950, found that due to the disruption of the war, 11-year-olds in 1948 were a year behind the cohort of 1938 in reading ability, while 15-year-olds in 1948 were 22 months behind the 1938 cohort.[71]

It was in the context of post-war unease about the implications of illiteracy that the idea of functional literacy crystallized.[72] This utilitarian concept had as its focus the ability to read well enough to perform job-related activities effectively and to comprehend written communications. Functional literacy was seen as essential for the conduct of economic activity; it equated reading to a technical skill, with applications limited to job-related pursuits.

Although policy-makers regarded the problem of literacy as one related to the demands of a modern industrial economy, they were also concerned about its implications for education and socialization. As I argue elsewhere, one of the main drivers of the recurring crisis in schooling and education is the difficulty that society experiences in the socialization of the young.[73] Debates about the crisis of reading and its teaching can be interpreted as an indirect reaction to these difficulties.

From the 1930s onwards, there is a perceptible transformation in the way that reading problems were conceptualized. Many of the old anxieties about the reading material available to the masses retained a degree of force, but the concern was increasingly directed at their low level of reading ability. This new narrative had, and continues to have, a twofold character. On the one hand doubts were raised about the level of literacy of adult readers. From a cultural standpoint the inability of the reading masses to engage with substantial texts was represented as a threat to cultural standards. Richard Altick notes that in the post-Second World War era 'this high incidence of semiliteracy was one reason why millions concentrated on papers like *News of the World*, the *Sunday Pictorial*, and *Picture Post* almost to the exclusion of more substantial reading matter.'[74] Fears about adult literacy were also raised by policy-makers who believed that an educated work force was essential for a productive and prosperous economy. But the new narrative was even more preoccupied by another problem: the difficulty that schools had turning a significant proportion of children into competent readers.

During the 1940s in the United States a public debate began around this problem. An article written in January 1946 by a high school principal,

George Henry, and published by *Harper's Magazine* under the title 'Can Your Child Really Read?', gained wide attention. Henry claimed that the fact that a third of school pupils were unlikely to become competent readers was an open secret amongst educators, and argued that the problem was not how the pupils were taught but that these children were 'simply, non-verbal'. He was pessimistic about solving this problem through remedial reading lessons, and argued that this 'non-verbal' third required a form of education not based on book-learning.

Henry made it clear that he was not referring to the far smaller group of 'mentally backward' children, who constituted 5 per cent of all pupils, but to a larger cohort who were mainly composed of 'normal, wholesome, even talented and responsible youth'.[75] In effect, he asserted that the low level of literacy attained by a substantial section of the population was an unalterable fact of life: 'Democracy is thus brought face to face with the cold fact that one-third of our citizens, although literate by census standards and able to read and write well enough to get along, are impervious to book learning.'[76]

Henry's call for a new form of education to help non-verbal students would, in the decades to come, crystallize into the pedagogy of multiple intelligences. The questions raised by Henry about the problem of non-verbal children became the point of departure for what would turn out to be, in the Anglo-American world, an ongoing debate around the crisis of reading. However, Henry's emphasis on identifying the natural endowment of the non-verbal child as the source of the problem went against prevailing assumptions about the potential of education to solve the problems of all in society, and he anticipated that his downbeat assessment of literacy education would face criticism.[77] American society was still relatively optimistic about the ability of educational authorities to deal with problems in the classroom. The failure to read was seen as a symptom of poor teaching practice.

Consequently, the crisis of reading was converted into a crisis about the way in which it was taught. This politicization of the teaching of reading ensured that differences of pedagogic style were expressed through a rhetoric of ideological conflict.

Since the 1920s, arguments between those who opted for the phonics method and those who preferred the whole-language approach of teaching reading acquired an increasingly zealous tone. In the 1950s this divisive controversy over the teaching of reading metamorphosed from a pedagogic to an openly political issue. The main catalyst for the launching in the United States of what has been referred to as the 'Reading Wars' was the publication in 1955 of the best-selling book by Rudolf Flesch, *Why Johnny Can't Read*. Flesch's target was the prevailing look-and-say method of teaching reading, and what he characterized as the accommodation of the teaching profession to low standards. He stated that for educators:

> [F]ailure in reading is *never* caused by poor teaching. Lord no, perish the thought. Reading failure is due to poor eyesight, or a nervous stomach, or poor posture, or heredity, or a broken home, or undernourishment, or a wicked stepmother, or an Oedipus complex, or sibling rivalry, or God knows what.[78]

Although Flesch's polemic against the whole-language approach had only a minimal impact on reading pedagogy, his criticism resonated with the American imagination and from this point onwards the diagnosis of crisis would be frequently applied to the state of reading.

That competent reading is no longer an attribute of modern adulthood is continually confirmed by reports – many of which are highly alarmist – about the state of public literacy. According to the French National Agency Against Functional Illiteracy, 9 per cent of the population between 18 and 65 of people living in France and who have received schooling are functionally illiterate.[79] A study reported on by the *Times Education Supplement* in 2010 found that around a fifth of pupils leaving school in England were functionally illiterate.[80] The US Education Department estimates that around 14 per cent of the American population lack basic prose literacy skills, which means they cannot read a newspaper or, say, instructions on a bottle of pills.[81]

These disturbing reports on levels of literacy need to be seen in a historical context. Estimates of literacy rates vary wildly and are frequently disputed; arguments about whether levels of literacy are in decline or improving are invariably politicized, and comparing levels of literacy between the present and the past is fraught with difficulty.[82] Over the past century, definitions of literacy and illiteracy have changed dramatically, and the meaning of functional literacy has altered in line with the demands of a complex economy. One sociological inquiry into this issue pointed out that there is 'no evidence that actual levels of literacy have declined, although it is clear that our standards for judging literacy have risen'.[83]

What is indisputable is that the enduring character of this debate, and the emotional intensity with which it is often conducted, indicates that reading has a social, economic and cultural significance transcending that of a skill. Reading often serves as a proxy for deliberations about education and socialization. Whatever its causes, the crisis of literacy is at least indirectly the outcome of the earlier acceptance of the claim that reading is an unnatural and complicated activity. If reading is indeed unnatural, then the acquisition of literacy will be very difficult.

Instead of getting bogged down in competing claims about rates of literacy, it is more useful to interpret the debate about the reading crisis as a sublimated discussion around the wider question of the meaning of education, socialization and the moral order. The very term in which the debate is conducted is reminiscent of the intemperate tone of historic exchanges about the perils of reading in the eighteenth and nineteenth centuries. American supporters of the whole-language movement casually demonize their critics; they argue that those who support the teaching of phonics are 'in bed with the Far Right' and that the promotion of phonics teaching is part of a conspiracy to 'discredit, control, and privatise American schools'.[84] In turn, some advocates of phonics condemn their opponents as mean-spirited subversives who are determined to lower the standards of American education.

Like their predecessors in the past, both sides of the reading wars use the analogy of health and medicine to legitimate their claims. One critic of phonics questions his opponents for alleging that the literacy crisis in the United States is a 'significant health problem' – only to respond with medicalized insults. Writing of 'Phonics Toxicity and Other Side Effects', Steven Strauss asserts that phonics turns children off from reading and leads to 'all sorts of emotional and psychological distress'.[85] The reader has become medicalized to the point that therapeutic intervention is called for.

In response, two proponents of teaching phonics justify their approach on the grounds that it is an effective antidote to the 'epidemic of reading disabilities' haunting society, claiming that 35 per cent of the population is affected by this disability and that it is 'the leading cause of emotional problems in children and adolescents in North America':

> Consider also that this epidemic is a major etiological factor in school-dropouts and in juvenile delinquency. Furthermore, although a definitive study has not yet been done, it seems likely that teenagers who can't read or spell and who consequently hate school are easy targets for drug dealers.

'Today's educators also are destroying the innocent,' they conclude. 'They are killing the hopes, and the potential, and the mental health of the children who are victims of the reading disability epidemic. How long must these children wait?'[86]

Whatever these exchanges represent, they are unlikely to reveal very much about the reality of reading and the meaning that individuals give to this experience. It is far more probable that the debate mystifies and further complicates the practice of reading.

REALITY CHECK

With so much energy devoted by experts to the complications of reading, it is easy to overlook the fact that reading is not nearly as unnatural as some make it out to be.

Despite the lament of cultural pessimists about the dangers posed by the reading masses, the aspiration for acquiring literacy was deeply entrenched in modern society. Consequently, in the Western world reading became an everyday, taken-for-granted activity.

Throughout most of the twentieth century, and especially during the first half, millions of people sought to develop and enhance their identities as readers. This was the golden age of the mass reading of books. Despite concerns about the state of 'semi-literacy' of the masses in England, it was widely reported that the reading of books flourished during the Second World War.[87] During the 1950s 'more books than ever before were produced and sold to growing numbers of educated consumers in the United States'.[88] A similar pattern was evident throughout most of the Western world.

The case of Mortimer Adler's publication of *How to Read a Book* in 1940 serves as evidence of the public's appetite for reading. Adler's championing of serious reading found an enthusiastic audience in people who were interested in improving their level of literacy. The book became an instant hit, sold millions of copies, and remained at the top of America's best-seller list for more than a year. Rudolf Flesch's *Why Johnny Can't Read*, published in 1955 and already alluded to, also became a widely known and popularly acclaimed best-seller. Its cover stated that the book was 'Endorsed by *Reader's Digest*', indicating that this commercially minded mass publication took the view that there existed a substantial audience receptive to purchasing a text on the crisis of teaching reading.

It is useful to recall that the validation of literacy is a relatively recent development. Only in the nineteenth century did the idea that literacy was 'good in itself' become accepted,[89] and it is remarkable that literacy has become, since that time, so swiftly and widely embraced. Despite the claim that it was not a natural activity, reading became integrated relatively easily into people's everyday experiences. If there is a problem, it clearly does not lie with the capacity of the human species to read: rather, it stems from the tendency to perceive so many of society's social and moral problems through the prism of literacy.

Continual references to the crisis of reading signify the importance that modern society attaches to the practice of literacy. But as we shall see, the way in which society regards reading remains highly contradictory. Although the validation of literacy retains its dominant influence, since the 1960s it has also become questioned by critics who believe that the significance of reading is overrated.

8

From Enchantment to Disenchantment

As we have seen, since the days of Socrates apprehensions about the impact of literacy on the individual and the wider community have coexisted with enthusiastic endorsements of its positive benefits for society. By the twentieth century, mass literacy was considered an indispensable skill for individuals attempting to make their way in the modern world, and only a handful of jeremiads still noted that society would be better off without it. Whereas in previous eras mass literacy had frequently been depicted as an ominous threat to the social order, during the last century illiteracy and poor reading habits came to be seen as dangerous, with the non-reader and the poor reader becoming the focus of unease.

At the turn of the twentieth century, policy-makers and educators were, on balance, upbeat about the capacity of education to raise the level of literacy. It was believed that the 'combination of school policies, pedagogical experiments and scientific discourses had virtually eliminated illiteracy', and that 'they would certainly overcome reading disabilities'.[1] Optimism about the advance of literacy and belief in the advantages it represented to cultural and economic life were sometimes challenged by sceptics. Concerns around mass culture and the gullibility of public opinion occasionally led to outbursts of disquiet about the influence of the press and media on its uncritical audience. But such reactions were motivated by a desire to improve the quality of literacy, rather than restrain access to it.

At least until the 1960s, the status of literacy within Western society enjoyed an unprecedented level of cultural affirmation. The positive endorsement of reading often accompanied eruptions of anxiety about the influence of mass culture and the newest forms of popular media such as radio and television. From the 1950s onwards, this anxiety was expressed through a narrative about the precarious cultural status of the reading public. The decline of reading became a recurrent theme of the Western cultural landscape, highlighting the fact that what readers chose to read or not to read could not be taken for granted. In the post-Second World War era, education and literacy became caught up in the Cold War, as global rivalries forced policy-makers to take a special interest in the promotion of literacy.

During the 1960s the contradictions inherent in reading assumed a new form. It was not the traditional conservative elites but counter-cultural radicals who raised new arguments that questioned the value of reading, informed by a sentiment of disenchantment with the promise of the Enlightenment education. While counter-cultural radicals declared that literacy was overrated, mainstream commentators and policy-makers were convinced that society faced a crisis of reading. The metamorphosis of the cultural devaluation of literacy into the current perception that literacy is in crisis is the subject of this chapter.

UNESCO'S LITERACY CAMPAIGN

Discussions during the Second World War that led to the establishment of the United Nations Educational, Scientific and Cultural Organization (UNESCO) concluded that the main goal of this international body was to eradicate illiteracy. UNESCO's founders were convinced that ignorance and illiteracy assisted the rise of fascist and other totalitarian movements, and perceived literacy and education as the prerequisite for the foundation of a progressive democratic international order. In 1946 Léon Blum, president of UNESCO's First General Conference, highlighted this emphasis by asking:

> How can UNESCO hope to operate satisfactorily in a world *more than half* of whose inhabitants cannot even read or write, and are without the

basis of ideas upon which there can be built healthy living or prosperous agriculture, and in general any rational application of science?[2]

The international delegates responded by establishing a global literacy campaign with the title 'Fundamental Education', which undertook to launch an 'attack upon ignorance'.

UNESCO's statement on Fundamental Education expressed an optimistic belief in the power of literacy to promote progress and development. The biologist Julian Huxley, Director General of UNESCO, embraced an enthusiastic Enlightenment belief in the contribution that reading could make to the advancement of humanity, presenting the literacy campaign as an attempt to lighten the 'dark zones' of the world. Although he argued that literacy was in and of itself not enough to transform the world, he stated that it was the prerequisite for 'scientific and technical advance' and for 'full intellectual awareness and mental development'.[3]

From an historical perspective, the UNESCO initiative represents one of the most ambitious attempts to promote a humanist culture of reading. Huxley argued that the future of humanity depended on the development of a common outlook – what he called a 'common scale of values' – and claimed that 'mass campaigns against illiteracy and for a common fundamental education' were the precondition for realizing this objective. Huxley maintained that it 'will be impossible for humanity to acquire a common outlook' if large sections of it remain illiterate.[4]

The early founders of UNESCO thought that its campaign for Fundamental Education would foster a climate of international understanding and promote economic development. However, the hopes invested in this initiative soon came up against the *realpolitik* of the Cold War. Bitter rivalries and mutual recrimination between East and West served to derail the campaign for literacy. Education and literacy were regarded as policy instruments for gaining global influence, particularly in the Third World; all sides regarded literacy as a weapon with which to beat each other. The success of Fidel Castro's literacy campaign in Cuba made many Western leaders reluctant to support mass literacy campaigns.

In the late 1950s the idealism of the early founders of UNESCO gave way to a narrow instrumental approach that relegated literacy to a skill necessary for economic development. Delegates at UNESCO's Tenth General Conference in 1958 decided to abandon the humanist conception of Fundamental Education. From this point onwards literacy ceased to be regarded as a medium through which humanity could achieve a common set of values. Seven years later, in 1965, UNESCO codified this approach by embracing the concept of *functional literacy*, a skill exclusively linked to economic performance. 'Literacy was no longer to be seen as a lauded humanitarian goal, but rather as an investment in human capital that would produce capitalist growth', observes one study of the global politicization of literacy.[5] By the 1970s 'functional literacy became synonymous with literacy for work'.[6]

The disassociation of functional literacy from the wider ambition of humanist education was paralleled by a tendency to represent illiteracy as a medical rather than a cultural problem. UNESCO documents described illiteracy as a 'form of blindness',[7] and it was treated as if it were 'an epidemic disease like malaria'. According to one account, illiteracy was 'seen as a kind of cultural pathogen susceptible to complete eradication by the widespread administration of a standardised educational treatment'.[8]

In 1976, when UNESCO evaluated its work, it was evident that this reorientation of international literacy campaigns 'produced few tangible results'.[9] For some, the lack of success of UNESCO's literacy campaign served as proof that the optimism of the organization's founders was based on unrealistic expectations. The experience of its campaign and the Cold War politicization of literacy led critics, particularly from the United States, to question the basic values of humanistic education.

One important legacy of the UNESCO experience was to encourage the idea that literacy was a skill bound up with what was increasingly termed 'human capital'. Organizations such as the World Bank conceptualized reading as a 'mechanism, for developing human capital in the form of cognitive skills and linguistic skills'.[10] Whatever the merits of the strategy of developing human capital, it has little to do with the cultivation of a culture of reading. The skill required to decode writing is essential for the performance of a variety of routine tasks in modern society; but once such skills become the main purpose of schooling, it is easy to lose sight of the broader intellectual and cultural potential of reading. The uneasy tension between a skills-based and humanistic approach towards the teaching of reading continues to prevail in education.

One of the perverse outcomes of UNESCO's literacy campaign was to strengthen disenchantment with the Enlightenment's vision of reading. In previous times, it was elitist traditionalists who voiced suspicion and cynicism about the celebration of mass literacy. From the 1960s onwards such views began to be voiced by critics who identified with the traditions of the Left. One leading representative of this trend was the social historian Harvey J. Graff, who developed the concept of 'The Literacy Myth'. Graff dismissed the numerous claims made about the positive contributions of literacy to social, cultural and economic development. His 1978 critique of a UNESCO 'Report on Literacy' conceded that literacy could be a 'tool for liberation', but concluded that it was in 'most cases used for conservative ends'.[11]

Losing sight of its transformative potential, Graff was drawn towards emphasizing the role of literacy as a medium of social control and warned against its 'overestimation' in education. Not content with criticizing UNESCO's narrow-minded instrumental approach to literacy, Graff widened his critique to dismiss the humanist cultural valuation of reading. 'The purpose of literacy, in the past as in the present, was to integrate society and to foster progress by binding men and women in its web,' he stated. He concluded that 'the importance of print and the concomitant ability to read and write were grasped by those most interested in social order'.[12]

Historically the elitist representatives of high culture regarded themselves as the only true readers. In a roundabout way, radical critics of UNESCO echoed this sentiment by portraying the validation of reading as an outlook held by those 'most interested in social order'. The reaction of Graff and other critics of the literacy myth represented a radical departure from the enthusiastic manner with which previous generations of left-wing commentators had idealized mass literacy. The narrow instrumental approach of UNESCO's literacy campaign made it an irresistible target for numerous critics. But the unexpected conversion of leftist and radical thinkers towards opposition to the Enlightenment's optimistic celebration of reading was not simply a reaction to UNESCO. The moral status of reading was also called into question by powerful counter-cultural forces operating at this time.

THE DISENCHANTMENT WITH READING

From the 1960s onwards, those disenchanted with reading maintained that claims about its positive benefits were exaggerated. One proclaimed, 'for the first time, many scholars are thinking the unthinkable: is it possible that literacy is over-rated'.[13] Scepticism towards the cultural status of literacy was echoed by educationalists who maintained that 'there is an unusually keen awareness, based on some startling and some profound recent research, that the importance of literacy, not only in education, but in the formation of culture, has been overestimated'.[14] Pointing to the sense of disappointment about the result of the spread of literacy, Elizabeth Eisenstein notes that 'Gutenberg's invention was less likely to be celebrated for its contributions to a peaceful knowledge industry and more likely to be condemned for promoting hysteria, unreason, and world wars'.[15]

An impulse to debunk the so-called myth of literacy led some historians to project their outlook back into the past, and to minimize the historic significance of reading. David Cressey's account of *Reading and Writing in Tudor and Stuart England* exemplifies this approach, with its rhetorical question: 'finally, we must ask what good literacy did for the people who possessed it', anticipated by the answer 'very little'.[16] Cressey's response to his own question assigns an unexceptional role to the contribution of literacy to the well-being of society:

> It should be stressed that people were capable of rational action, of acquiring and digesting information, and of making well-founded political and religious decisions without being able to read or write. Illiteracy was not necessarily a bar to economic advancement nor did it stand in the way of common sense.[17]

Cressey recognizes that literacy possesses a 'liberating potential', but suggests that this potential must be weighed up against its 'mundane reality'.[18] Others simply regarded literacy's liberating potential as an illusion and perceived reading as an over-hyped and unexciting social construct.

Since the 1960s, the validation of the historical significance of literacy has become a frequent target of criticism. Advocates of what came to be known as the New Literacy Studies represent reading as an ideologically shaped activity that is deeply implicated in coercive power relations. Brian Street, one of New Literacy's leading voices, criticized what he called 'autonomous' theories of literacy as ideologically motivated attempts to maintain social order, arguing that 'the actual examples of literacy in different societies that are available to us suggest that it is more often "restrictive" and hegemonic, and concerned with instilling discipline and exercising social control'.[19]

From the standpoint of the New Literacy Studies, the very validation of literacy and the celebration of reading is not only ideological, but also motivated by narrow self-interest. The educational psychologist David Olson has argued that 'the significance of a universal high degree of literacy is grossly misrepresented' and 'overvalued', in part 'because literate people, such as educators, knowing the value of their own work, fail to recognize the value of anyone else's'.[20] What is remarkable about the claim that reading is overvalued is its implicit assumption that it ought to be judged as on a par with non-literacy. As we go on to note, the accommodation to non-literacy has in recent decades acquired its most grotesque manifestation in the tendency to minimize the difference between the value of the oral and the written word.

One interesting development in the 1960s was the apparent reversal of roles between Left and Right in their attitudes towards reading. Historically the Left was at the forefront of advocating the social benefits of mass literacy. But during the past 50 years the growing antagonism of sections of the cultural Left to the values of the Enlightenment has extended into cynicism towards the idealization of literacy. Brian Street was even critical of the radical pedagogue Paulo Freire for his support of the literacy campaigns in Cuba and Nicaragua. According to Street, Freire had not entirely shrugged off the assumptions of the '"autonomous" model'[21] – in other words, Freire took literacy far too seriously as a value in its own right.

The emergence of a cultural critique of Enlightenment assumptions regarding reading was integral to a wider movement of unease and estrangement from the ideals of progress and modernity. During the 1960s the ideals of modernization and technological and economic development came under fire from advocates of the emerging counter-culture.[22] The cultural elites, overwhelmed by a crisis of self-belief, reacted to this mood of scepticism in a hesitant and defensive manner.

It was in the context of the development of a counter-culture that literacy was redefined as more a tool of oppression than an instrument of liberation. From this point onwards the history of reading was often represented as a story about how a privileged and educated elite used literacy to impose its authority. The historian Keith Thomas portrays literacy in early modern England as an instrument of ruling–class oppression, asserting that literacy consolidated 'the authority of the educated classes over their inferiors' and served to 'impoverish and disparage other forms of expression'.[23] Commentators disenchanted with literacy frequently reiterate this claim.

The 1960s' mood of estrangement from modernity went so far as to encourage a romantic reversion to the ancient Socratic glorification of orality. Criticism of the 'mythology' of literacy was accompanied by acclamation of the 'sophistication' of oral cultures.[24] David Olson takes exception to the tendency 'to distinguish alphabetic from non-alphabetic cultures'.[25] The twin project of rehabilitating oral culture and diminishing the value of literacy was connected to a wider mood of disillusionment in which Western civilization, with its unique acclamation of the written word, was accused of losing touch with its soul.

The propensity to reduce reading to a relatively unimportant act called into question the authority of the book and the cultural values associated with it. Writing in the mid-1980s, Kenneth Levine observes that the 'very generalised and culturally diffuse respect for the written word and the skills for handling it has long been on the wane on account of the erosion of traditional supports such as deference to the educated elites that historically monopolised it, and the special awe emanating from sacred religious texts and legal codes'. He predicts that 'this diminution is likely to continue', adding that 'in a social environment containing so many textual varieties and formats in circulation, the pre-eminence of the book as a repository of distilled knowledge and an exemplar of "complete" literacy cannot be taken for granted'.[26]

Levine is right to point out that the authority of the written word had lost some of its force, and that the book faced competition from other forms of knowledge and communication. However, the disenchantment with the value of literacy did not simply represent a reaction to the educated elites – indeed, significant sections of the educated elites were themselves in the forefront of distancing themselves from their literary legacy. In many respects, the changing status of literacy and reading was bound up with the wider cultural tensions that erupted within the dominant institutions.

Disenchantment with the value of reading was an indirect expression of a wider climate of disillusionment with many of the fundamental values that Western civilization claimed to uphold. The ideals of progress, the assertion that modernization represented a superior alternative to the pre-modern traditional world, and the contention that the literate culture of the West represented a qualitative advance over the pre-literate communities of the past, were all called into question by critics of modern industrial society.

One unexpected consequence of the reaction against the cultural authority of Western civilization was not only that the significance of literacy was minimized. The claim that it represented a qualitative advance on non-literacy was also disputed. Unlike UNESCO's campaign for Fundamental Education, which regarded illiteracy as a form of blindness, many post-1960s commentators belittled the problems associated with it. Keith Thomas's study of early modern England warned that 'it would be wrong to think that illiterates lived in some sort of mental darkness, debarred from effective participation in the great events of their time'.[27] Others went a step further, and imagined that pre-literate oral cultures possessed important virtues that literate societies had lost.

THE MCLUHAN MOMENT

The connection between disenchantment with the value of reading and the wider mood of estrangement from modern society was most strikingly expressed in the early 1960s with the rediscovery and acclamation of oral culture.[28] The name most associated with this unexpected adulation of pre-Gutenberg oral culture was that of Marshall McLuhan. In a series of path-breaking essays, McLuhan distilled the essential anti-modern and counter-cultural sentiments of the early 1960s and directed them against the rationality of the Enlightenment culture of literacy. His anti-modernist sentiments were channelled through a moral critique of the Gutenberg culture of printing. McLuhan tended to regard the reader as a passive consumer, believing that the culture of print had a distorting and constricting effect on human consciousness. Those who took their reading seriously were likely to be unimaginative, conformist and isolated individuals. McLuhan hoped that the narrow print mode of consciousness would give way to the richer non-linear form of communication made available through the electronic media of radio and television.

McLuhan indicted the culture of literacy for endowing 'men with the means of repressing their feelings and emotions when engaged in action'. In contrast to previous forms of moral condemnation of reading, which warned about its capacity to enhance the emotional involvement of the reader, McLuhan put forward the very opposite argument – that it suppressed human expressiveness. According to McLuhan's analysis, the consumption of the printed text rendered readers passive and alienated.[29]

McLuhan's romanticization of pre-literate cultures was underpinned by the conviction that the historical development of reading and writing had, on balance, a regressive impact on the human condition, and the belief that modernity threatened the spiritual soul of the individual. He supposed that literacy created individuals who were morally inferior to 'oral man'. According to McLuhan:

> Literacy creates very much simpler kinds of people than those that develop in the complex web of ordinary tribal and oral societies. For the fragmented man creates the homogenized Western world, while oral societies are made up of people differentiated, not by their specialist skills or visible marks, but by their unique emotional mixes.[30]

McLuhan's preference for pre-literate culture was justified on the grounds that writing and reading were unnatural and artificial activities that distorted the complexity and unique quality of human individuality.

The association of pre-literate community with complexity and modern society with homogeneity may come across to the historically informed reader as curious. It is likely that McLuhan's distorted narrative of the fall of pre-literate complex man was influenced by the prevailing cultural reaction against the conformist imperatives of mass consumer society. In line with the spirit of his time, McLuhan was drawn towards the romanticized narrative about wholesome pre-industrial community life.

As we noted in previous chapters, the claim that reading was unnatural was frequently asserted in previous debates touching on the difficulties associated with learning to read. In the early 1960s, McLuhan and other advocates of orality went a step further and contended that reading and writing were also inherently inferior to spoken language. The philosopher and historian Walter Ong stated that 'all reductions of the spoken word to non-auditory media, however necessary they may be, attenuate and debase it, as Plato so intensely felt'.[31] At times, Ong's apotheosis of the oral bestowed on the spoken word the character of the sacred. For him, 'the word in its purest form, in its human and most divine form, in its holiest form' was 'the word which passes orally between man and man to establish and deepen human relations'.[32]

Despite his palpable sense of hostility to modernity, McLuhan looked to the new non-print electronic and digital media to correct the distortions caused by the reading of printed texts, hoping that these new media could overcome the fragmentation and alienation of the post-Gutenberg era. He characterized the printed text as an individualized and low-participatory 'hot media', which would be transcended by a multi-sensory and participatory electronic 'cool media'.[33]

McLuhan's enthusiasm for the electronic media of his time was based on the conviction that it would help overcome the fragmentary and distorting effect of print culture and contribute to creating the kind of communities associated with pre-literate oral societies. He famously speculated that the alienating and isolating culture of print would soon be transcended by what he foresaw as *electronic interdependence*. According to McLuhan, the new media would foster a new sense of community leading to the retribalization of humanity and the establishment of what he characterized as the *global village*. In this, his writings could be seen to anticipate the attitude and behaviour of internet enthusiasts who regard the digital world as a territory for building robust online communities, seeing it as providing the technological foundation for returning to a more natural and interactive pre-Gutenbergian way of life.

In his introduction to McLuhan's *Understanding Media*, the journalist Lewis Lapham explains the author's thesis in the following terms:

> Believing that it was the grammar of print that divided mankind into isolated factions of selfishly defined interests, castes, nationalities, and provinces of feeling, McLuhan also believes that the unifying networks of electronic communication might restore mankind to a state of bliss not unlike the one said to have existed within the Garden of Eden.[34]

McLuhan's tendency to invest salvationist hopes in the electronic media was shared by Walter Ong, who developed the concept of *second orality* to argue for the superiority of the community sensibility created through the use of electronic media. For Ong the 'age of secondary orality' resembled the old 'in its participatory mystique, its fostering of a communal sense'. However, it was 'a more deliberate and self-conscious orality, based permanently on the use of writing and print, which are essential for the manufacture and operation of the equipment and for its use as well'. Ong also believed that through the use of electronic communication, secondary orality 'generates a sense for groups immeasurably larger than those of primary oral culture – McLuhan's "global village".[35] The concept of secondary orality retains influence to this day, and serves to support the glorification of internet communities.

The reactionary implications of the belittling of literacy in the 1960s were self-consciously emphasized in McLuhan's writing. Unlike most of his colleagues, who were sceptical about the value of reading, McLuhan expressly acknowledged the connection between his views on the media and his religious, traditional, conservative inclinations, assuming that the new media would encourage a more positive attitude towards the values of traditionalism:

> [W]e have seen in this century the changeover from the debunking of traditional myths and legends to their reverent study. As we begin to react in depth to the social life and problems of our global village, we become reactionaries. Involvement that goes with our instant technologies transforms the most 'socially conscious' people into conservatives.[36]

McLuhan's yearning after community led him back to a mythical past that bore little resemblance to the realities of existence in pre-literate communities, and combined a rejection of the authority of the book with a reverence for pre-literate traditions. McLuhan had no doubt that 'a culture based upon the printed book' ought 'to be cast aside'; the reading of books had little place in the Brave New World of his Global Village. Paradoxically, the very instrument through which this project of cultural recovery was to be realized was the very modern technology driving the electronic media.

THE LOSS OF JUDGEMENT

The sense of cultural loss and the disposition to mythologize the virtues of pre-literate communities exercised significant influence over academic discourse and popular culture during the post-1960s decades. In intellectual and cultural life, proponents of humanist and Enlightenment ideals were conspicuously on the defensive, and in academic circles concepts like progress and universalism were increasingly dismissed with scorn. One of the few significant attempts to counter this trend and restate the argument for the progressive validation of literacy was provided by the anthropologist Jack Goody and his literary historian colleague, Ian Watt. Published in 1963, their essay 'The Consequences of Literacy' offered an eloquent defence of the humanist support for reading.

Goody and Watt's essay was a riposte to what they saw as the displacement of the 'Enlightenment's attack on myth as irrational superstition' by a 'regressive yearning for some modern equivalent of the unifying function of myth'.[37] They feared that the tendency towards 'diffuse relativism and sentimental egalitarianism' would undermine the progressive achievement gained through the practice of literacy,[38] and were particularly perturbed by the growing influence of a school of thought that refused to acknowledge the positive transformative impact that literacy had on human cognition. Goody and Watt argued that though there were no 'radical differences between the mental attributes of literate and non-literate peoples', there were likely to be important differences between literate and non-literate societies.

Goody and Watt insisted that writing facilitated the development of abstract thought. The written word was 'less closely connected with the particularities of person, place and time than it obtains in oral communication'.[39] One of the consequences of literacy was the emergence of an 'impersonal mode of discourse', which in turn assisted the birth of logical thought. Such an impersonal discourse supported the clarification of an epistemology oriented towards objectivity, which helped people to draw a distinction between myth and history. According to this thesis, the capacity to perceive the past as logically different from the present was one of the historical outcomes of literacy.[40]

Goody and Watt claimed that the rise of literacy provided the cultural foundation for the development of science and philosophy in ancient Greece, and that furthermore 'alphabetic reading and writing was probably an important consideration in the development of political democracy in Greece'.[41] Free citizens of Greece could read laws and play an informed role in public life. The written codification of cultural tradition 'brought about an awareness of two things: of the past as different from the present; and of the inherent inconsistencies in the picture of life as it was inherited by the individual from the cultural tradition in its recorded form'.[42] The ability to perceive inconsistencies encouraged the attitude of questioning, which in turn fostered a disposition towards critical thought. The development of printing served to amplify these attitudes and from this perspective reading and writing had a major influence on the development of human consciousness.

The strong case that Goody and Watt advanced regarding the transformative historical impact of literacy on cognition and culture provoked a backlash in intellectual circles. Critics labelled Goody and Watt's contribution a 'Great Divide theory', on the grounds that it supposedly created an unbridgeable dichotomy between oral and literate societies. At a time when the Enlightenment ideal of progress and the Western model of development were dismissed as hopelessly ideological, the claim that literate society represented an advance over pre-literate ones was criticized for its allegedly ethnocentric bias. In this climate of cultural conservatism and relativism, the claim that the form of thought encouraged by literacy was superior to what preceded it was often denounced as prejudiced. As one critic of the so-called Great Divide theory explained, 'the arguments about literacy have been important politically because they involve claims about "Great Divides", that is, about essential differences in humankind, in particular in the cultural and cognitive development of literates and nonliterates'.[43]

The debate around the relationship between oral and literate societies had become politicized to the point that ideological posturing meshed with intellectual exchanges about reading and literacy. For some, the historical claims for the progress of science, technology and intellectual life represented an apology for the oppressive and exploitative practices that underpinned the rise of modern capitalism. Objectivity was often decried as an ideological construct and increasingly discussions around the role of literacy sought to avoid making distinctions or judgements about its value. The reluctance to make such judgements meant that there was neither a common nor an objective basis on which reading and its teaching could be assessed or discussed.

The reluctance to make judgements was accompanied in the 1960s by a cultural relativist epistemology that sought to eradicate distinctions between illiteracy and literacy, as well as to oppose the establishment of a common standard in the teaching of reading. Attempts to develop authoritative definitions of literacy were often disparaged as an attempt to impose Western values on other societies. Levine's relativist definition of functional literacy is paradigmatic in this respect, justifying his approach on the grounds that it avoids 'applying the cultural tastes and standards of highly literate social strata on everyone in the community'. His opposition to the standards of the highly literate was also motivated by the desire to minimize the sense of failure of those who would be defined as illiterate. He criticized fixed standards of literacy on the grounds that they generate 'a false sense of security for those who achieve them and inflict an unnecessary burden of failure on those who do not'.[44]

The well-meaning attempt to protect non-readers and illiterates from social stigma extended into the field of education. Influential figures in the area of literacy studies were often stating that the kind of theories put forward by Goody and Watt were ideological and the attempts to put them into practice in schools represented a form of social control.[45]

The principal argument against the attempt to formalize common standards of literacy was the assertion that reading could not be separated from the context within it was conducted. The context-dependent thesis of literacy was often articulated through opposition to what it described as 'autonomous models' of literacy, and served to legitimate the claim that literacy could not be assessed according to a common standard. The advocacy of context-dependent literacy was also hostile to abstract thought: Brian Street, along with other supporters of the New Literacy Studies, dismissed the view that literacy was 'the source of significant cognitive differences' as ideological.[46]

The reluctance to make judgements about how to value reading had profound implications for the way in which its teaching in schools was conceptualized. Indirectly the criticism by New Literacy Studies of abstract thought and its rejection of the maintenance of authoritative standards as an elitist project encouraged the pedagogy of relevance.[47] According to this pedagogy, children come to school with their own literacy, which schools devalue and disrupt; as a result, the *common-sense* literacy of the child becomes challenged and destabilized by the *schooled* literacy of the classroom. Critics of schooled literacy argue that the curricula 'tend to concentrate on decontextualized language skills that will necessarily separate children's naturally developed (or innate) competencies'.[48] Such views are often accompanied by the suggestion that what children need is an affirmation of the type of literacy relevant to their lives.

This accommodation to common-sense literacy was paralleled by the embrace of the pedagogy of relevance. As I argue elsewhere, teaching children topics supposedly relevant to their lives was underpinned by the belief that this was the most effective way of motivating them. Motivation became the primary theme of pedagogy and the teaching of a knowledge-based curriculum was often criticized for teaching subjects not directly 'relevant' to children's lives and experience.[49]

The aforementioned romanticizing of pre-literate culture was paralleled by the propensity to criticize schooling on the grounds that its elitist practices undermined the authentic literacy of young people. Some even went so far as to criticize schooled literacy on the grounds that it differentiated children's language from the everyday use of language and therefore undermined popular culture.[50] Sylvia Scribner and Michael Cole argued that the kind of literacy attained outside school is different but equivalent to what is taught in the classroom, and cautioned against upholding what they perceived as the academic essayist's notion of literacy as the model for all. They warned that 'the assumption that logicality is in the text and the text is in school can lead to a serious underestimation of the cognitive skills involved in non-school, non-essay writing, and reciprocally to an overestimation of the intellectual skills that the essayist test "necessarily" entails.'[51]

In recent decades, influenced by the work of the anthropologist Clifford Geertz, the emphasis of literacy scholars on cultural context has become even more one-sided. Their context-specific approach directly challenges the important work of the Russian psychologist Lev Vygotsky, who highlighted the significance of the way in which human consciousness is altered by literacy. Vygotsky's compelling analysis showed that through learning to read and write, pupils assimilate the logic of general and abstract concepts, which allows them to be aware of 'language in its own right and as an object of thought, thereby bringing thought and language under conscious and deliberate control.'[52] Although literacy has a distinctive conceptual quality, through formal education children can become conscious of its rules and learn to use it for their own purposes.

The reluctance to judge and evaluate according to a common standard has encouraged a pedagogy that prefers context-specific knowledge to what it dismisses as canonical abstract knowledge. From this standpoint, street knowledge and street literacy are but variants of what children learn in school.[53] One of the most important legacies of the assault against the formulation of a common standard of literacy was its pluralization into different forms. Having established that literacy should not be bound by common rules and assessed according to a shared criteria, it was asserted that there were in fact numerous types of literacies.

A CRISIS IN READING?

The narrative of disenchantment with reading discussed above coexisted with an alarmist *cri de coeur* about the crisis facing reading. Remarkably, these two contrasting narratives rarely engaged with one another. The sense that society faced a crisis in reading was underpinned by unease about the authority of Western culture and the book, and the effectiveness of institutions of education. Levels of literacy, its teaching, the authority of the texts associated with Western civilization – the so-called Western Canon – seamlessly meshed to produce a diffuse sense of crisis about reading.

The public manifestation of the crisis of reading first surfaced in the United States in the 1950s around Rudolf Flesch's *Why Johnny Can't Read*. However, a far more expansive current of alarm about the state of education gained a powerful momentum with the launching of Sputnik by the Soviet Union in October 1957. Western policy-makers and commentators claimed that standards of educational attainment had fallen behind the Soviet Union. The cover of *Life* magazine on 14 March 1958 declared 'CRISIS IN EDUCATION', headlining the first in an 'urgent' five-part series of essays arguing that 'the schools are in terrible shape, what has long been an ignored national problem, Sputnik has made a recognized crisis.'[54]

Since the late nineteenth century, the difficulties facing society have often been interpreted as the outcome of a failed system of education. Such crisis is often accompanied by soul-searching about the state of literacy and society's ability to transmit its cultural legacy to a new generation of readers. This point was specifically raised in an editorial in the *Saturday Review*, pointing to the decline of reading as the chief means of transmitting cultural heritage.[55]

In his 1963 address to the conference of the American Historical Association, Carl Bridenbaugh, its president, explicitly linked fears about the decline of reading to nervousness around the challenge of retaining historical memory. Warning about worrying 'material and spiritual changes in the condition of human existence', he stated that mankind is faced with 'the loss of its memory, and this memory is history'. For Bridenbaugh, one disturbing symptom of this development was the 'decline of reading'. He told his audience that 'on the educational and cultural side, perhaps nothing so marks the age as the decline in reading, especially reading for enjoyment, and with it, a shrinking of the imagination that reading has always stimulated'.[56]

In an essay published a year later, Marshall McLuhan responded to the fears regarding the disruption that the electronic media could cause to the print-based moral order. He appeared to take delight in drawing attention to 'the current anxieties of civilized man concerning the written word', which he believed were for 'some Westerners' a 'very touchy subject', because this 'ancient technology of literacy built on the phonetic alphabet' appeared to be threatened by the electronic media.[57]

The evolution of new media is frequently paralleled by the contestation of values. McLuhan stated that 'Our Western values, built on the written word have already been considerably affected by the electric media of telephone, radio, and TV. Perhaps that is the reason why many highly literate people in our time find it difficult to examine this question without getting into a moral panic.'[58]

McLuhan's characterization of the cultural elites' anxiety towards the future of reading as a moral panic is important for two reasons. It was the first time that the now widely used term 'moral panic' had been deployed by a media theorist to describe an outbreak of anxiety.[59] McLuhan had also succeeded in linking the cultural elite's unease about the effects of the electronic media to a wider defensive attitude about the status of the written word.

Evan Brier's study of the post-war American book trade has drawn attention to an important contradiction between the perception and the reality of reading. He observes that the '1950s is likely the time during which alarm over the fate of both reading in general and high literature in particular was at its apex'. When, in 1956, the *Saturday Review* asked 'who is to blame' for the 'plight of contemporary reading', there was little public recognition that sales of books were flourishing and that, despite the advent of television, reading remained a popular pastime. In 1959 *Publishers Weekly* reported the pleasing news that book publishing was 'approaching a billion-dollar level'.[60]

The disconnect between references to the 'plight of reading' and the growth in book sales indicated that through it wider uncertainties about the moral order were channelled via the narrative of crisis. Some commentators have blamed anti-communist paranoia during the Cold War as one possible explanation for the alarmist accounts of the decline of reading in the 1950s and 1960s.[61] Others argue that such reactions were manifestations of apprehension towards the rise of electronic media, particularly television. However, the crisis narrative of reading does not appear to be tied to any specific experience or historical context. It is much more useful to diagnose McLuhan's characterization of 'moral panic' as a symptom of the uneasy relationship between cultural authority and the moral order.

Since the invention of writing, reading has become the principal source of moral knowledge. That is why, throughout history, reading had served as a focus for controversy. During the 1950s and 1960s, the ascendancy of new media complicated the role and cultural status of reading. The narrative of a decline in reading standards indicated that the previous tensions and anxieties that had been directed towards mass reading were now displaced and sublimated through problems raised about the new media. From this point onwards, the preoccupation with the media effect tended to be directed at electronic or digitally assisted media.

A series of reports published by the National Endowment for the Arts (NEA) in recent decades argues that book reading has declined amongst the American public, especially the young.[62] Dire predictions about the 'End of the Book' have blamed the growth of electronic media for what the NEA described as 'drawing Americans away from reading'. Yet some surveys indicate that many intensive users of the new media – particularly the internet – read more than the average person. The sense of unease and gloom that pervades reports of the supposed decline of reading is likely to be an outcome of a more general concern with the fragility of cultural authority. It is difficult to avoid the conclusion that the defensive manner in which the state and status of reading are discussed indicates uneasiness about a world where disenchantment regarding the authority of literacy continues to influence cultural life.

WHAT CRISIS? VOICES OF COMPLACENCY

The idea that reading is in decline has become a focus of debate between supporters of traditional cultural authority and those inclined to challenge it. Those associated with the New Literacy Studies approach have tended to dismiss claims that reading and or its teaching faces a crisis. From their perspective, literacy was in any case overrated by the ideology that glorified it, and those who lament its decline are simply muddying the waters. In an essay written in 1981, Harvey Graff stated that 'our comprehension of this crisis and decline is no more firm than that of the historical relevance of literacy itself'.[63] Others suggested that claims about a literacy crisis and 'negative views of schooling achievements' were a consequence of the way in which literacy was defined.[64] According to this argument, the application of elite standards of literacy to a broader group of students inevitably created problems mistakenly interpreted as those of declining standards of reading.

Debates about the decline of reading seamlessly converged with apprehension about the quality of its teaching. By the 1970s, the debate between those who argued that schools were failing to teach children to read and those who insisted that there was no crisis to worry about had hardened into intractable ideological positions. In October 1975 an editorial in *The Times Educational Supplement* noted that 'it almost seems as if it is no longer possible for good men and women to agree to disagree amicably', and that the hostile debate over reading skills had polarized along the lines of Left and Right.[65] A special issue of the *Cambridge Journal of Education* in 1993 featured the title 'The politics of reading'; its editorial poured scorn on those who tried to incite a climate of crisis around the teaching of reading.

In the United States, the argument that there was a crisis of literacy was frequently dismissed by anti-traditionalist educators and academics, who argued that the call for the raising of standards of literacy teaching, particularly through the use of phonics, was part of a right-wing agenda. The suggestion that there was a literacy crisis in US schools was dismissed as a manufactured crisis that aimed to subvert public education.[66] Two opponents of the charge that the classroom teaching of reading was inadequate responded by blaming religious fundamentalists for creating an atmosphere of crisis: 'The preservation of standards is consistent with fundamentalists' belief in absolutes, stemming from the belief in God as the absolute, supreme being.'[67] That was enough to indict all those who sought to improve standards of literacy as supporters of a dangerous conspiracy designed to sabotage the good work of the whole-language movement. Those who believed that there was no crisis of literacy also regularly raised the idea that right-wing scaremongers were behind the campaign to raise the quality of reading attained by British pupils in schools in the UK.[68]

CONFUSION ON BOTH SIDES

The debate between those disenchanted with the promise of literacy and their opponents, as well as the controversy surrounding its teaching in schools, sheds little light on what readers actually do and what reading means to them. Towards the end of the twentieth century, 'authoritative' estimates of the extent of illiteracy among American adults ranged from 'less than 1 percent to as much as 50 percent'.[69] At the same time the intensely polarized debate about the teaching of reading in classrooms varied from complacent reassurance that all was well to the claim that poor pedagogy was normalizing illiteracy.

A Special Edition of the *Peabody Journal of Education* devoted to the theme of literacy in the twenty-first century observed that 'literacy education and the preparation of literacy educators has long been marked by variant and extreme philosophies'. It also noted that literacy instruction was 'inextricably interwoven with the sociopolitical context in which it exists and perhaps even creates'.[70] Pointing to the 'acrimony of this debate', John Miller commented that the 'near-incessant bickering within the literacy community over what constitutes best practice not only does nothing to advance the field but has led to "closed-circuit" discussion among proponents of a particular perspective, individuals who are typically content to talk among themselves'.[71]

Commentaries on the acrimonious and dogmatic rhetoric through which the question of literacy is debated rarely attempt to account for the drivers of this phenomenon. Yet for some time it has been evident to astute observers that there must be something more than technical issues at stake in this confusing and intemperate clash of views on the teaching of reading. Referring to the controversy and publicity surrounding Rudolf Flesch's best-selling critique, Hannah Arendt pointedly remarked that 'certainly more is involved here than the puzzling question of why Johnny can't read'.[72] In her 1958 essay 'The Crisis in Education' she linked the disquiet regarding the question of 'why Johnny can't read' to the more profound problem of uncertainty about just what it is that society wants Johnny to read.

Arendt took the view that the debate on literacy bypassed the more fundamental question of what constituted the content and purpose of education. This point was also stressed by the philosopher of education Richard Stanley Peters. Peters asserted that the teaching of reading and writing is merely a means – an instrument – for the attainment of fundamental educational objectives:

> If anything in education is purely instrumental the basic skills of reading and writings are. They give access to and make participation possible; but they have no content built into them. Everything depends on what is read or written.[73]

In other words, what is important about reading is the content transmitted to the reader and more broadly to the younger generations that are being educated. The importance of content was also affirmed by E. D. Hirsch's argument that literacy is 'no autonomous empty skill but depends on literate culture' – that is, the transmission of a shared knowledge and cultural values.[74]

But shared values and knowledge presuppose that they enjoy the affirmation of cultural authority. The question of content directly relates to the knowledge and ideas that society sees as authoritative and significant. This is the question that the main protagonists in the literacy debate tend to evade.

It is likely that both the sense of disorientation that haunts the literate elites and the disenchantment that motivated critics of the printed text are fuelled by the absence of consensus on common values. That is why cultural fragmentation and divisions have so readily converged with discords that surround literacy and its teaching in schools. One consequence is that the confusion surrounding the meaning of reading has intensified. The problems associated with reading have acquired an unprecedented intensity, to the point where the reader is sometimes cast in the role of an endangered species.

CONCLUSION: THE FLIGHT FROM CONTENT

Thousands of years after the invention of writing, reading continues to be a cause of concern and a subject of controversy. The contradictory narratives of reading, which since the 1960s assumed the form of disenchantment with literacy or apprehension about its future, have, if anything, acquired a more polarized dimension.

Today, disenchantment with the Enlightenment conception of literacy is often articulated through an uncritical celebration of digital technology. Post-McLuhan technophiles praise the internet's potential for subverting the undesirable authority of the text. One digital media expert, Clay Shirky, proclaims that there was no need to mourn the demise of deep reading since it was, in any case, something of a con. Pointing to Leo Tolstoy's masterpiece *War and Peace*, he appears delighted that 'no one' reads the novel anymore: it was 'too long and not so interesting', and people have 'increasingly decided that Tolstoy's sacred work isn't actually worth the time it takes to read it'.[1] The philistine sentiments expressed by Shirky resonate with the current *Zeitgeist* — to the point where the journal *Foreign Policy* even named him as one of their 'Top 100 Global Thinkers' in 2010.

Celebrations of the supposed death of Gutenberg's print culture coexist with lamentation by commentators who fear that society faces a crisis of literacy and an irreversible decline of the Literary Canon. Stories about the failure of schools to teach a significant minority of their pupils how to read erupt frequently into angry exchanges about who to blame. Warnings about the decline of the literate mind extend to the argument that in the current era serious reading is faced with unprecedented obstacles, with technophobes complaining that serious reading has fallen victim to the distractions of the internet.[2] Whereas literary confessionals in the past noted the difficulties that their authors had in restraining their passion for reading, today's commentators offer personal accounts of the extraordinary trials they face when attempting to read serious literature in a distracted age.[3]

For one side of the debate, technology appears as the saviour and for the other as the culprit. Despite their different emphasis, both narratives appear to ascribe the changing meaning and status of reading to the emergence of the digital media. Yet history indicates that most of the outcomes attributed to the internet and digital technology have served as topics of concern in previous centuries. Stories of information overload, media distraction and loss of attention are far from new developments. Contributions on the current challenges facing readers recycle an age-old mantra that there is too much choice, too much information and too much change. 'Awed and intimidated by the availability of texts, faced with the all but impossible task of discriminating among them, the reader tends to move across surfaces, skimming, hastening from one site to the next without allowing the words to resonate inwardly,' states one recent critic of the digital form of extensive reading.[4]

We can conclude from this that the source of our current predicament is not the availability of powerful and exciting new technologies of communication, but an uncertainty about what to communicate. In such circumstances, reading inevitably acquires a new meaning.

THE FLIGHT FROM CONTENT

Literacy comes into its own when what people read matters to them. Writing and reading are not simply techniques of communication, and reading is not purely a skill that allows individuals to decode a text. Readers gain meaning from their experience through engaging with the content, and how people read is influenced by the wider cultural attitudes towards literacy. The prevailing intellectual climate, and the significance that ideas and texts possess for communities, shapes such attitudes. The sacralization of reading and the text by religions such as Judaism and Christianity was connected to the conviction that it provided an access to the Truth and to a greater understanding of God's purpose for humanity. The Reformation helped launch a veritable literacy campaign as thousands of hitherto non-literate believers sought to read the vernacular Bible. The rise in literacy rates was closely connected to the spread of the Reformation.

The eighteenth-century Enlightenment took ideas and education seriously and helped encourage an environment where reading was highly valued. It was during this century that the idiom of 'love of reading' emerged and gained influence. Not everyone who learned how to read was interested in the finer points of philosophy, but in circumstances where reading was celebrated as a fundamental cultural accomplishment, it became a medium for enhancing knowledge, intellectual and aesthetic pleasure, and self-improvement. Learning how to read did not pose a serious problem. As Jonathan Rose points out in *The Intellectual Life of the British Working Class*, numerous working-class people during the nineteenth century learned to read on their own because they believed that self-education was important. The energy and devotion of these autodidacts demonstrates that when it is seen to matter, people readily embrace the practice of reading.

As I have argued in my study of intellectual life, contemporary society finds it difficult to take ideas and the authority of knowledge seriously.[5] Ours is an Information Age, not an Age of Ideas. In a climate where the status of ideas and the objective significance of knowledge claims are regarded casually, literacy itself will be seen as no big deal. The disenchantment with literacy reviewed in the previous chapter is but one symptom of this cultural predicament. Another indication, arguably even more disconcerting, is the apparent loss of a language with which to express the virtues of reading. Literacy advocates often adopt the approach of public-health campaigners to gain the attention of would-be readers, arguing, for example, that reading serves as a useful stress-relieving therapy.[6]

Take the well-intentioned report published in 2012 by the UK's Department of Education, *Research Evidence on Reading for Pleasure*. This report on 'reading for pleasure' cannot actually bring itself to state that the pleasure of reading is good in and of itself. Instead it offers such anodyne conclusions as 'evidence suggests that reading for pleasure is an activity that has emotional and social consequences', and is also 'associated with higher scores in reading assessments'.[7] This contrived manner with which the case for reading for pleasure is stated is itself an indication that something has gone terribly wrong with the teaching of literacy. The absence of a normative language through which the pleasure of reading can be expounded suggests that the report's authors are struggling with the challenge of giving literacy meaning.

Well-meaning advocates of reading find it difficult to justify their cause in a language that draws attention to its transformative impact on readers. Their promotional material rarely adopts the humanist approach that regards reading as valuable; instead, they endorse literacy as a useful skill that provides the reader with important social and economic benefits. One group of campaigners contend that Britain's literacy deficit is linked to unemployment, and that the nation's Gross Domestic Product 'could be £32 billion higher if action had been taken to ensure all children were reading well by the age of 11'.[8]

The meaning of reading is gained through the subjective interaction with the content of the text, which serves as a catalyst for intellectually inspiring or emotionally arousing the reader. The range of reader reactions that have emerged throughout history were directly or indirectly an outcome of an interaction with the content of what they were reading. But what happens when society finds it difficult to give meaning to content?

Sven Birkerts's *The Gutenberg Elegies* offers a moving reminder of the significance of reading as an activity that, because it possesses metaphysical qualities such as the fashioning of the self, needs to be valued in its own right. He writes of how 'the stable hierarchies of the printed page' are 'being superseded by the rush of impulses through freshly minted circuits'.[9] Birkerts fears that this loss of authority of the text has important implications for 'an entire system of belief, values and cultural aspirations' because 'our entire collective subjective history – the soul of our societal body – is encoded in print'.[10]

Birkerts blames the rise of electronic media and the changes it unleashed for thrusting society into a 'place of unknowing',[11] and censures the rise of digital technology and media for rendering a 'vast part of our cultural heritage utterly alien'.[12] He is by no means alone in imagining that society has become alienated from the culture of print as a result of the revolutionary impact of digital technology: numerous commentators on culture and the media have as their premise the belief that the internet has led to the demise of the linear-thinking Gutenberg reader. They also assume that the form of reasoning associated with Enlightenment thought has given way to a new form of cognition.[13] Those who welcome the coming of the post-Gutenberg age are actually applauding the loss of the forms of rationality and knowledge associated with print culture.

Whatever the long-term changes brought about by the internet, it is not directly responsible for the estrangement of society from its cultural heritage or the problems associated with the crisis of literacy. As we have noted, discussions about the crisis of reading precede the emergence of the internet, and deliberations about society's uneasy relationship with its cultural heritage have been a perpetual source of debate since modern times. Authority in all of its forms has been contested to the point that, by the second half of the twentieth century, it was increasingly branded with negative connotations.[14]

The current tendency in debates about the trajectory of twenty-first-century society is to confuse the erosion of cultural authority with the effects of the rise of the new media. A fetishized orientation towards the impact of new technology and new media exercises significant influence on the cultural landscape. This outlook of technological determinism was most systematically expounded by McLuhan, who insisted that what mattered was the medium and not its content, which he characterized as merely 'the juicy piece of meat carried by the burglar to distract the watchdog of the mind'.[15]

But if content is indeed a distraction and the medium is 'the message', the relative importance of whatever is read becomes arbitrary. From this perspective the content – knowledge, wisdom and cultural legacy – developed through and embodied in print culture loses its authority to the new medium. This point is explicitly endorsed by supporters of the post-Gutenberg way of life. Katherine Viner, editor-in-chief of *The Guardian*, voiced her enthusiasm about the demise of '500 years of print dominated information', stating that:

> In fact, digital is a huge conceptual change, a sociological change, a cluster bomb blowing apart who we are and how our world is ordered, how we see ourselves, how we live. It's a change we're in the middle of, so close up that sometimes it's hard to see. But it is deeply profound and it is happening at an almost unbelievable speed.[16]

This fetishization of technological change does not simply lead to an underestimation of the cultural significance of content. It also represents a flight from it. So whereas someone like Birkerts laments the loss of cultural continuity implied by the arbitrary status of content, Viner celebrates it.

According to Viner, there was always something inhibiting about the stable and hierarchical format of the printed text. The ancient Socratic prejudice that the culture of reading is unnatural and therefore less pure than what preceded it was restated in the present-day critique of the stability of the text, which celebrates the digital because it allegedly allows people to break out of the restraints imposed by the rigid boundaries of the static text. Thus, the artificiality of the printed book can be transcended by a more natural and spontaneous attitude towards the content of what is read.

Along with other adherents of the idea of the 'Gutenberg Parenthesis', Viner anticipates a return to the more natural and participatory oral era that preceded the invention of the printing press. She claims that 'for 500 years, knowledge was contained, in a fixed format that you believed to be a reliable version of the truth; now, moving to the post-print era, we are returning to an age when you're as likely to hear information, right or wrong, from people you come across'.[17]

If Viner is right and a 'reliable version of the truth' can no longer be accessed through the reading of a published text, society faces a problem that is far graver than a mere 'crisis of literacy'. The history of reading has always been bound up with a search for meaning. And meaning – whether religious, philosophical, or scientific – acquires reality for the self through providing insight into what is true. When reading becomes divested of its truth-seeking potential it becomes a banal exercise. Relegated to an instrumental skill, the role of reading is limited to decoding text and accessing information. That was how the technocratic school of functional literacy regarded the purpose of reading in the post-war era, and in a roundabout manner, the McLuhan-inspired flight from content leads back to a similar conclusion.

The convergence of the technocratic school of literacy skills with the backward-looking reaction against the humanist approach to reading recurs in the domain of teaching. In schools, both sides of the reading wars fail to take seriously the content and the cultural meaning of reading. One side is concerned with ensuring that learning is natural and relevant to children's inclination, while the objective of the other is to train pupils to acquire the skill of literacy. Divested of its aesthetic and intellectual content, the teaching of reading risks becoming an exercise in the training of a skill.

THE FANTASY OF A RETURN TO THE PRE-GUTENBERG ERA

Those disenchanted with the culture of print believe that digitally mediated communication will help liberate readers from the unnatural confines of the stable and fixed printed text, and they represent this development as a transformation that is as far-reaching as the invention of writing. This belief is most systematically proclaimed by a group of commentators associated with the proposition that the 500-year-long era of print culture initiated around 1500 by Gutenberg's invention has given way to a new epoch of a more natural form of communication.

Lars Ole Sauerberg invented the term 'Gutenberg Parenthesis' to describe the period from the late Renaissance to the beginning of the twenty-first century. During this Parenthesis – from 1500 to 2000 – the print press and the mass production of books became synonymous with Western culture. Sauerberg argues that with the absorption of the printed book into an age of digital media, textually communicated knowledge has changed and opened up the possibility for the emergence of modes of communication that are more harmonious with the values of pre-modern oral cultures. This return to what Walter Ong has characterized as Secondary Orality means that the epoch of the book is represented as a transitional phase between the preceding oral tradition and the now emergent secondary form of orality.[18]

The idea that the Gutenberg era and its modernist intellectual tradition is a phase that has now been transcended combines McLuhan's veneration for the power of new technology with reverence for the medieval past. The Danish media theorist Thomas Pettitt, the leading exponent of the Gutenberg Parenthesis, believes that 'we are not just moving upwards and onwards, we are moving upwards and backwards', adding that though society is technologically sophisticated 'we are going back to the way things were long before'.[19] The new technologically mediated networks allegedly open up the possibility of recovering a more connected, community-oriented, participatory and less individualistic society. The theory strongly resembles nineteenth-century conservative social theories, from Edmund Burke to Ferdinand Tönnies, which posited organically connected communities as their ideal. But unlike the proponents of the Gutenberg Parenthesis, their nineteenth-century ancestors were pessimistic about the recovery of such communities.

Striking a light-hearted mystical tone, Pettitt observes that:

> With the right spelling, 'media studies' is contained within 'mediaeval studies'. One of those neat cabbalistic things that means nothing in itself but is useful for making you think: a medievalist can be a futurist because the Gutenberg Parenthesis tells us the future is medieval.[20]

Pettitt uses the phrase 'restoration' to signal the idea of a return to a less rationalized and more spontaneous form of communication. Another digital media enthusiast, Trent Batson, maintains that now that the Gutenberg Parenthesis has come to an end, 'humanity is beginning to understand once again, with the Internet, that knowledge is communal'. For Batson the Gutenberg era was an anomaly – a detour from the more natural, oral participatory culture that preceded it – and we are now in a period of secondary orality, which 'brings us back to the norms and processes of communications that humans have always sustained'.[21]

The fantasy of a return to a medieval past, where the production and communication of knowledge was more participatory and communal than in the days of the unnatural Gutenberg Parenthesis, is evoked to disparage the cultural authority of literacy and of the book. The authority of objective knowledge as codified through books – indeed any form of intellectual and cultural authority – is dismissed as an attempt to construct a rigid, anti-participatory hierarchy, while the negation of the authority of the book is presented as an anti-hierarchical and democratizing impulse that aims to liberate the reader. This devaluation of the content of the text and therefore also of its author is framed in a populist language that rejoices in the supposed empowerment of readers.

Adopting the modest tone that self-consciously eschews appearing as the possessor of any form of cultural authority, Viner states that 'we are no longer the all-seeing all-knowing journalists, delivering words from on high for readers to take in, passively'. On the contrary:

> [D]igital has wrecked those hierarchies almost overnight, creating a more levelled world, where responses can be instant, where some

readers will almost certainly know more about a particular subject than the journalist, where the reader might be better placed to uncover a story.[22]

But flattering readers does not mean that they are taken more seriously. The rhetorical erosion of the distinction between readers and authors and journalists does little more than foster the illusion of cultural levelling. The claim that readers are no longer 'just readers' but newsmakers and collaborators participating with professional journalists and authors has the perverse effect of devaluing the culture of reading, reintroducing the age-old caricature of a passive readership that possesses no inherent cultural values. Just sharing an anecdote with an online journalist will apparently turn the passive excluded reader into an active, culturally included citizen author.

The presumption that during the past 500 years of hierarchical print culture readers constituted a passive group of unthinking individuals who simply internalized the authoritative wisdom of 'all–knowing journalists' is a fantasy. The burning of tens of thousands of books, the institutionalization of state censorship, and officialdom's attempts to contain the political energies and emotions unleashed through reading, indicates that this practice was and remains a very serious activity. Viner's invitation to readers to be collaborators fails to understand that reading – especially serious reading – is itself a culturally beneficial activity.

Ever since 1967, when Roland Barthes declared 'the death of the author', the author's alleged demise has been advertised as the elevation of the status of the reader. But why should the death of the author – either existentially or digitally – possess any positive or liberating cultural attributes? Whatever one thinks of the authority of authors, they can be held to account – unlike the producers of the often anonymous and continually shifting content of a webpage. Readers can react to and engage with a fixed point of reference. It is not always easy or comfortable to wrestle with the powerful creative will of the author, but this experience is in part what gives reading its compelling power.

Those who rejoice in the death of the author allege that the deconstructed text has no permanent meaning and is therefore open to interpretation: 'any fixing of meaning is the property and prerogative of the reader'.[23] According to one account of deconstruction, 'with text (rather than book) in hand, the reader becomes the authoritative determiner, indeed the author, of meaning'.[24] In one sense, of course, readers have always been interpreters of the words of authors, and reading has always involved the search for meaning. The difference between the reading of a book and an inherently unstable text is that meaning acquires a different connotation. In the former, meaning is meshed with the search for the truth; in the latter it acquires a fragmented and arbitrary character.

The attempt to deconstruct the text and strip the book of its authority calls into question the very premise and cultural content of reading. As Birkerts notes, the attempt to 'liberate' the imagination 'from the constraint of being guided at every step by the author' means that 'necessity is dethroned and arbitrariness is installed in its place'.[25] Yet one of the most exhilarating and transformative dimensions of reading is that through the struggle to interpret and gain meaning, readers learn how to think critically and ultimately how to judge. As the poet Milton noted, it was through their capacity to judge that readers gained power and genuine authority.[26] When meaning is rendered arbitrary, it diminishes the potential of reading for developing the capacity to judge and clarify – effectively disempowering the reader.

SAME OLD, SAME OLD?

Looking back over the past two millennia, it appears that every generation has had to fight to preserve the integrity of reading from its detractors. Reading has always been indicted as unnatural and the reader has forever been the object of well-meaning moral and medical advice. In recent times the claim that reading is unnatural and therefore a risk to human health inevitably relies on the legitimacy of science and particularly that of neuroscience. 'We were never born to read', proclaims a study of the 'science of the reading brain', raising the unanswered question of what we were born to do.[27] Maryanne Wolf, the author of this study, claims that '[t]o acquire this unnatural process, children need instructional environments that support all the circuit parts that need bolting for the brain to read'.[28] One can only wonder how millions of children in candlelit rooms and overcrowded classes managed to deal with this highly 'unnatural process' throughout history.

Neuroscience, psychology, and a variety of other disciplines have contributed to the medicalization of reading to the point that its very acquisition is regarded as a complex and challenging accomplishment. Such expectations turn into a self-fulfilling prophecy when reading difficulty is normalized as a natural condition. Back in 1887, when the German physician Rudolf Berlin came up with the diagnosis of dyslexia to describe the difficulty that some people had in interpreting written characters, he would have been surprised and shocked to discover that a little over a century later tens of millions of children would be diagnosed with that condition. Today dyslexia is sometimes presented as the natural and even normal symptom of the functioning of the human brain. 'Dyslexia is our best, most visible evidence that the brain was never wired to read,' argues Wolf.[29]

The aetiology of reading problems remains a subject of controversy. It is far from evident how the interaction between social and cultural expectations interrelates with the way that human beings decode text. But the veritable epidemic of dyslexia and other reading-related symptoms is likely to be related to the lowering of educational and cultural expectations, the tendency to re-interpret the learning problems facing children in medical terms, and the expansion of the definition of medical diagnosis. In their recent study, Professor Julian Elliott of Durham University and Dr Elena Grigorenko of the Yale School of Medicine have concluded that as a diagnostic category, dyslexia is far too imprecise to capture the different challenges facing people. They rightly assert that more emphasis should be placed on helping children to read rather than focusing on finding a label to account for their difficulties.[30]

Reading disorders, like most anxieties concerning the use of today's media, are increasingly re-routed through the internet. As noted previously, both techno-utopians and techno-sceptics have adopted a deterministic orientation towards its power. Most contributions to the media effect of the internet have tended to transfer pre-existing offline anxieties to the online experience. Books with titles like *The Dumbest Generation: How the Digital Age Stupefies Young Americans and Jeopardizes Our Future* attribute problems that are fundamentally cultural in nature to the workings of digital technology.[31] The internet is held responsible – as was television previously – for distracting people from reading and indeed for making it almost impossible to study in a serious manner. Numerous surveys of teachers and educators appear to confirm the prejudice that the 'constant use of digital technologies by students is affecting their ability to concentrate.'[32]

The eighteenth-century diagnosis of reading addictions has been revived in the form of a new panic about 'internet addiction'. Internet addiction, like its predecessors, expresses the compulsion to recast the moral ambiguities surrounding use of the media in medical terms. However, unlike in medieval and early modern times, there is a constant attempt to justify this diagnosis on the basis of scientific evidence, despite the absence of sound evidence. As one meta-analysis of quantitative research on this subject concluded, studies have used 'inconsistent criteria to define Internet addicts, applied recruiting methods that may cause serious sampling bias, and examined data using primarily exploratory rather than confirmatory data analysis techniques to investigate the degree of association rather than causal relationships among variables.'[33]

The old Werther Effect has re-emerged as an online reading disorder, and cybersuicide is often presented as an inevitable consequence of the passions prompted by the reading of digital texts.[34] Cyberpanic often runs in parallel with neuro-panic about the effects of digitally mediated reading. Digital technology has even been blamed for the decline of empathy among Americans. The neuroscientist Susan Greenfield has warned that the human brain faces an unprecedented assault and that therefore 'there's a danger that that cherished sense of the self could be diminished or even lost.'[35]

Warnings about the power of digital technology to rewire the brain coexist with the opposite tendency to acclaim its allegedly beneficial effects. Both sides of the argument beg the question of why a change to the workings of the brain is either a problem or a solution. As the Australian neuroethicist Neil Levy maintains, 'brains are supposed to change in response to experiences; that's a sign they're working as they are designed to.'[36] Moreover, how the brain responds to a particular text or technology of communication is mediated through cultural and social influences.

It is worth noting that while technophobes fear that the internet leads to the weakening of the sense of self, the romantic upholders of the fantasy of a return to a pre-Gutenberg oral age celebrate its assistance in strengthening an ethos that helps transcend the individual self. Their decoupling of literacy from its cultural content leads both parties to technologically deterministic conclusions.

THE INFANTILIZATION OF THE READER

For those who celebrate its demise, reading is not a serious issue. This casual attitude is most systematically expressed through the relativization of literacy, namely decoupling reading from literacy and recasting the latter in a pluralized form. In recent times, 'much of the literature of the past decade speaks of a multiplicity of literacies'.[37] In a world of pluralized literacies – emotional literacy, sexual literacy, computer literacy, visual literacy, digital literacy – reading is regarded as a skill on a par with that of managing information.

Supporters of the New Literacies believe that literacy is more than just reading and writing,[38] claiming that in the digital age multiple, dynamic and malleable communication practices require cognitive skills that are more sophisticated than what is required for old-school reading. Yet the literacy that emerged through the history of reading and writing still remains the unacknowledged foundation on which its pluralized imitators rest. The new rhetoric of *literacies* uses the authority of literacy to legitimate itself.

The loss of authority on the part of literacy and the book represents one side of the reaction to the uncertainties surrounding cultural authority. In their heart of hearts, most educators understand that reading and writing have a foundational significance for society. Attempts to avoid the problem of education through turning schools into sites for skills training have done little to reassure society that the question of cultural authority can be bypassed with technical solutions. Unfortunately, what is lacking is a language through which the humanist valuation of reading can be expressed in a twenty-first-century context.

The fundamental reading problem confronting society today is not that books have become marginalized and will soon disappear. Nor does the digital media represent a threat to reading: a significant proportion of serious readers of books are also actively engaged with the internet.[39] People read for enjoyment on Kindles, and e-books are widely used by academic libraries, providing greater access to students. The specific form that the problem of reading assumes today is society's tendency to infantilize the reader. Superficially, the age of the internet is represented as the empowerment of the status of the reader. Readers are constantly flattered as authors, active collaborators and autonomous agents who are free to shape and react to content in accordance with their inclinations. However, a narrative that highlights the unnatural features of reading and complicates the acquisition of literacy contradicts the glorification of reader empowerment.

Lurking behind the rhetoric of reader empowerment is the conviction that readers need expert guidance and support. The tendency to define human beings as vulnerable rather than resilient exercises a remarkable influence over the manner in which readers are perceived. Such sentiments have percolated into the way that the teaching of children to read is conceptualized. Children are often represented as vulnerable readers who are at risk from potentially dangerous teaching practices. According to Durham University academic Andrew Davis, imposing synthetic phonics on children who can already read when they start school is 'almost a form of abuse'.[40]

The tendency to liken certain teaching practices to a type of abuse is founded on the idea that young people are at risk of being psychologically damaged by them. In an essay entitled 'Phonics Toxicity and Other Side Effects' one vociferous opponent of this practice asks why children and their parents are not provided with a health warning about its risks, warning that children may become 'emotionally damaged'.[41] The evolutionary biologist Richard Dawkins even worries about the allegedly pernicious effects of fairy tales on youngsters.[42]

The language of reader vulnerability has expanded beyond childhood. In some American universities there have been calls to introduce 'trigger warnings' as a routine practice, which are designed to protect readers from the unsettling and potentially traumatizing consequences of the material they read. Those who support the call for trigger warnings believe that readers need to be protected from ideas, views, images and attitudes that may make them feel uncomfortable and possibly traumatized. One American academic at the City University of New York has argued that trigger warnings are 'sound pedagogy'.[43]

Reading is indeed a risky activity. Yet it was the psychologically disturbing impact of the written text and the upheavals that it caused that gave reading its authoritative power and appeal. Readers can explore the world, and through that journey explore themselves. In contrast to the vulnerable child in need of trigger warnings, Milton posited the ideal of the fit reader. He believed that readers 'possessed a fundamental capacity to judge, endowing them with importance and dignity'.[44] The infantilized reader who needs to be protected from the potentially damaging consequences of disturbing literature has displaced the fit reader who could be trusted to take on the world. Rediscovering the virtues of reading through cultivating the exercise of judgement constitutes one of the most significant cultural challenges of the present era.

NOTES

INTRODUCTION

1   See the discussion in Bratlinger (1998), p. 214.
2   See Plato (1997), *Phaedrus*, 275.
3   See Plato (1997), *Phaedrus*, 275.
4   Plato (1997a), *Republic*, 341d.
5   Plato (1997a), *Republic*, 341e.
6   Eisenstein (1979), p. 19.
7   Cited in Carr (2010), p. 168.
8   Sir Thomas Browne as cited by Eisenstein (1979), p. 19.
9   Seneca's 'On discursiveness in reading' can be found at http://www.stoics.
    com/seneca_epistles_book_1.html, accessed 3 May 2014.
10 For an example of this form of advice in the nineteenth century, see Philes
    (1873). archive.org/details/howtoreadabooki00phigoog; see Mikics (2013)
    for a current version of such advice.
11 Fischer (2005), p. 214.
12 Marius (1985), p. 428.
13 Cited in Furedi (2013), p. 39.
14 Seneca's 'On discursiveness in reading' can be found at http://www.stoics.
    com/seneca_epistles_book_1.html, accessed 3 May 2014.
15 See the discussion in Van Horn Melton (2001), pp. 94–100.
16 Bratlinger (1998), p. 96.
17 See, for example, 'Moral poisons: The antidote', part two, by F. C. W., *The
    Mother's Magazine* (June 1845), pp. 184–8.
18 Leavis (1968), p. 50.
19 Matthews (1966), p. 190.
20 Jackson (2008), p. 166.
21 Jackson (2008), p. 171.
22 Andrew Solomon, 'The closing of the American book', *The New York Times*
    (10 July 2004).

23 http://www.huffingtonpost.com/2013/10/06/mind-reading-skills-read-literature_n_4044507.html

24 'Reading can help reduce stress', *The Daily Telegraph* (30 March 2009).

25 http://www.huffingtonpost.com/2013/10/12/health-benefits-reading_n_4081258.html

26 Carr (2010), p. 214.

CHAPTER 1

1   Enzensberger and Lipson (1986), p. 88.

2   Enzensberger and Lipson (1986), p. 88.

3   Ortega y Gasset (1959), p. 15.

4   Ortega y Gasset (1959), p. 16, fn. 26.

5   Wolf (2010), pp. 77–8.

6   Wolf (2010), p. 70.

7   See Strauss (1993), p. 83.

8   Plato (1997a), II, 377, p. 1,016.

9   Plato (1997a), II, 378, p. 1,017.

10 Plato (1997a), II, 378, p. 1,016.

11 Plato (1997a), II, 386, p. 1,022.

12 Plato (1997a), III, 387, p. 1,024.

13 Plato (1997a), X, 606, pp. 1,210–11.

14 Ife (1985), p. 31.

15 Plato (1997a), X, 595, p. 1,200.

16 Derrida (1981), p. 71.

17 Plato (1997a), 341d.

18 Ong (2002), p. 164.

19 Ong (2002), p. 79.

20 Ong (2002), pp. 31–2.

21 See Thomas (1996) for a discussion of the role of writing in ancient Greece.

22 Derrida (1981), pp. 99–100.

23 See Lyons (2010), p. 18.

24 Thomas (1996), p. 35.

25 Thomas (1995), p. 59.

26 Thomas (1996), p. 35.

27 Greene (1951), p. 25.

28 Greene (1951), p. 52.

29 'Alcidamas, the sophist', translated by LaRue Van Hook, was originally published in 1919 in *The Classical Weekly*, no. 12. It is available on http://www.classicpersuasion.org/pw/alcidamas/alcsoph1.htm, accessed 20 September 2014.

30 Havelock (1999), p. 57.

31 Derrida (1981), pp. 106 and 149.
32 Greene (1951), p. 51.
33 Fischer (2005), p. 51.
34 Goody and Watt (1963), p. 328.
35 Fischer (2005), p. 54.
36 Levine, Locke, Searls and Weinberger (2001), p. xxxi.
37 Levine, Locke, Searls and Weinberger (2001), p. 164.
38 Levine, Locke, Searls and Weinberger (2001), p. iv.
39 Ong (2002), p. 8.
40 Hall (1901), p. 16.
41 Huey (1910), p. 8.
42 Huey (1910), p. 302.
43 See Maryanne Wolf, 'Socrates' nightmare', *The New York Times* (6 September 2007).
44 Hall (1901), p.16.
45 McLuhan (1994), p. 86.
46 McLuhan (1962), p. 2.
47 Havelock (1986), p. 24.
48 Ong (1982), p. 170.
49 For example, see Graff (1987).
50 McLuhan (1994), p. 84.
51 McLuhan (1994), p. 84.
52 Levine (1986), p. 187.
53 Ong (2002), p. 171.
54 See Umberto Eco, 'From Internet to Gutenberg 1996', a lecture given on 12 November 1996, http://www.umbertoeco.com/en/from-internet-to-gutenberg-1996.html.
55 On the rise of the idea of the love of reading, see Mäkinen (2013).
56 Fischer (2005), p. 41.

CHAPTER 2

1 Plato (1997), *Phaedrus*, 274e, p. 551.
2 Fischer (2005), p. 32.
3 Cited in Watson (2005), p. 209.
4 Robert Kintgen cited in Dobranski (2005), p. 21.
5 Sharpe (2000), pp. 65 and 83.
6 Fischer (2005), p. 33.
7 See Watson (2005), p. 207.
8 Watson (2005), p. 210.
9 Watson (2005), p. 210.
10 See Seneca's advice to Lucilius, http://www.stoics.com/seneca_epistles_book_1.html, accessed 10 November 2014.

11 See his 'Moral letters to Lucilius', available on http://www.stoics.com/seneca_epistles_book_1.html.

12 Carcopino (1991), p. 216.

13 This version of Martial's epigram 3.44 is cited in http://www.believermag.com/issues/200309/?read=article_perrottet, accessed 10 November 2014.

14 Furedi (2013), p. 62.

15 Watson (2005), p. 208.

16 See the *OED*, available online at http://www.oed.com.chain.kent.ac.uk/view/Entry/158857?redirectedFrom=reader#eid, accessed 7 October 2014.

17 Lyons (2011), p. 21.

18 Jeffrey (1996), p. xiii.

19 Fischer (2005), p. 60.

20 Jacobs (2011), p. 19.

21 Stock (1998), p. 5.

22 Stock (1998), p. 1.

23 See Jeffrey (1996), pp. 79–89.

24 Saint Augustine (1961), p. 224.

25 Stock (1998), p. 5.

26 See Jeffrey (1996), p. xviii.

27 Saint Augustine (1961), p. 186.

28 Saint Augustine (1961), p. 156. Paul appraised himself as the 'least of your apostles' in Corinthians 15:9.

29 Stock (1998), p. 53.

30 Saint Augustine (1961), p. 60.

31 Saint Augustine (1961), p. 117.

32 Saint Augustine (1961), pp. 116–17.

33 Saint Augustine (1961), p. 117.

34 Jeffrey (1996), p. 11.

35 Saint Augustine (1961), p. 156.

36 K. F. Morrison is cited in Olson (1994), p. 143.

37 Olson (1994), p. 147.

38 Stock (1998), pp. 54–5.

39 Burckhardt (1990), p. 98.

40 Manguel (1997), p. 86.

41 Saint Augustine (1961), p. 208.

42 Stock (1995), p. 717.

43 Stock (1995), p. 718.

44 Saint Augustine (1961), p. 114.

45 Saenger (1982), p. 377.

46 Saenger (1982), p. 384.

47 Amtower (2000), p. 9.

48 Amtower (2000), p. 38.

49 Amtower (2000), p. 43.

50 See Bosmajian (2006), pp. 59 and 66.

51 Cited in Olson (2003), p. 69. *Liber Confortatorius* is translated into English as *The Book of Encouragement and Consolation*; see its online review at https://scholarworks.iu.edu/dspace/bitstream/handle/2022/5837/05.08.23.html?sequence=1, accessed 26 September 2014.

52 See the discussion on Goscelin in Canatella (2010).

53 Olson (2003), p. 72.

54 Cited in Olson (2003), p. 72.

55 Olson (2003), p. 73.

56 See Kahn (1985) for a discussion of the *Secretum*.

57 Amtower (2000), p. 85.

58 http://www.fordham.edu/halsall/source/petrarch-ventoux.asp, accessed 12 November 2014.

59 Amtower (2000), p. 205.

60 Stock (1995), p. 725.

61 Saint Augustine (1961), p. 116.

62 Olson (1994), p. 144.

63 Olson (1994), p. 145.

64 Olson (1994), p. 148.

65 Olson (1994), p. 147.

66 Olson (1994), p. 143.

67 Saint Thomas Aquinas (2008), 1a1.10, online edition at http://www.newadvent.org/summa/1001.htm, accessed 12 July 2014.

68 Olson (1994), p. 144.

69 Olson (1994), p. 93.

70 Graff (1987b), pp. 138–9.

71 Amtower (2000), pp. 5–6.

72 Machiavelli's letter is available online at http://faculty.cua.edu/pennington/churchhistory220/Lecture13/MachiavelliStudy.htm, accessed 4 October 2014.

73 See Kahn (1985), pp. 154–6.

74 Amtower (2000), p. 5.

75 The image of this portrait is available on http://www.artble.com/artists/agnolo_bronzino/paintings/portrait_of_laura_battiferri.

76 The allegorical portrait of Dante can be accessed at http://www.artble.com/artists/agnolo_bronzino/paintings/allegorical_portrait_of_dante.

77 Amtower (2000), p. 85.

78 Thomas à Kempis in his *Doctrinale Juvenum*.

79 *The Life of Solitude* can be found at http://www.humanistictexts.org/petrarch.htm, accessed 4 November 2014.

80 http://www.poetryintranslation.com/PITBR/English/GoodWomen.htm, accessed 15 October 2014.

81 Lubbock (2005), 'A song of books', in Emerson and Lubock (2005), p. 31.
82 See E. C. Thomas, 'Preface' to *Philobiblion*, at https://ebooks.adelaide.edu.au/b/bury/
richard/philo/preface.html, accessed 5 November 2014.
83 'Prologue' to *Philobiblion*, at https://ebooks.adelaide.edu.au/b/bury/richard/philo/
preface.html, accessed 5 November 2014.
84 Levine (2006), p. 63.
85 See Fischer (2005), p. 253, and Mäkinen (2013).

CHAPTER 3

1   Eisenstein (1979), p. 7.
2   Abel (2012), p. 79.
3   Eisenstein (1979), p. 304.
4   Martin (1996), p. 12.
5   Furet and Ozouf (1982), p. 58.
6   See Martin (1996), p. 13.
7   Blair (2010), p. 47.
8   See the discussion in Abel (2012), pp. x–xi.
9   Abel (2012), p. xi.
10 Abel (2012), p. 121.
11 Bosmajian (2006), p. 65.
12 Himmelfarb (1997), p. 198.
13 Achinstein (2001), p. 52.
14 Joseph Hall cited in Bushnell (1996), p. 119.
15 Achinstein (2001), p. 52.
16 Achinstein (2001), p. 51.
17 Blair (2010), p. 59.
18 Francis Bacon, 'Of studies' (1625), is available online at http://www.authorama.com/
essays-of-francis-bacon-50.html, accessed 13 November 2014.
19 Cited in Dobranski (2005), p. 30.
20 Francis Bacon, 'Of studies' (1625), is available online at http://www.authorama.com/
essays-of-francis-bacon-50.html, accessed 13 November 2014.
21 Milton cited in Achinstein (1994), p. 3.
22 Olson (1994), p. 3.
23 Johansson (2003), p. 33.
24 Graff (2003), p. 263.
25 Graff (1988), p. 89.
26 Graff (1988), p. 89.
27 Furet and Ozouf (1982), p. 58.
28 Furet and Ozouf (1982), p. 58.
29 Furet and Ozouf (1982), p. 308.
30 Luther cited in Dobranski (2005), p. 27.

31 Marius (1985), p. 428.

32 Hill (1986), p. 41.

33 Hill (1986), p. 25.

34 Erasmus cited in Bushnell (1996), p. 127.

35 Sharpe and Zwicker (2003a), p. 4.

36 Cited in Sharpe (2000), p. 340.

37 Eisenstein (1979), p.133.

38 Hobbes (1985), chapter 29. Also available online at https://ebooks.adelaide.edu.au/h/hobbes/thomas/h68l/chapter29.html, accessed 10 January 2015.

39 Eisenstein (1979), p. 303.

40 For a discussion of the constitution of public opinion see Furedi (2013), pp. 222–34 and 247–72.

41 Zaret (1996), p. 1,532.

42 Zaret (1996), p. 1,499.

43 Zaret (1996), p. 1,532.

44 Zaret and Brown (2001), p. 61.

45 Achinstein (1994), p. 39.

46 Dobranski (2005), p. 45.

47 Sharpe (2003), p. 138.

48 Achinstein (1994), p. 15.

49 Achinstein (1994), p. 58.

50 Milton (1999), p. 15.

51 Milton (1999), pp. 15 and 16.

52 Milton (1999), p. 31.

53 Achinstein (1994), p. 65.

54 Milton (1999), p. 23.

55 Achinstein (1994), p. 68.

56 Achinstein (1994), p. 58.

57 Stone (1986), p. 96.

58 Wilson (2009), p. 16.

59 Sharpe (2000), p. 31.

60 See Lake and Pincus (2007).

61 See Achinstein (1996), p. 1.

62 Altick (1957), p. 26.

63 Raymond (2003), p. 186.

64 Raymond (2003), p. 186.

65 See Bosmajian (2006), p. 59.

66 Raymond (2003), p. 188.

67 Cited in Raymond (2003), p. 188.

68 Vives cited in Bushnell (1996), p. 118.

69 Blair (2010), p. 48.

70 Blair (2010), p. 57.

71 Blair (2010), p. 58.
72 Lyons (2010), p. 28.
73 Chapter 3 of Lyons (2010) offers a clear statement of these criticisms directed at the notion of a printing revolution.
74 Lyons (2010), p. 28.
75 Lyons (2010), pp. 27 and 35.
76 Bushnell (1996), p. 119.
77 Abel (2012), p. 10.
78 Johns (2002), p. 106.
79 Eisenstein (2002), p. 128.
80 This argument is echoed by Thomas (1986), pp. 119 and 121.

CHAPTER 4

1   See the classic account in *The Age of Improvement* by Briggs (1979).
2   Blair's *Sermons* (1790) are available online at https://archive.org/details/sermonsby-hughbl00conggoog, accessed 11 December 2014.
3   Towsey (2007), p. 262.
4   Van Horn Melton (2001), p. 93.
5   Fischer (2005), p. 257.
6   See the chapter on 'Eighteenth-Century Attitudes' in Eisenstein (2011).
7   For an interesting overview of this discussion see Mason (1999).
8   Hohendahl cited in Eagleton (1984), p. 10.
9   Eagleton (1984), p. 10.
10 Cragg (1964), p. 2.
11 Baker (1994), p. 186.
12 See Habermas (1992).
13 Eisenstein (2011), p. 136.
14 Benedict (2001), pp. 382–3.
15 Van Horn Melton (2001), pp. 116–17.
16 Cited in Eisenstein (2011), p. 120.
17 Beljame is cited in Eagleton (1984), p. 14.
18 Eagleton (1984), p. 14.
19 Collins (1989), p. 4.
20 Eagleton (1984), pp. 51–2.
21 Cited in Van Horn Melton (2001), p. 117.
22 Dr Johnson is cited in Collins (1926), p. 429.
23 Cited in Collins (1926), p. 430.
24 Outram (2013), p. 16.
25 Wittmann (1999), p. 285.
26 See Engelsing (1974).
27 Van Horn Melton (2001), pp. 89–90.

28 Van Horn Melton (2001), p. 91.

29 Van Horn Melton (2001), p. 92.

30 See DeMaria (1997).

31 Hall (1999), p. 234.

32 Fischer (2005).

33 Curran (2005), p. 696.

34 Mäkinen (2013), p. 128.

35 Mäkinen (2013), p. 134.

36 Mäkinen (2013), p. 134.

37 See Brewer (1997), p. 128.

38 Addison is cited in Van Horn Melton (2001), p. 96.

39 Locke's *New Method* is available online at https://archive.org/details/gu_newmethod-maki00lock, accessed 4 June 2014.

40 Bell is cited in Towsey (2007), p. 191.

41 See the discussion of these distinctions in DeMaria (1997).

42 Cited in Fischer (2005), p. 365.

43 Brewer (1997), pp. 191–2.

44 Benedict (2001), pp. 389–90.

45 Brewer (1997), p. 194.

46 Bratlinger (1998), p. 17.

47 Cited in Jackson (2004), p. 1,046.

48 Wittmann (1999), p. 288.

49 Wittmann (1999), p. 291.

50 Van Horn Melton (2001), p. 113.

51 Cited in Small (1996), p. 264.

52 One advocate of conversation was Lord Chesterfield, who in 1752 advised his son 'you should now read very little, but converse a great deal'; see http://www.gutenberg.org/files/3361/3361-h/3361-h.htm, accessed 21 July 2014.

53 See 'On Studies' by Samuel Johnson, which first appeared in the journal *The Adventurer* in 1753. Available online at http://grammar.about.com/od/classicessays/a/JohnsonStudies.htm, accessed 2 December 2014.

54 Eisenstein (2011), p. 99.

55 Baker (1975), p. 298.

56 Malesherbes is cited in Eisenstein (2011), p. 137.

57 Cited in Eisenstein (2011), p. 138.

58 Cited in Hanvelt (2010), p. 13.

59 Cited in Porter (2000), p. 192.

60 Haakonssen (1994), p. 3.

61 Cited in Hanvelt (2010), p. 3.

62 Haakonssen (1994), p. 5.

63 Altick (1957), p. 76.

64 Burke (2009), pp. 112–13.

65 Eisenstein (2011), p. 144.

66 Cited in Keen (1999), p. 28.

67 Keen (1999), p. 32.

68 Altick (1957), pp. 76 and 104.

69 For a discussion of the reaction of the middle-class elite to these cheap short pamphlets, see Pendersen (1986).

70 Pendersen (1986), p. 106.

71 Bratlinger (1998), p. 5.

CHAPTER 5

1 Vincent (1993), p. 6.

2 See *Oxford English Dictionary*, online edition, accessed 4 November 2014.

3 Burke (2009), p. 117.

4 Van Horn Melton (2001), p. 112.

5 Cited in Van Horn Melton (2001), p. 113.

6 Woodmansee (1988–9), p. 206.

7 Woodmansee (1988–9), p. 208.

8 Woodmansee (1988–9), p. 208.

9 See Alexander Innes Shand, 'Contemporary literature, VII; Readers', *Blackwood's Magazine*, vol. 126 (August 1879), pp. 238–9.

10 Bell (2011), p. 98.

11 See 'Letter to Nathaniel Burwell', Monticello, 14 March 1818, available online at http://www.let.rug.nl/usa/presidents/thomas-jefferson/letters-of-thomas-jefferson/jefl251.php, accessed 23 November 2014.

12 'Letter to Nathaniel Burwell', Monticello, 14 March 1818, available online at http://www.let.rug.nl/usa/presidents/thomas-jefferson/letters-of-thomas-jefferson/jefl251.php, accessed 23 November 2014.

13 Bratlinger (1998), p. 12.

14 Pearson (1999), p. 27.

15 Gettelman (2011), p. 64.

16 See letter to H. S. Sutton (24 May 1848) at http://www.forgottenbooks.org/readbook_text/Memoirs_and_Correspondence_of_Coventry_Patmore_v2_1000500613/179, accessed 12 September 2014.

17 'Confessions of a novel reader', by A, *Southern Literary Messenger* (March 1839), pp. 179–93, available online at http://www.merrycoz.org/books/CONFESSN.HTM, accessed 23 May 2014.

18 Ife (1985), p. 12.

19 Littau (2006), p. 64.

20 Samuel Johnson writing in the fourth number of *The Rambler* (31 March 1750), to be found at http://www.english.upenn.edu/~mgamer/Etexts/johnson.rambler.html, accessed 27 April 2014.

21 See the discussion on the 'taming of public opinion' in Chapter 11 of Furedi (2013).
22 Hume's 'Of Suicide' is available online at http://www.davidhume.org/texts/suis.html, accessed 12 January 2015.
23 Moore (1790), vol. 2, pp. 68–70.
24 Moore (1790), vol. 2, p. 125.
25 Moore (1790), vol. 2, p. 341.
26 Moore (1790), vol. 2, p. 153.
27 Moore (1790), vol. 2, pp. 121–2.
28 Moore (1790), vol. 2, p. 153.
29 Moore (1790), vol. 2, p. 123.
30 Swales (1987), p. 94.
31 Goeze cited in Swales (1987), pp. 95–6.
32 Thorson and Öberg (2003), p. 70.
33 Thorson and Öberg (2003), p. 70.
34 Batley (1992), p. 870.
35 Appel is cited in Thorson and Öberg (2003), p. 71.
36 McGuire (2011), p. 59.
37 Parisot (2014), p. 277.
38 Long (1915), p. 171.
39 Long (1915), p. 170.
40 *Gentleman's Magazine*, vol. LIV (November 1784), p. 876.
41 *Gentleman's Magazine*, vol. LIV (November 1784), pp. 965–6.
42 *European Magazine*, vol. VII (February and April 1785), pp. 107–12, 261–3.
43 *Analytical Review*, vol. I (1788), p. 95.
44 Moore (1790), vol. 2, p. 147.
45 McGuire (2011), p. 62.
46 See Minois (1999), pp. 267–8.
47 Cited in Bell (2012), p. 56.
48 Bell (2011), p. 106.
49 Bell (2012), p. 55.
50 Bell (2012), p. 80.
51 Moore (1790), vol. 2, p. 147.
52 Tierney (2010), p. 368.
53 Moore (1790), vol. 2, pp. 156–7.
54 See McGuire (2011), p. 67.
55 Pearson (1999), p. 99.
56 Pearson (1999), p. 111.
57 Schiffman (2010), pp. 217–18.
58 Bell (2012), p. 58.
59 Schiffman (2010), p. 216.
60 Cited in Bell (2012), p. 58.
61 Bell (2012), p. 60.

62 Long (1916), p. 203.
63 Brown (1969), p. 5.
64 Brown (1969), p. xxxv.
65 Bell (2012), p. 59.
66 Cited in Bell (2012), p. 60.
67 Bell (2012), p. 60.
68 The concept of rhetorical idiom is discussed in Furedi (2007).
69 Cited in Schiffman (2010), p. 214.
70 See Georg Lukacs (1936) 'The Sorrows of Young Werther', published online at https://www.marxists.org/archive/lukacs/works/1936/young-werther.htm, accessed 17 December 2014.
71 Littau (2006), p. 20.
72 See Littau (2006), p. 11.
73 Anonymous, *The New England Quarterly Magazine* (1802), p. 173.
74 Pearson (1999), p. 24. Those who perceived *Julie* as justifying adultery as well as advocating political revolution considered this novel as even more dangerous than *Werther*.
75 Gettelman (2011), p. 57.
76 Gettelman (2011), p. 55.
77 W. Collins, 'The Unknown Public', *Household Words*, vol. 18 (21 August 1858), p. 218.
78 Altick (1957)
79 'The literature of the streets', *Edinburgh Review*, vol. 165 (January 1887).
80 See Drotner (1999).
81 Bratlinger (2008), p. 26.
82 Cited in Jones (1996), p. 83.
83 Starker (1990), p. 44.
84 Trollope (1879), pp. 202–3.
85 Walpole (1913), p. 252.
86 Jones (1996), p. 132.
87 Cited in Bratlinger (1998), p. 63.
88 Bell (2012), p. 61.
89 Phillips (1974), p. 341.
90 Coleman (2004), p. 2.
91 See Ferreday (2010).
92 Schiffman (2010), p. 216.
93 Schiffman (2010), p. 216.

CHAPTER 6

1 Pearson (1999), p. 99.
2 See for example F. C. W., 'Moral poisons: The antidote', part two, *The Mother's Magazine* (June 1845), pp. 184–8.

3   Richards (1929), p. 320.

4   Steiner (1985), p. 29.

5   Johns (1996), p. 141.

6   Johns (1996), p. 147.

7   Schoenfeldt (2003), p. 218.

8   Johns (2000), p. 292.

9   Boyle is cited in Johns (1996), p.146.

10   Johns (1996), p. 153.

11   *Of Studies* is available online at http://www.authorama.com/essays-of-francis-bacon-50.html, accessed 12 January 2015.

12   Schoenfeldt (2003), p. 220.

13   Cited in Littau (2006), p. 41.

14   Cited in Schoenfeldt (2003), p. 328.

15   See A. L. Maycock, 'Bibliophobia', *Blackwood's Magazine* (October 1929), pp. 175–6.

16   See 'Devouring books', *American Annals of Education* (January 1835), pp. 30–32.

17   Ruskin (1902), p. 163.

18   Ruskin (1902), p. 163.

19   Ruskin (1902), p. 163.

20   Mays (1995), p. 173.

21   Vogrinčič (2008), p. 109.

22   Leeds (1985), p. 9.

23   See *Daily Chronicle* (30 June 1890); a review is reprinted online at http://www.gutenberg.org/files/33689/33689-h/33689-h.htm, accessed 2 September 2014.

24   Wynne (2001), p. 6.

25   Mansel is cited in Wynne (2001), p. 5.

26   Cited in William Dean Howells, 'Is the reading habit a vice', *The Review of Reviews* (December 1901).

27   In *The Characteristics of the Present Age* by Johann Gottlieb Fichte, trans. from the German by William Smith Chapman; review in *The Spectator* (30 October 1847) at http://archive.spectator.co.uk/article/30th-october-1847/15/spectators-library.

28   Anonymous, 'The Literature of the Streets', *Edinburgh Review*, vol. 165 (January 1887).

29   See discussion in Furedi (2014), pp. 140–41.

30   Austin (1874), 'The vice of reading', *Temple Bar*, no. 42 (September 1874), p. 253.

31   Leavis (1968), p. 50.

32   Priestley cited in McAleer (1992), p. 98.

33   Iremonger cited in McAleer (1992), p. 159.

34   See discussion in Bosmajian (2006), p. 76.

35   For an illustration see F. C. W., 'Moral poisons: The antidote', from *The Mother's Magazine* (May 1845), pp. 148–52.

36   Schopenhauer (1851), letter LXI.

37   Dark (1922), p. 11.

38   Leeds (1985), pp. 8 and 17.

39 Reports cited in Beisel (1997), pp. 70, 57–8.

40 J. Douglas, 'A book that must be suppressed', *Sunday Express* (19 August 1928).

41 Dames (2007), p. 18.

42 *Annual Report of the Regents of the University of the State of New York*, vol. 79 (1866), p. 133.

43 Austin (1874), 'The Vice of Reading', *Temple Bar*, no. 42 (September), pp. 252–6.

44 Austin (1874), 'The Vice of Reading', *Temple Bar*, no. 42 (September), p. 256.

45 http://www.stoics.com/seneca_epistles_book_1.html, accessed 3 May 1914.

46 Littau (2006), p. 46.

47 Dames (2007), p. 18.

48 Dames (2007), p. 81.

49 Mikics (2013), p. 12.

50 See Daniel J. Levitin, 'Why the modern world is bad for your brain', *The Observer* (18 January 2015).

51 Mikics (2013), p. 12.

52 Dames (2007), p. 207.

53 For example see Osol and Pratt (1851), p. 392.

54 Cited in Leavis (1968), p. 51.

55 Dames (2007), p. 20.

56 Daniel J. Levitin, 'Why the modern world is bad for your brain', *The Observer* (18 January 2015).

57 Daniel J. Levitin, 'Why the modern world is bad for your brain', *The Observer* (18 January 2015).

58 Mikics (2013), p. 3.

59 Rose (1992), p. 56.

60 Allen (1991), pp. 124–5.

61 Cited in Emerson and Lubbock (2005), letter LXI.

62 Edward Bulwer-Lytton's essay, *The Hygienic Chemistry of Books*, is available online, http://laudatortemporisacti.blogspot.co.uk/2013_09_01_archive.htm, accessed 12 February 2015.

63 See Ralph Waldo Emerson's essay 'The poet' in *Essays, Second Series* (1844), http://www.gutenberg.org/files/2945/2945-h/2945-h.htm, accessed 15 February 2015.

64 Nietzsche (2007), p. 52.

65 Walpole (2004), p. 43.

66 Jackson (2001), p. 38

67 Jackson (1932), p. 45.

68 Jackson (1932), p. 44.

69 Cited in Jackson (1932), p. 58.

70 Jackson (2001), p. 237.

71 Schroeder (1906), p. 56.

72 Schroeder (1906), p. 56.

73 Bonomi, Nemeth, Attenburger, Anderson, Snyder and Dotto (2014), p. 721.

74 Bonomi, Nemeth, Attenburger, Anderson, Snyder and Dotto (2014), p. 721.

CHAPTER 7

1   Marden and Devitt (1907), pp. 493 and 512.
2   Anonymous, 'What Books to Read and How to Read Them' (1859), *The Scottish Review* (October 1985), p. 368.
3   Lubbock (2005a), p. 43.
4   Carlyle's address is reprinted online at http://www.bartleby.com/268/5/2.html.
5   Cited in Jackson (1950), p. 99.
6   Mao Zedong, 'Remarks at the spring festival' (13 February1964), at http://www.marxists.org/reference/archive/mao/selected-works/volume-9/mswv9_14.htm
7   Mao Zedong, 'Remarks at the spring festival' (13 February 1964), at http://www.marxists.org/reference/archive/mao/selected-works/volume-9/mswv9_14.htm.
8   http://www.oed.com.chain.kent.ac.uk/view/Entry/54060?redirectedFrom=discrimination#eid, accessed 26 March 2015.
9   See Wharton (1903), p. 515.
10 Virginia Woolf (1932), p. 3.
11 Bloom (2001), p. 23.
12 Jacobs (2011), p. 88.
13 Hoggart (1992), pp. 196–7.
14 Price (2004), p. 315.
15 Adler and Van Doren (1972), p. ii.
16 Adler and Van Doren (1972), p. 1.
17 Griswold, Lengahan and Naffziger (2011), p. 23.
18 See Cieslik and Simpson (2015) at http://www.socresonline.org.uk/20/1/7.html#fn1.
19 Jackson (2001), p. 39.
20 Escarpit (1971), pp. 17–18.
21 Price (2004), p. 310.
22 Bourdieu (2010), p. 49.
23 Hoggart (1992), p. 341.
24 Hoggart (1992), p. 183.
25 Griswold, McDonell and Wright (2005), p. 139.
26 Goffman is cited in Levine (1986), p. 4.
27 Seneca cited in Fischer (2005), p. 78.
28 Jackson (2001), p. 40.
29 Jackson (2001), p. 40.
30 Carey (1992), p. 94.
31 Escarpit (1971), p. 87.
32 Mays (1995), p. 180.
33 Cavallo (1999), p. 67.
34 Goethe in a letter to J. F. Rochlitz, 13/6/1819, cited in Leenhardt (1980), p. 205.
35 Coleridge (1811–12), *Lectures on Shakespeare and Milton*, cited in Jackson (2001), p. 269.

36 Hall (1849), p. 154.

37 Wilkie Collins, 'The unknown public', *Household Words*, 21 August 1858, p. 221.

38 Wilkie Collins, 'The unknown public', *Household Words*, 21 August 1858, p. 221.

39 Wilkie Collins, 'The unknown public', *Household Words*, 21 August 1858, p. 222.

40 See Furedi (2013), pp. 354–5.

41 Vincent (1993), p. 89.

42 Anonymous review of *Lessons and Tales: A Reading Book for the Use of Children: chiefly intended for the junior classes in elementary schools*, ed. the Rev. Richard Dawes, Dean of Hereford, *The Gentleman's Magazine* (July 1856), p. 643.

43 Davidson (1986), p. 61.

44 Furet and Ozouf (1982), p. 1.

45 See Stahl (1999), p. 18.

46 Turner (1994), p. 124.

47 Turner (1994), p. 127.

48 See Johns (1998), p. 407.

49 Mathews (1966), p. 9.

50 Vincent (1993), p. 54.

51 Levine (1987), p. 93.

52 Mathews (1966), p. 18.

53 Vincent (1993), p. 273.

54 Wilderspin (1832), p. 56.

55 Cited in Vincent (1993), p. 73.

56 Cited in Vincent (1993), p. 73.

57 Anonymous (1857), p. 175.

58 Cited by Flesch (1986), p. 14.

59 Styles and Drummond (1993), p. 2.

60 Huey (1910), pp. 8 and 302.

61 Hall (1901), p. 1.

62 Hall (1901), p. 12.

63 Carmichael and Dearborn (1948), p. 1.

64 Monaghan (2007), p. 16.

65 Monaghan (2007), p. 21.

66 See Winzer (2002), p. 339.

67 Winzer (2002), p. 339.

68 E. Morpurgo (1958), 'Books for the new reading public', *The UNESCO Courier*, no. 3 (March), p. 26.

69 Chartier (2004), p. 534.

70 McArthur (1998), 'Functional literacy', *Concise Oxford Companion to the English Language*. 1998. *Encyclopedia.com*. http://www.encyclopedia.com, accessed 12 March 2015.

71 Diack (1965), p. 105.

72 See discussion in Levine (1982), pp. 250–1.

73 See Furedi (2009), Chapter 4.

74 Altick (1957), p. 366.

75 Henry (1946), p. 73.

76 Henry (1946), p. 73.

77 Henry (1946), p. 73.

78 Flesch (1986), p. 18.

79 http://www.readspeaker.com/functional-illiteracy-in-france-a-case-study, accessed 12 January 2015.

80 See 'Functionally illiterate and innumerate', *Times Educational Supplement* (7 May 2010).

81 http://www.livescience.com/3211-14-percent-adults-read.html, accessed 21 November 2014.

82 See Stedman and Kaestle (1991).

83 Best (2011), p. 24.

84 Altwerger (1998), p. 175.

85 Strauss (2010), pp. 67–8.

86 Carl Kline and Carolyn Lacey Kline, 'The epidemic of reading disabilities', http://www.readingstore.com/EPIDEMIO.HTM, accessed 4 May 2014. It is worth noting that one of these authors, Carl Kline, was an adolescent psychiatrist and the other, Carolyn Lacey Kline, a language disabilities consultant.

87 Altick (1957), p. 366.

88 Brier (2009), p. 7.

89 See Stone (1969), p. 89.

CHAPTER 8

1   Chartier (2004), p. 534.

2   Cited in Dorn and Ghodsee (2012), p. 377.

3   UNESCO (1946), p. 14.

4   Huxley (1946), p. 17.

5   Dorn and Ghodsee (2012), p. 392.

6   Levine (1986), p. 32.

7   UNESCO (1970), 'Introduction' to *Functional Literacy: Why and How*, p. 8.

8   Levine (1986), p. 27.

9   Dorn and Ghodsee (2012), p. 397.

10 Griswold, Lenaghan and Naffziger (2011), p. 25.

11 Graff (1987b), p. 62.

12 Graff (1987b), p. 53.

13 Olson (1994), p. 13.

14 Solomon (1986), p. 37.

15 Eisenstein (2011), p. 214.

16 Cressey (1980), p. 189

17 Cressey (1980), p. 189.

18 Cressey (1980), p. 189.

19 Street (1984), p. 4.

20 Olson is cited in Graff (1987a), pp. 17–18.

21 Street (1984), p. 14.

22 See Furedi (2014), Chapter 6, for a discussion of this development.

23 Thomas (1986), p. 121.

24 Olson (1994), p. 11.

25 Olson (1994), p. 4.

26 Levine (1986), p. 187.

27 Thomas (1986), p. 105.

28 See Eric Havelock's essay, 'The modern discovery of orality', in which he noted that around 1963 a 'modern consciousness' of orality 'appears to burst' on the scene. Havelock (1986), p. 24.

29 McLuhan (1994), p. 86.

30 McLuhan (1994), p. 50.

31 Ong (1967), p. 322.

32 Ong (1967), p. 2.

33 McLuhan (1964), p. 23.

34 Cited in McLuhan (1994), p. xviii.

35 Ong (2002), pp. 123–4.

36 McLuhan (1994), p. 34.

37 Goody and Watt (1963), p. 338.

38 Goody and Watt (1963), p. 344.

39 Goody and Watt (1963), p. 321.

40 Goody and Watt (1963), p. 321.

41 Goody and Watt (1963), p. 332.

42 Goody and Watt (1963), p. 333.

43 Collins (1995), p. 76.

44 Levine (1986), p. 45.

45 See for example Street (1984).

46 Street (1984), p. 23.

47 For a critique of the education of relevance see Furedi (2009).

48 Cook-Gumperz (2006a), p. 2.

49 See Furedi (2009).

50 Cook-Gumperz (2006b), p. 34.

51 Scribner and Cole (1988), p. 61.

52 Vygotsky cited in Brockmeier and Olson (2002), p. 5.

53 See Erickson (1988), p. 205.

54 See http://www.pbs.org/wnet/need-to-know/the-daily-need/our-sputnik-moment-then-and-now/7286/.

55 Editorial cited in De Boer and Dallmann (1960), p. vi.

56 Bridenbaugh (1963), p. 318.

57 McLuhan (1994), p. 82.

58 McLuhan (1994), p. 82.

59 Since the late 1960s the concept of moral panic has gained widespread currency in the social sciences to the point that it has extended into wider everyday usage.

60 Brier (2010), pp. 7–8.

61 See Brier (2010), pp. 8–9.

62 See   http://arts.gov/publications/reading-risk-survey-literary-reading-america-0, accessed 3 May 2014.

63 Graff (1987), p. 16.

64 Cook-Gumperz (2006a), pp. 22–3.

65 See 'Broomsticks and bedknobs and witch hunts galore', *TES* (31 October 1975).

66 See contributions to Poynor and Wolfe (2010).

67 Brinkley and Weaver (2010), p. 95.

68 Stannard and Huxford (2007).

69 Best (2011), p. 23.

70 Miller (1998), pp. 1–2.

71 Miller (1998), p. 7.

72 Arendt (2006), p. 171.

73 Peters (1996), p. 53.

74 Hirsch (1988), p. xvii.

CONCLUSION

1 Shirky is cited in Carr (2010), p. 111.

2 Ulin (2010), p. 34.

3 Tim Parks, 'Reading the struggle', *The New York Review of Books* (10 June 2014), http://www.nybooks.com/blogs/nyrblog/2014/jun/10/reading-struggle, accessed 24 October 2014.

4 Birkerts (1994), p. 73.

5 See Furedi (2006).

6 Jeanne Whalen, 'Read slowly to benefit your brain and cut stress', *The Wall Street Journal* (16 September 2014).

7 Department of Education (2012), *Research Evidence on Reading for Pleasure*, at https://www.gov.uk/government/uploads/system/uploads/attachment_data/file/284286/reading_for_pleasure.pdf, accessed 12 February 2015.

8 Patrick Wintour, 'Poor reading "could cost UK £32bn in growth by 2025"', *The Guardian* (8 September 2014).

9 Birkerts (1994), p. 3.

10 Birkerts (1994), pp. 19 and 20.

11   Birkerts (1994), p. 21.

12   Birkerts (1994), p. 19.

13   See for example Carr (2010).

14   See Furedi (2014).

15   McLuhan (2003), p. 31.

16   See http://www.theguardian.com/commentisfree/2013/oct/09/the-rise-of-the-reader-katharine-viner-an-smith-lecture, accessed 15 November 2014.

17   See http://www.theguardian.com/commentisfree/2013/oct/09/the-rise-of-the-reader-katharine-viner-an-smith-lecture, accessed 15 November 2014.

18   See Sauerberg (2009).

19   See Dean Starkman, 'The future is medieval', *Columbia Journalism Review*, 7 June 2013, http://www.cjr.org/the_audit/the_future_is_medieval.php?page=all, accessed 2 April 2015.

20   See Dean Starkman, 'The future is medieval', *Columbia Journalism Review*, 7 June 2013, http://www.cjr.org/the_audit/the_future_is_medieval.php?page=all, accessed 2 April 2015.

21   Trent Batson, 'Web 2.0, secondary orality and the Gutenberg Parenthesis', 3 May 2008, http://campustechnology.com/Articles/2008/03/Web-20-Secondary-Orality-and-the-Gutenberg-Parenthesis.aspx?p=1, accessed 3 November 2014.

22   See http://www.theguardian.com/commentisfree/2013/oct/09/the-rise-of-the-reader-katharine-viner-an-smith-lecture, accessed 15 November 2014.

23   Sharpe and Zwicker (2003a), p. 1.

24   Sharpe and Zwicker (2003a), p. 1.

25   Birkerts (1994), p. 163.

26   See the discussion in Achinstein (1994), p. 65.

27   Wolf (2010), p. 3.

28   Wolf (2010), p. 19.

29   Wolf (2010), p. 19.

30   See Sarah Knapton, 'Dyslexia may not exist, warn academics', *The Daily Telegraph* (2 February 2014).

31   See Bauerlein (2009).

32   See Mikics (2013), p. 10.

33   Byun, Ruffini, Mills, Douglas, Niang, Stepchenkova, Lee, Loutfi, Atallah and Blanton (2009), p. 203.

34   See Ferreday (2010).

35   http://www.smh.com.au/federal-politics/society-and-culture/how-digital-culture-is-rewiring-our-brains-20120806-23q5p.html#ixzz2uF4tvG3s, accessed 23 March 2014.

36   Neil Levy, 'Your brain on the internet: A response to Susan Greenfield', in the *Conversation* (7 August 2012), http://theconversation.com/your-brain-on-the-internet-a-response-to-susan-greenfield-8694, accessed 24 April 2015.

37   Cook-Gumperz (2006a), p. 2.

38 See the website http://www.ncte.org/governance/literacies for an example of how so-called twenty-first-century literacy is presented.

39 See Griswold, McDonnell and Wright (2005), pp. 136–7.

40 Helen Ward, 'Imposing synthetic phonics "is almost abuse" says academic', *The Times Educational Supplement*, 28 January 2014.

41 Strauss (2010), pp. 67–8.

42 Charlotte Eyre, 'Richard Dawkins renews attack on fairy tales', *The Daily Telegraph* (5 June 2014).

43 Angus Johnson, 'Why I'll add a trigger warning', *Inside Higher Education* (29 May 2014).

44 Achinstein (1994), p. 65.

BIBLIOGRAPHY

Abel, R. (2012), *The Gutenberg Revolution: A History of Print Culture*. New Brunswick, NJ: Transaction Publishers.

Achinstein, S. (1994), *Milton and the Revolutionary Reader*. Princeton: Princeton University Press.

—— (1996), 'Milton's spectre in the Restoration: Marvell, Dryden, and literary enthusiasm', *Huntington Library Quarterly*, vol. 59, no. 1, pp. 1–29.

—— (2001), 'Texts in conflict: The press and the Civil War', in N. H. Keeble (2001) (ed.), *The Cambridge Companion to Writing of the English Revolution*. Cambridge: Cambridge University Press.

Adler, M. J. and Van Doren, C. (1972), *How to Read a Book: A Classic Guide to Intelligent Reading*. New York: Touchstone.

Allen, J. S. (1991), *In the Public Eye: A History of Reading in Modern France, 1800–1940*. Princeton: Princeton University Press.

Allington, R. L. and Woodside-Jiron, H. (1999), 'The politics of literacy teaching: How "research" shaped educational policy', *Educational Researcher*, vol. 28, no. 4.

Altick, R. D. (1957), *The English Common Reader: A Social History of the Mass Reading Public, 1800–1900*. Chicago: The University of Chicago Press.

Altwerger, B. (1998), 'Whole language as decoy: The real agenda behind the attacks', in Goodman (1998).

—— (2010), 'The push of the pendulum', in Poynor and Wolfe (2010) (eds).

Amtower, L. (2000), *Engaging Words: The Culture of Reading in the Later Middle Ages*. New York: Palgrave.

Annual Report of the Regents of the University of the State of New York (1866), vol. 79, p. 133. Albany, NY: G. Wendell Printers.

Anonymous (1802), 'Novel reading, a cause of female depravity', *The New England Quarterly Magazine*, no. 2, p. 173, originally published in the *Monthly Mirror*, November 1797.

Anonymous (1856), Review of *Lessons and Tales: A Reading Book for the Use of Children: Chiefly Intended for the Junior Classes in Elementary Schools*, ed. Rev. Richard Dawes, Dean of Hereford, *The Gentleman's Magazine*, July, pp. 643–53.

Anonymous (1857), *Reading Without Tears, or, A Pleasant Mode of Learning to Read*. London: Hatchard.

Arendt, H. (2006), 'The crisis in education', in H. Arendt (2006a), *Between Past and Future*. New York: Penguin Books.

Austin, A. (1874), 'The vice of reading', in *Temple Bar*, September, no. 42, pp. 251–7.

Baker, K. M. (1975), *Condorcet: From Natural Philosophy to Social Mathematics*. Chicago: University of Chicago Press.

Baker, M. K. (1994), *Inventing the French Revolution*. Cambridge: Cambridge University Press.

Barnard, J. (2002), 'Introduction', in J. Barnard and D. F. McKenzie (2002), *The Cambridge History of the Book in Britain: Volume IV, 1557–1695*. Cambridge: Cambridge University Press.

Batley, E. (1992), 'Werther's final act of alienation: Goethe, Lessing, and Jerusalem on the poetry and the truth of suicide', *Modern Language Review*, vol. 87, no. 4, pp. 868–78.

Bauerlein, M. (2009), *The Dumbest Generation: How the Digital Age Stupefies Young Americans and Jeopardizes Our Future*. London: Penguin.

Beisel, N. (1997), *Imperilled Innocents: Anthony Comstock and Family Reproduction in Victorian America*. Princeton: Princeton University Press.

Bell, D. A. (1999), 'Why books caused a revolution: A reading of Robert Darnton', in Mason (1999).

Bell, R. (2011), 'In Werther's thrall: Suicide and the power of sentimental reading in early national America', *Early American Literature*, vol. 46, no. 1, pp. 93–120.

——— (2012), *We Shall Be No More: Suicide and Self-Government in the Newly United States*. Cambridge, MA: Harvard University Press.

Benedict, B. (1994), *Framing Feeling: Sentiment and Style in English Prose Fiction, 1745–1800*. New York: AMS Press.

——— (2001), 'The eighteenth-century anthology and the construction of the expert reader', *Poetics*, vol. 28, pp. 377–397.

Bernstein, B. (2003), *Class, Codes and Control. Volume 4: The Structure of Pedagogic Discourse*. Abingdon: Routledge.

Best, J. (2011), *The Stupidity Epidemic: Worrying About Students, Schools and America's Future*. New York: Routledge.

Birkerts, S. (1994), *The Gutenberg Elegies: The Fate of Reading in an Electronic Age*. London: Faber and Faber.

Blair, A. M. (2010), *Too Much to Know: Managing Scholarly Information before the Modern Age*. New Haven, CT: Yale University Press.

Bloom, H. (1994), *The Western Canon: The Books and School of the Ages*. New York: Harcourt Brace and Co..

——— (2001), *How to Read and Why*. London: Fourth Estate.

Bonomi, A., Nemeth, J., Attenburger, L., Anderson, M., Snyder, A. and Dotto, I. (2014), 'Fiction or not? *Fifty Shades* is associated with health risks in adolescent and young adult females', *Journal of Women's Health*, vol. 23, no. 9.

Bosmajian, H. (2006), *Burning Books*. Jefferson, NC: McFarland and Co..

Bourdieu, P. (2010), *Distinction: A Social Critique of the Judgment of Taste*. London: Routledge.

Bowman, A. K. and Woolf, G. (1996) (eds), *Literacy and Power in the Ancient World*. Cambridge: Cambridge University Press.

Boyson, R. (1975), *The Crisis In Education*. London: The Woburn Press.

Brandt, D. and Clinton, K. (2002), 'Limits of the local: Expanding perspectives on literacy as a social practice', *Journal of Literacy Research*, vol. 34, pp. 337–56.

Bratlinger, P. (1998), *The Reading Lesson: The Threat of Mass Literacy in Nineteenth-Century Fiction*. Bloomington, IN: Indiana University Press.

Brewer, J. (1997), *The Pleasures of the Imagination: English Culture in the Eighteenth Century*. London: Harper Collins.

Bridenbaugh, C. (1963), 'The great mutation', *The American Historical Association*, vol. 68, no. 2, pp. 315–31.

Brier, E. (2010), *A Novel Marketplace: Mass Culture, the Book Trade, and Postwar American Fiction*. Philadelphia: University of Pennsylvania Press.

Briggs, Asa (1979), *The Age of Improvement, 1783–1867*. London: Longman.

Brinkley, E. and Weaver, C. (2010), 'Phonics, literalism and futuristic fiction: Religious fundamentalism and education policy', in Poynor and Wolfe (2010).

Brockmeier, J. and Olson, D. R. (2002), 'What is a culture of literacy?', in J. Brockmeier, M. Wang and D. R. Olson (eds) (2002), *Literacy, Narrative and Culture*. Richmond, UK: Curzon.

Brown, W. H. (1969), *The Power of Sympathy*. Columbus, Ohio: Ohio State University Press.

Bulwer-Lytton, E. (1870), *England and the English*. Chicago, IL: University of Chicago Press.

Burckhardt, J. (1990), *The Civilization of the Renaissance in Italy*. London: Penguin Books.

Burke, E. (2009), *Reflections on the Revolution in France*. Oxford: Oxford University Press.

Bushnell, R. W. (1996), *The Culture of Teaching: Early Modern Humanism in Theory and Practice*. Ithaca, NY: Cornell University Press.

Byun, S., Ruffini, C., Mills, J. E., Douglas, A. C., Niang, M., Stepchenkova, S. and Blanton, M. (2009). 'Internet addiction: Metasynthesis of 1996–2006 quantitative research', *CyberPsychology & Behavior*, vol. 12, no. 2, pp. 203–7.

Canatella, H. M. (2010), 'Long-distance love: The ideology of male-female spiritual friendship in Goscelin of Saint Bertin's *Liber confortatorius*', *Journal of the History of Sexuality*, vol. 19, no. 1, pp. 35–53.

Capel, A. (Hon.) (1856), *Few Words on Every Man's Right to Possess and Read the Scriptures*. London: William and Frederick G. Cash.

Carcopino, J. (1991), *Daily Life in Ancient Rome: The People and the City at the Height of the Empire*. London: Penguin.

Carey, J. (1992), *The Intellectuals and the Masses? Pride and Prejudice among the Literary Intelligentsia, 1880–1939*. London: Faber and Faber.

Carmichael, L. and Dearborn, W. F. (1948), *Reading and Visual Fatigue*. London: George Harrap.

Carr, N. S. (2010), *The Shallows*. London: Atlantic Books.

Castell, de S. and A. Luke (1988), 'Defining "literacy" in North American schools: Social and historical consequences', in Kintgen, Kroll and Rose (1988).

Cavallo, G. and Chartier, R. (1999), *A History of Reading in the West*. Cambridge: Polity Press.

Chall, J. (1967), *Learning to Read: The Great Debate*. New York: McGraw-Hill.

Chartier, A. M. (2004), 'Teaching reading: A historical approach', in T. Nunes and A. Bryant (2004) (eds), *Handbook of Children's Literacy*. New York: Springer.

Chartier, R. (2002), 'The practical impact of writing', in D. Finkelstein and A. McCleery (2002) (eds), *The Book History Reader*. London: Routledge.

Cieslik, M. and Simpson, D. (2015), 'Basic skills, literacy practices and the "hidden injuries of class"', *Sociological Research Online*, vol. 20, no. 1.

Clanchy, M.T. (1979), *From Memory to Written Record: England 1066–1307*. London: Edward Arnold.

—— (1998), 'Hearing and seeing *and* trusting writing', in Kintgen, Kroll and Rose (1988).

Coleman, L. (2004), *The Copycat Effect: How the Media and Popular Culture Trigger the Mayhem in Tomorrow's Headline*. New York: Paraview Pocket Books.

Collins, A. S. (1926), 'The growth of the reading public during the eighteenth century', *The Review of English Studies*, vol. 2, no. 8, pp. 428–38.

Collins, J. (1995), 'Literacy and literacies', *Annual Review of Anthropology*, vol. 24, pp. 75–93.

Collins, J. (1989), *Uncommon Cultures: Popular Culture and Post-Modernism*. New York: Routledge.

Cook-Gumperz, J. (2006) (ed.), *The Social Construction of Literacy*. Cambridge: Cambridge University Press.

—— (2006a), 'The social construction of literacy', in Cook-Gumperz (2006).

—— (2006b), 'Literacy and schooling: An unchanging equation?', in Cook-Gumperz (2006).

Cox, M. (1968) (ed.), *The Challenge of Reading Failure*. Slough, Buckinghamshire: National Foundation for Educational Research.

Cragg, G. R. (1964), *Reason and Authority in the Eighteenth Century*. Cambridge: Cambridge University Press.

Cressey, D. (1980), *Reading and Writing in Tudor and Stuart England*. Cambridge: Cambridge University Press.

Curran, J. (2005), 'Oral reading, print culture, and the German Enlightenment', *The Modern Language Review*, vol. 100, no. 3, pp. 695–708.

Cvetkovich, A. (1992), *Mixed Feelings: Feminism, Mass Culture, and Victorian Sensationalism*. New Brunswick, NJ: Rutgers University Press.

Dames, N. (2007), *The Physiology of the Novel: Reading, Neural Science, and the Form of Victorian Fiction*. New York: Oxford University Press.

Dark, S. (1922), *The New Reading Public*. London: George Allen and Unwin.

Darnton, R. (1971), 'Reading, writing, and publishing in eighteenth-century France: A case study in the sociology of literature', *Daedalus*, vol. 100, no. 1, pp. 214–56.

—— (1982), 'What is the history of books?', *Daedalus*, vol. 111, no. 3, pp. 65–83.

—— (1984a), 'Readers respond to Rousseau: The fabrication of Romantic sensitivity', in R. Darnton (1984), *The Great Cat Massacre: And Other Episodes in French Cultural History*. London: Allen Lane.

Davidson, C. N. (1988), 'Towards a history of books and readers', *American Quarterly*, vol. 40, no. 1, pp. 7–17.

De Boer, J. J. and Dallmann, M. (1960), *The Teaching of Reading*. New York: Holt.

DeMaria, R. (1997), *Samuel Johnson and the Life of Reading*. Baltimore, MD: The Johns Hopkins University Press.

Derrida, J. (1981), *Dissemination*. London: The Athlone Press.

Diack, H. (1965), *In Spite of the Alphabet: A Study of the Teaching of Reading*. London: Chatto and Windus.

Dobranski, S. B. (2005), *Readers and Authorship in Early Modern England*. Cambridge: Cambridge University Press.

Docherty, T. (1987), *On Modern Authority: The Theory and Condition of Writing. 1500 to the Present Day*. Brighton: The Harvester Press.

Dolin, T. (2011), 'Fiction and the Australian reading public, 1888–1914', in Palmer and Buckland (2011).

Dorn, C. and Ghodsee, K. (2012), 'The Cold War politicization of literacy: Communism, UNESCO, and the World Bank', *Diplomatic History*, vol. 36, no. 2.

Dromi, S. and Illouz, E. (2010), 'Recovering morality, pragmatic sociology and literary studies', *New Literary History*, vol. 41, no. 2, pp. 351–69.

Drotner, K. (1999), 'Dangerous media? Panic discourses and dilemmas of modernity', *Paedagogica Historica: International Journal of the History of Education*, vol. 35, no. 33, pp. 593–619.

Dunstan, V. S. (2010), *Reading Habits in Scotland: circa 1750–1820*. PhD Thesis, University of Dundee.

Eagleton, T. (1984), *The Function of Criticism: From* The Spectator *to Post-Structuralism*. London: Verso.

Edelsky, C. (2010), 'Relatively speaking: McCarthyism and teacher-resisters', in Poynor and Wolfe (2010).

Eisenstein, E. L. (1979), *The Printing Press as an Agent of Change: Communications and Cultural Transformations in Early Modern Europe*. Cambridge: Cambridge University Press.

—— (2002), 'A reply', *American Historical Review* (February), vol. 107, no. 1.

—— (2011), *Divine Art, Infernal Machine*. Philadelphia, PA: University of Pennsylvania Press.

Emerson, R. W. and Lubbock, J. (2005) (originally published 1901), *In Praise of Books*. New York: Cosimo Classics.

Engelsing, R. (1974), *Der Burger als Leser: Lesergeschichte in Deutschland, 1500–1800*. Stuttgart: Metzler.

English, J. F. (2010), 'Everywhere and nowhere: The sociology of literature after "the sociology of literature"', *New Literary History*, vol. 41, no. 2, pp. v–xxiii.

Enzensberger, H. and Lipson, M. (1986), 'In praise of illiteracy', *Grand Street*, vol. 5, no. 4, pp. 88–96.

Erickson, F. (1988), 'School literacy, reasoning, and civility: An anthropologist's perspective', in Kintgen, Kroll and Rose (1988).

Escarpit, R. (1971), *Sociology of Literature*. London: Frank Cass and Co.

Ferreday, D. (2010), 'Reading disorders: Online suicide and the death of hope', *Journal for Cultural Research*, vol. 14, no. 4.

Fischer, S. R. (2005), *A History of Reading*. London: Reaktion Books.

Flesch, R. (1986), *Why Johnny Can't Read – And What You Can Do About It*. New York: Harper and Row.

Flint, K. (1993), *The Woman Reader: 1837–1914*. Oxford: Clarendon Press.

Freeman, H. E. and Kassebaum, G. G. (1955), 'The illiterate in American society: Some general hypotheses', *Social Forces*, vol. 34, no. 1, pp. 371–5.

Freire, P. (1987), 'The importance of the act of reading', in Freire and Macedo (1987).

—— (1987a), 'Literacy and critical pedagogy', in Freire and Macedo (1987).

—— and Macedo, D. (1987), *Literacy: Reading the Word and the World*. London: Routledge and Kegan Paul.

Furedi, F. (2006), *Where Have All the Intellectuals Gone?* London: Continuum Press.

—— (2007), 'From the narrative of the Blitz to the rhetoric of vulnerability', *Cultural Sociology*, vol. 1, no. 2, pp. 235–54.

—— (2009), *Wasted: Why Education is Not Educating*. London: Bloomsbury.

—— (2013), *Authority: A Sociological History*. Cambridge: Cambridge University Press.

Furet, F. and Ozouf, J. (1982), *Reading and Writing: Literacy in France from Calvin to Jules Ferry*. Cambridge: Cambridge University Press.

Gallaway, W. F. (1940), 'The conservative attitude toward fiction, 1770–1830', *PMLA*, vol. 55, no. 4, pp. 1,041–55.

Gettelman, D. (2011), '"Those Who Idle over Novels": Victorian critics and post-Romantic readers', in Palmer and Buckland (2011a), 'Introduction', in Palmer and Buckland (2011).

Giroux, H. A. (1987), 'Introduction: Literacy and the pedagogy of political empowerment', in Freire and Macedo (1987).

Goodman, K. S. (1998) (ed.), *In Defense of Good Teaching*. York, ME: Stenhouse Publishers.

—— (1998a), 'Who's afraid of whole language? Politics, paradigms, pedagogy, and the press', in Goodman (1998).

Goody, J. and Watt, I. (1963), 'The consequences of literacy', *Comparative Studies in Society and History*, vol. 5, no. 30, pp. 304–45.

Gordon, D. (1999), 'The great Enlightenment massacre', in Mason (1999).

Gough, K. (1988), 'Implications of literacy in traditional China and India', in Kintgen, Kroll and Rose (1988).

Graff, H. J. (1987), *The Labyrinths of Literacy: Reflections on Literacy Past and Present*. London: The Falmer Press.

—— (1987a), 'Reflections on the history of literacy: Overview, critique, and proposals', in Graff (1987).

—— (1987b), 'On literacy in the Renaissance: Review and reflections', in Graff (1987).

—— (1988), 'The legacies of literacy', in Kintgen, Kroll and Rose (1988).

—— (2003) 'Assessing the history of literacy; Theme and questions', in Graff, Mackinnon, Sandin and Winchester (2003).

——, Mackinnon, A., Sandin, B. and Winchester, I. (2003) (eds), *Understanding Literacy in its Historical Contexts*. Lund: Nordic Academic Press.

Greene, W. C. (1951), 'The spoken and written word', *Harvard Studies in Classical Philology*, vol. 60, pp. 23–59.

Griswold, W., McDonnell, T. and Wright, N. (2005), 'Reading and the reading class in the twenty-first century', *Annual Review of Sociology*, pp. 127–41.

Griswold, W., Lenaghan, E. and Naffziger, M. (2011), 'Readers as audiences', in V. Nightingale (2011), *The Handbook of Media Audiences*. Oxford: Blackwell Publishing Ltd.

Grogan, C. (1999), 'The politics of seduction in British fiction of the 1790s: The female reader and *Julie, ou La Nouvelle Héloïse*', *Eighteenth-Century Fiction*, vol. 11, no. 4.

Haakonssen, K. (1994) (ed.), *Hume: Political Essays*. Cambridge: Cambridge University Press.

Habermas, J. (1992), *The Structural Transformation of the Public Sphere*. Cambridge: Polity Press.

Hackel, H. B. (2003), '"Boasting of silence": Women readers in a patriarchal state', in Sharpe and Zwicker (2003).

Hall, A. (1849), *Manual of Morals for Common Schools*. Andover: John P. Jewett.

Hall, D. D. (1994), 'Readers and reading in America: Historical and critical perspectives', *American Antiquarian Society*, pp. 337–57.

Hall, G. S. (1901), *How to Teach Reading: And What to Read in School*. Boston, MA: Heath.

Hampton, M. (2001), '"Understanding media": Theories of the press in Britain, 1850–1914', *Media, Culture and Society*, vol. 23, no. 2, pp. 213–31.

Hanvelt, M. (2010), 'Pluralism, politeness, and the public sphere: Hume on the liberty of the press', for delivery at the 2010 Canadian Political Science Annual Conference, 1–3 June 2010, Concordia University, Montreal.

Havelock, E. (1986), *The Muse Learns to Write: Reflections on Orality and Literacy from Antiquity to the Present*. New Haven, CT: Yale University Press.

—— (1988), 'The coming of literate communication to Western culture', in Kintgen, Kroll and Rose (1988).

—— (1999), 'The Greek legacy', in D. Crowley and P. Heyer, *Communication in History: Technology, Culture, Society*. New York: Longman.

Henry, G. H. (1946), 'Can Your Child Really Read?', *Harper's Magazine*, 1 January, pp. 72–6.

Hill, C. (1986), 'The problem of authority', in C. Hill, *The Collected Essays of Christopher Hill*, vol. 2. Brighton: The Harvester Press.

Himmelfarb, G. (1997), 'Revolution in the library', *The American Scholar*, pp. 197–204.

Hirsch, E. D. (1988), *Cultural Literacy: What Every American Needs to Know*. New York: Vintage Books.

Hoggart, R. (1992), *The Uses of Literacy*. London: Penguin Books.

Huey, E. B. (1910), *The Psychology and Pedagogy of Reading*. New York: The Macmillan Co.

―――― (1912), *Backward and Feeble-Minded Children: Clinical Studies in the Psychology of Defectives, with a Syllabus for the Clinical Examination and Testing of Children*. Baltimore, MD: Warwick and York.

Huxley, J. (1946), *UNESCO: Its Purpose and its Philosophy*, Preparatory Commission of the United Nations Educational, Scientific and Cultural Organization: UNESCO Archives, Paris, available online, http://unesdoc.unesco.org/images/0006/000681/068197eo. pdf.

Ife, B. W. (1985), *Reading and Fiction in Golden-Age Spain*. Cambridge: Cambridge University Press.

Iotti, G. (2009), 'Voltaire as story-teller', in N. Cronk (2009) (ed.), *The Cambridge Companion to Voltaire*. Cambridge: Cambridge University Press.

Iser, W. (1978), *The Act of Reading: A Theory of Aesthetic Response*. London: Routledge and Kegan Paul.

Israel, S. E. and Monaghan, E. J. (2007) (eds), *Shaping the Reading Field: The Impact of Early Reading Pioneers, Scientific Research and Progressive Ideas*. Newark, DE: International Reading Association.

Jackson, H. (1932), *The Fear of Books*. London: The Soncino Press.

―――― (1950), *The Anatomy of Bibliomania*. London: Faber and Faber.

―――― (2001), *The Reading of Books*. Urbana, IL: University of Illinois Press.

Jackson, I. (2004), 'Approaches to the history of readers and reading in the eighteenth century', *The Historical Journal*, vol. 47, no. 4, pp. 1,041–54.

Jackson, M. (2008), *Distracted: The Erosion of Attention and the Coming Dark Age*. Amherst, NY: Prometheus Books.

Jacobs, A. (2011), 'Christianity and the future of the book', *The New Atlantis* (Autumn), pp. 19–36.

―――― (2011a), *The Pleasures of Reading in an Age of Distraction*. Oxford: Oxford University Press.

Jast, L. S. (1927), *The Child as Reader*. London: Libraco.

Jeffrey, D. L. (1996), *People of the Book: Christian Identity and Literary Culture*. Grand Rapids, MI: Wm. B. Eerdmans Publishing Co.

Johansson, E. (2003), 'The history of literacy in Sweden', in Graff, Mackinnon, Sandin and Winchester (2003).

Johns, A. (1996), 'The physiology of reading and the anatomy of enthusiasm', in O. P. Grell and A. Cunningham (1996), *Religio Medici: Medicine and Religion in Seventeenth-Century England*. Aldershot: Scolar Press.

—— (1998), *The Nature of the Book: Print and Knowledge in the Making*. Chicago, IL: The University of Chicago Press.

—— (2000), 'The physiology of reading', in M. Frasca-Spada and N. Jardine (2000) (eds), *Books and the Sciences in History*. Cambridge: Cambridge University Press.

—— (2002), 'How to acknowledge a revolution', *American Historical Review*, February.

Johnson, W. A. (2000), 'Toward a sociology of reading in classical antiquity', *The American Journal of Philology*, vol. 121, no. 4, pp. 593–627.

Jones, A. (1996), *Power of the Press: Newspapers, Power and the Public in Nineteenth-Century England*. Aldershot: Scolar Press.

Kahn, V. (1985), 'The figure of the reader in Petrarch's *Secretum*', *Publications of the Modern Language Association of America*, vol. 100, no. 2, pp. 154–66.

Keen, P. (1999), *The Crisis of Literature in the 1790s: Print Culture and the Political Sphere*. Cambridge: Cambridge University Press.

Kintgen, E. R., Kroll, B. M., Rose, M. (eds) (1988), *Perspectives on Literacy*. Carbondale, IL: Southern Illinois University Press.

Kloek, J. (1999), 'Reconsidering the reading revolution: The thesis of the "reading revolution" and a Dutch bookseller's clientele around 1800', *Poetics*, vol. 26, pp. 289–307.

Lake, P. and Pincus, S. (2007),*The Politics of the Public Sphere in Early Modern England*. Manchester: Manchester University Press.

Lambirth, A. (2011), *Literacy on the Left: Reform and Revolution*. London: Continuum.

Larson, M. (1976), 'Science fiction, the novel, and the continuity of condemnation', *The Journal of General Education*, vol. 28, no. 1, pp. 63–74.

Leavis, Q. D. (1968), *Fiction and the Reading Public*. London: Chatto and Windus.

Leeds, J. W. (1885), *Concerning Printed Poison*. Philadelphia, PA: printed for the author.

Leenhardt, J. (1980), 'Towards a sociology of reading', in S. R. Suleiman and I. Crosman (1980) (eds), *The Reader in the Text: Essays on Audience and Interpretation*. Princeton, NJ: Princeton University Press.

Leigh, J. G. (1904), 'What the masses read', *Economic Review*, vol. 7, pp. 166–77.

LeMahieu, D. L. (1988),*A Culture for Democracy: Mass Communication and the Cultivated Mind in Britain Between the Wars*. Oxford: Clarendon Press.

Lemmings, D. (2009), 'The *London Journal*, moral panics and the law', in Lemmings and Walker (2009).

—— and Walker, C. (2009), *Moral Panics, the Media and the Law in Early Modern England*. Houndmills, Basingstoke: Palgrave Macmillan.

Leonard, R. M. (1911), *The Book-Lovers' Anthology*. London: Oxford University Press.

Levine, K. (1986), *The Social Context of Literacy*. London: Routledge and Kegan Paul.

Levine, R., Locke, C., Searls, D. and Weinberger, D. (2001), *The Cluetrain Manifesto: The End of Business as Usual*. New York: Perseus Publishing.

Littau, K. (2006), *Theories of Reading: Books, Bodies and Bibliomania*. Cambridge: Polity.

Long, O. W. (1915), 'English translations of Goethe's *Werther*', *The Journal of English and Germanic Philology*, vol. 14, no. 2, pp. 169–203.

—— (1916), 'English and American imitations of Goethe's "Werther"', *Modern Philology*, vol. 14, no. 4, pp. 193–216.

Lovell, T. (1987), *Consuming Fiction*. London: Verso.

Lowenthal, L. and Fiske, M. (1956), 'Reaction to mass media growth in 18th-century England', *Journalism and Mass Communication Quarterly*, vol. 33, no. 4, pp. 442–55.

Lubbock, Sir J. (2005), 'A song of books', in R. W. Emerson and J. Lubbock (2005) (originally published 1901), *In Praise of Books*. New York: Cosimo Classics.

—— (2005), 'The choice of books', in R. W. Emerson and J. Lubbock (2005) (originally published 1901), *In Praise of Books*. New York: Cosimo Classics.

Lyons, M. (2010), *The History of Reading and Writing*. Houndmills, Basingstoke: Palgrave Macmillan.

—— (2011), *Books: A Living History*. London: Thames and Hudson.

McAleer, J. (1992), *Popular Reading and Publishing in Britain, 1914–1950*. Oxford: Clarendon Press.

McArthur, T. (1998), 'Functional literacy', *Concise Oxford Companion to the English Language*. http://www.encyclopedia.com, accessed 12 March 2015.

MacDonald, M. (1986), 'The secularization of suicide in England, 1660–100', *Past and Present*, vol. 111, pp. 50–100.

McGuire, K. (2011), 'True crime: Contagion, print culture and Herbert Croft's *Love and Madness; or, A Story Too True*', *Eighteenth-Century Fiction*, vol. 24, no. 1, pp. 55–75.

McLuhan, M. (1962), *The Gutenberg Galaxy: The Making of Typographic Man*. Toronto: University of Toronto Press.

—— (1994), *Understanding Media: The Extensions of Man*. Cambridge, MA: MIT Press.

Mäkinen, I. (2013), *Why People Read: Jean-Jacques Rousseau on the Love of Reading*. Helsinki: Essays on Libraries, Cultural Heritage and Freedom of Information.

Manguel, A. (1997), *A History of Reading*. London: Flamingo.

Mann, P. H. and Burgoyne, J. L. (1969), *Books and Reading*. London: André Deutsch.

Marden, O. S. and Devitt, G. R. (1907), *The Consolidated Library*, vol. 8. Washington, DC: Bureau of National Literature and Art.

Marius, R. (1985), *Thomas More: A Biography*. London: J. M. Dent and Son.

Martin, H.-J. (1996), *The French Book: Religion, Absolutism, and Readership, 1585–1715*. Baltimore, MD: The Johns Hopkins University Press.

Mason, H. T. (1999) (ed.), *The Darnton Debate: Books and Revolution in the Eighteenth Century*. Oxford: Voltaire Foundation.

Mathews, M. M. (1966), *Teaching to Read: Historically Considered*. Chicago, IL: The University of Chicago Press.

Matthews, S. (2010), 'Who gets to play? How and why reading researchers were left out of the No Child Left Behind Act', in Poynor and Wolfe (2010).

Mays, K. (1995), 'The disease of reading and Victorian periodicals', in J. H. Jordan and R. L. Platten (1995) (eds), *Literature in the Marketplace: Nineteenth-Century British Publishing and Reading Practices*. Cambridge: Cambridge University Press.

Mikics, D. (2013), *Slow Reading in a Hurried Age*. Cambridge, MA: Harvard University Press.

Miller, J. W. (1998), 'Literacy in the 21st century: Emergent themes', *Peabody Journal of Education*, vol. 73, nos. 3–4, pp. 10–14.

Milton, J. (1999), *Areopagitica and other Political Writings of John Milton*. Indianapolis, IN: Liberty Fund.

Minois, G. (1999), *History of Suicide: Voluntary Death in Western Culture*. Baltimore, MD: Johns Hopkins University Press.

Monaghan, E. J. (2007), 'Scientific research and progressive education: Contexts for the early reading pioneers, 1870–1956', in Israel and Monaghan (2007).

Moore, C. (1790), *A Full Inquiry into the Subject of Suicide*, vol. 2.

Morpurgo, J. E. (1958), 'Books for the new reading public', *The UNESCO Courier*, no. 3, pp. 26–8.

Nell, V. (1988), *Lost in a Book: The Psychology of Reading for Pleasure*. New Haven: Yale University Press.

Nietzsche, F. (2007), *Twilight of the Idols*. London: Wordsworth Edition, Ltd.

O'Hara, K. (2004), 'Socrates, trust and the internet', in *Proceedings of the 2nd International Conference on Speech, Writing and Context*. Kansaigaidai University, http://eprints.soton.ac.uk/id/eprint/265836.

—— (2004a), *Trust: From Socrates to Spin*. Cambridge: Icon Books.

Olson, D. (1975–6), 'Toward a literate society', *Proceedings of the National Academy of Education, 1975–1976*.

—— (1988), 'From utterance to text: The bias of language in speech and writing', in Kintgen, Kroll and Rose (1988).

—— (1994), *The World on Paper: The Conceptual and Cognitive Implications of Writing and Reading*: Cambridge: Cambridge University Press.

Olson, L. (2003), 'Did medieval English women read Augustine's *Confessiones*? Constructing feminine interiority and literacy in the eleventh and twelfth centuries', in S. T. Jones (2003) (ed.), *In Medieval England and Abroad*. Turnhout, Belgium: Brepols Publishers.

Ong, W. J. (1967), *The Presence of the Word: Some Prolegomena for Cultural and Religious History*. New Haven: Yale University Press.

—— (1998), 'Some psychodynamics of orality', in Kintgen, Kroll and Rose (1988).

—— (2002), *Orality and Literacy*. New York: Routledge.

Ortega y Gasset, J. (1959), 'The difficulty of reading', *Diogenes*, vol. 7, no. 28, pp.1–17.

——, Lewis, J. and Carpenter, R. (1961), 'The mission of the librarian', *The Antioch Review*, vol. 21, no. 2 (Summer), pp. 133–54.

Osol, A. and Pratt, R. (1851), *The United States Dispensator*. New York: J. B. Lippincott Co.

Outram, D. (2013), *The Enlightenment*. Cambridge: Cambridge University Press.

Palgrave, F. T. (1860), 'On readers 1760 and 1860', *Macmillan's Magazine* (April), p. 488.

Palmer, B. and Buckland, A. (2011), *A Return to the Common Reader: Print Culture and the Novel, 1850–1900*. Farnham, Surrey: Ashgate.

—— (2011a), 'Introduction', in Palmer and Buckland (2011).

Parisot, E. (2014), 'Suicide notes and popular sensibility in the eighteenth-century British press', *Eighteenth-Century Studies*, vol. 47, no. 3 (Spring), pp. 277–91.

Pearson, J. (1999), *Women's Reading in Britain*. Cambridge: Cambridge University Press.

Pendersen, S. (1986), 'Hannah More meets simple Simon: Tracts, chapbooks, and popular culture in late eighteenth-century England', *Journal of British Studies*, vol. 25.

Peters, R. S. (1966), *Ethics and Education*. London: George Allen and Unwin Ltd.

Philes, G. (1873), *How to Read a Book the Best Way*. New York: George Philes. archive.org/details/howtoreadabooki00phigoog.

Phillips, D. P. (1974), 'The influence of suggestion on suicide: Substantive and theoretical implications of the Werther effect', *American Sociological Review*, vol. 39, no. 3, pp. 340–54.

Plato (1997), *Phaedrus*, in J. M. Cooper (ed.) (1997), *Plato: Complete Works*. Indianapolis, IN: Hackett, pp. 506–56.

—— (1997a), *Republic*, in J. M. Cooper (ed.) (1997), *Plato: Complete Works*. Indianapolis, IN: Hackett.

—— (1997b), 'Letter VII', in J. M. Cooper (ed.) (1997), *Plato: Complete Works*. Indianapolis, IN: Hackett.

Poggioli, R. (1957), 'Tragedy or romance? A reading of the Paolo and Francesca episode in Dante's *Inferno*', in *Publications of the Modern Language Association of America*, pp. 313–58.

Porter, R. (2000), *Enlightenment: Britain and the Creation of the Modern World*. Allen Lane: London.

Poynor, L. and Wolfe, P. M. (2010) (eds), *Marketing Fear in America's Public Schools*. New York: Routledge.

Price, L. (2004), 'Reading: The state of the discipline', *Book History*, vol. 7, pp. 303–20.

Quindlen, N. (1998), *How Reading Changed My Life*. New York: The Ballantine Publishing Group.

Rabbås, O. (2010), 'Writing, memory, and wisdom: The critique of writing in the *Phaedrus*', *Symbolae Osloenses: Norwegian Journal of Greek and Latin Studies*, vol. 84, no. 1, pp. 26–48.

Raven, J., Small, H. and Tadmor, N. (1996), 'Introduction: The practice and representation of reading in England', in Raven, Small and Tadmor (1996a).

—— (1996a), *The Practice and Representation of Reading in England*. Cambridge: Cambridge University Press.

Ravitch, D. (2001), 'It is Time to Stop the War', in T. Loveless (2001) (ed.), *The Great Curriculum Debate: How Should We Teach Reading and Math?* New York: Brookings Institution Press.

Ray, W. (1994), 'Reading women: Cultural authority, gender, and the novel: The case of Rousseau', *Eighteenth-Century Studies*, vol. 27, no. 3, pp. 421–47.

Raymond, J. (2003), 'Irrational, impractical and unprofitable: Reading the news in seventeenth-century Britain', in Sharpe and Zwicker (2003).

Resnick, D. (1990), 'Historical perspectives on literacy and schooling', *Daedalus*, vol. 119, no. 2, pp. 15–31.

—— and Resnick, L. (1977), 'The nature of literacy: An historical explanation', *Harvard Educational Review*, 47, pp. 370–85.

Richards, I. A. (1929), *Practical Criticism: A Study of Literary Judgment*. London: Routledge and Kegan Paul.

Robins, E. (2010), *Beginning Reading: Influences on Policy in the United States and England, 1998–2010*. Dissertation for Degree of Doctor in Education, Aurora University, Aurora, IL.

Robinson, R. D., Baker, E. and Clegg, L. (1998), 'Literacy and the pendulum of change: Lessons for the 21st century', *Peabody Journal of Education*, vol. 73, nos 3–4, pp. 15–30.

Rose, J. (1992), 'Rereading the English Common Reader: A Preface to a History of Audiences', *Journal of the History of Ideas*, vol. 53, no.1, pp. 47–70.

—— (2007), 'The history of education as the history of reading', *History of Education*, vol. 36, nos 405, pp. 595–605.

Rowe, D. (2009), 'The concept of the moral panic: An historico-sociological positioning', in Lemmings and Walker (2009).

Ruskin, J. (2009), *Fors Clavigera: Letters to the Workmen and Labourers of Great Britain*. London: BiblioLife.

Saenger, P. (1982), 'Silent reading: Its impact on late medieval script and society', *Viator*, vol. 13, no. 1, pp. 367–414.

Saint Augustine (1961), *Confessions*, trans. R. S. Pine-Coffin London: Penguin Books.

Saint Thomas Aquinas (2008), *The Summa Theologica of St Thomas Aquinas*, online edition by Kevin Knight, *Saint Thomas Aquinas* (2008) 1a1.10, online edition http://www.newadvent.org/summa/1001.htm, accessed 12 July 2014.

Sauerberg, L. A. (2009), 'Preface to The Gutenberg Parenthesis – Print, Book and Cognition', *Orbis Litterarum*, vol. 64, no.2, pp.79–80.

Schiffman, R. L. (2010), 'A concert of Werthers', *Eighteenth-Century Studies*, vol. 43, no. 2, pp. 207–22.

Schoenfeldt, M. (2003), 'Reading bodies', in Sharpe and Zwicker (2003).

Schopenhauer, A. (1851), 'On reading and books', in *Essays of Schopenhauer*, eBooks @ Adelaide: Adelaide. https://ebooks.adelaide.edu.au/s/schopenhauer/arthur/essays/chapter3.html, accessed 13 January 2014.

Schroeder, T. (1906), *Freedom of the Press and 'Obscene' Literature*. New York: Free Speech League.

Schucking, L. L. (1966; original 1931), *The Sociology of Literary Taste*. London: Routledge and Kegan Paul.

Scribner, S. (1988) 'Literacy in Three Metaphors', in Kintgen, E.R., Kroll, B.M., Rose, M. (eds) (1988).

—— and Cole, M. (1988), 'Implications of literacy in traditional China and India', in Kintgen, Kroll and Rose (1988).

Shannon, P. (1989), *Broken Promises: Reading Instruction in Twentieth-Century America*. Granby, MA: Bergin and Garvey Publishers.

Sharpe, K. (2000), *Reading Revolutions: The Politics of Reading in Early Modern England*. New Haven, CT: Yale University Press.

—— and Zwicker, S. N. (2003), *Reading, Society and Politics in Early Modern England*. Cambridge: Cambridge University Press.

—— and Zwicker, S. N. (2003a), 'Introduction: Discovering the Renaissance reader', in Sharpe and Zwicker (2003).

Small, H. (1996), 'Dickens and a pathology of the mid-Victorian reading public', in Raven, Small and Tadmor (1996a).

Solar, J. and Oppenshaw, R. (2006), *Literacy Crises and Reading Policies: Children Still Can't Read*. London: Routledge.

Solomon, R. C. (1986), 'Literacy and the education of the emotions', in S. de Castell, A. Luke and K. Egan (1986), *Literacy, Society, and Schooling: A Reader*. Cambridge: Cambridge University Press.

Springhall, J. (1998), *Youth, Popular Culture and Moral Panics: Penny Gaffs to Gangsta-Rap, 1830–1996*. Houndmills, Basingstoke: Macmillan Press.

Stahl, S. A. (1998), 'Understanding shifts in reading and its instruction', *Peabody Journal of Education*, vol. 73, nos 3–4, pp. 31–67.

—— (1999), 'Why innovations come and go (and mostly go): The case of whole language', *Educational Researcher*, vol. 28, no. 12.

Stannard, J. and Huxford, L. (2007), *The Literacy Game: The Story of the National Literacy Strategy*. London: Routledge.

Starker, S. (1990), 'Fear of fiction: The novel', *Book Research Quarterly*, vol. 6, no. 2.

Stedman, L. C. and Kaestle, C. F. (1991), 'Literacy and reading performance in the United States from 1880 to the present', in C. F. Kaestle, H. Damon-Moore, L. C. Stedman, K. Tinsley and W. V. Trollinger (1991) (eds), *Literacy in the United States*. New Haven, CT: Yale University Press.

Steiner, G. (1985), *Language and Silence: Essays 1958–1966*. London: Faber and Faber.

Stierer, B. (1994), 'Simply doing their job? The politics of reading standards and "real books"', in Stierer and Maybin (1994).

—— and Maybin, J. (1994) (eds), *Language, Literacy and Learning in Educational Practice*. Clevedon: The Open University.

Stock, B. (1983), *The Implications of Literacy: Written Language and Models of Interpretation in the Eleventh and Twelfth Century*. Princeton, NJ: Princeton University Press.

—— (1994), 'The self and literary experience in late antiquity and the Middle Ages', *New Literary History*, pp. 839–52.

—— (1995), 'Reading, writing, and the self: Petrarch and his forerunners', *New Literary History*, vol. 26, no. 4, pp. 717–30.

—— (1998), *Augustine the Reader: Meditation, Self-Knowledge and the Ethics of Interpretation*. Cambridge, MA: Harvard University Press.

Stone, L. (1969), 'Literacy and education in England, 1640–1900', *Past and Present*, no. 42, pp. 69–139.

—— (1986), *The Causes of the English Revolution, 1529–1642*. London: ARK.

Strauss, B. S. (1993), *Fathers and Sons: Ideology and Society in the Era of the Peloponnesian War*. London: Routledge.

Strauss, S. L. (2010), 'Warning: Curent federal education policy may be hazardous to your health', in Poynor and Wolfe (2010).

Street, B. V. (1984), *Literacy in Theory and Practice*. Cambridge: Cambridge University Press.

Styles, M. and Drummond, M. (1993), 'The politics of reading', *Cambridge Journal of Education*, vol. 23, no. 1, pp. 3–13.

Sumpter, C. (2006), 'The cheap press and the "reading crowd"', *Media History*, vol. 12, no. 3, pp. 233–52.

Swaine, L. A. (1998), 'A paradox reconsidered: Written lessons from Plato's *Phaedrus*', *Educational Philosophy and Theory*, vol. 30, no. 3, pp. 259–73.

Swales, M. (1987), *Goethe: The Sorrows of Young Werther*. Cambridge: Cambridge University Press.

Swidler, A. and Ariditi, Y. (1994), 'The new sociology of knowledge', *Annual Review of Sociology*, vol. 20, pp. 305–29.

Thomas, K. (1896), 'The meaning of literacy in early modern England', in Gerd Baumann (1986) (ed.), *The Written Word: Literacy in Transition*. Oxford: Clarendon Press.

Thomas, R. (1995), 'Written in stone? Liberty, equality, orality and the codification of law', *Bulletin of the Institute of Classical Studies*, vol. 40, no. 1, pp. 59–74.

—— (1996), 'Literacy and the city-state in archaic and classical Greece', in Bowman and Woolf (1996).

Thorson, J. and Öberg, P. A. (2003), 'Was there a suicide epidemic after Goethe's *Werther*?', *Archives of Suicide Research*, vol. 7, pp. 69–72.

Thurlow, C. (2006), 'From statistical panic to moral panic: The metadiscursive construction and popular exaggeration of new media language in the print media', *Journal of Computer-Mediated Communication*, vol. 11, pp. 667–701.

Tierney, T. F. (2010), 'The governmentality of suicide: Peuchet, Marx, Durkheim, and Foucault', *Journal of Classical Sociology*, vol. 10, no. 4, pp. 357–89.

Towsey, M. R. (2007), *Reading and the Scottish Enlightenment: Libraries, Readers and the Intellectual Culture in Provincial Scotland, 1740–1820*. PhD Thesis, University of St Andrews.

Trollope, A. (1879), *Thackeray*, 'English men of letters series'. London: Macmillan. Web. Project Gutenberg. E-text prepared by Barbara Tozier, Bill Tozier and Lisa Reigel, 4 August 2013, at http://www.victorianweb.org/authors/trollope/moralteaching.html, accessed 8 April 2014.

Turner, M. (1994), 'Sponsored reading failure', in Stierer and Maybin (1994).

Ulin, D. L. (2010), *The Lost Art of Reading: Why Books Matter in a Distracted Time*. Seattle, WA: Sasquatch Books.

UNESCO (1946), *Fundamental Education: Common Ground for All People*. New York: The Macmillan Co.

Van Horn Melton, J. (2001), *The Rise of the Public in Enlightenment Europe*. Cambridge: Cambridge University Press.

Vincent, D. (1993), *Literacy and Popular Culture: England 1750–1914*. Cambridge: Cambridge University Press.

Vogrinčič, A. (2008), 'The novel-reading panic in the 18th century in England: An outline of an early moral media panic', *Medijska Istrazivanja/Media Research*, vol. 14, no. 2, pp. 103–24.

Vries, G. J. de (1969), *Commentary on the* Phaedrus *of Plato*. Amsterdam: Adolf M. Hakkert.

Walpole, H. (2004), *Reading: An Essay*. Whitefish, MO: Kessinger Publishing.

Walpole, S. (1913), *History of England: From the Conclusion of the Great War in 1815*, vol. 1. London: Longman, Green and Co.

Watson, P. (2005), *Ideas: A History of Thought and Invention*. London: Weidenfeld and Nicolson.

Weaver, C. and Brinkley, E. H. (1998), 'Phonics, whole language, and the religious and political right', in Goodman (1998).

Wharton, E. (1903), 'The Vice of Reading', *The North American Review*, vol. 177, no. 563, pp. 513–21.

Wilderspin, S. (1832), *The Infant System for Developing the Physical, Intellectual and Moral Powers of All Children from One to Seven Years of Age*. London: W. Simpkin and R. Marshall.

Willinsky, J. (1994), 'Introducing the new literacy', in Stierer and Maybin (1994).

Wilson, B. (2009), *What Price Liberty?* London: Faber and Faber.

Winzer, M. A. (2002), *The History of Special Education: From Isolation to Integration*. Washington, DC: Gallaudet University Press.

Wittmann, R. (1999), 'Was there a reading revolution at the end of the eighteenth century?', in Cavallo and Chartier (1999).

Wolf, M. (2010), *Proust and the Squid: The Story and Science of the Reading Brain*. Thriplow, Cambridge: Icon Books.

Wood, P. (2011), 'A virtuoso reader: Thomas Reid and the practices of reading in eighteenth-century Scotland', *The Journal of Scottish Thought*, vol. 4, pp. 33–74.

Woodmansee, M. (1988–9), 'Toward a genealogy of the aesthetic: The German reading debate of the 1790s', *Cultural Critique*, no. 11, pp. 203–21.

Woolf, V. (1932), *The Common Reader: Second Series*. London: The Hogarth Press.

Wynne, D. (2001), *The Sensation Novel and the Victorian Family Magazine*. Houndmills, Basingstoke: Palgrave Macmillan.

Yatvin, J. (2010), 'Making whole language disappear: How the national reading panel worked its magic', in Poynor and Wolfe (2010).

Zaret, D. (1996), 'Petitions and the "invention" of public opinion in the English Revolution', *The American Journal of Sociology*, vol. 101, no. 6, pp. 1,497–1,555.

—— and Brown, S. (2001), 'Origins of Democratic Culture: Printing, Petitions, and the Public Sphere in Early-Modern England', Renaissance and Reformation/Renaissance et Réforme, vol. 25, no.3, pp. 61–63.

Zwicker, S. N. (2003), 'The constitution of opinion and the pacification of reading', in Sharpe and Zwicker (2003).

INDEX